# THE SECRETARY-GENERAL
# OF THE UNITED NATIONS

# The Secretary-General of the United Nations

## HIS POLITICAL POWERS AND PRACTICE

### Stephen M. Schwebel

GREENWOOD PRESS, PUBLISHERS
NEW YORK

TO HONEY, DAD, AND JACK

# Preface

The importance of our subject is in fact our subject and so will not lengthily be dealt with in the preface. A single sentence will place it in rough context: It is apparent that the future, if there is to be one, belongs to international organization; that the primary international organization of the present is the United Nations; and that the chief permanent officer of that organization necessarily occupies a unique and strategic position meriting the fullest study.

This work is not that full study. It is rather a consideration of one aspect, and the most significant aspect, of the Secretaryship General: its political powers and practice. All phases of the Secretaryship General which are analyzed are approached only so as to extract their political elements; the administrative, technical, personnel, coördinating, and financial functions of the office are treated only insofar as they bear upon the Secretary-General's political authority.

Our approach is further qualified by unorthodox usage of the term, "Secretary-General." The term as officially employed by the United Nations embraces the totality of the activity of the Secretariat in the Organization. Little is done in the Secretariat's name; virtually nothing is done in the name of any member of the Secretariat other than the Secretary-General. It is the Secretary-General who is at once in Geneva and New York, who simultaneously lunches with the Secretary of State and sifts data on tribal autonomy in Togoland, who is legal adviser to the Security Council and the prolific author of a vast number of economic and social studies.

"Secretary-General" as herein employed does not denote all that. Rather, we consider the political activity of the Secretary-General himself and that of his senior associates which is under his direction. Thus, for the purposes of this study, the "Secretary-General" includes the occupant of the office, his Executive Assistant, and the ranking members of the Executive Office, as well as the Assistant Secretaries-General, the General Counsel, and certain miscellaneous officers of the Secretariat who carry out political assignments at the Secretary-General's personal or quasi-personal instructions (such as the Principal Secretaries of United Nations Missions).

A final reservation. Much of the material of the study has been drawn from interviews which I have been privileged to enjoy with numerous well-informed persons, the majority in official position. In certain cases, information which they have imparted cannot be specifically employed. In other cases, sources cannot be disclosed. I wish to assure the reader that some of the generalizations which follow and which seem but sparsely supported with facts are in reality factually based; the generalizations, as far as it is within my ability to make them so, are rooted in facts which for evident reasons themselves cannot be cited.

The number of persons to whom I am indebted is agreeably large. To none of them can be attributed any particular bit of data, unless specifically so indicated. Who has said what has been too often surprising to lend any validity to such a process. And of course no one but the author bears responsibility for the product.

I wish to thank first of all Secretary-General Trygve Lie: for providing invaluable background information on three occasions, each of generous length; for several briefer conversations of equal pleasure; and for an early and steadily encouraging interest in this study which has been gracious and warm.

May I further thank the Earl of Perth (formerly Sir Eric Drummond), first Secretary-General of the League of Nations, for his extreme courtesy in providing an otherwise unavailable insight into the political activities of the League Secretary-General, both in a long conversation and by his preparation, for the purposes of this study, of Notes describing the nature of his political work. I also should like to express my great appreciation to M. Joseph Avenol, second Secretary-General of the League,

for affording me, in the course of two revealing interviews, access
to original material concerning his political activities.

I have been greatly assisted throughout by the discerning and
informed instruction of my former tutor, Dr. Rupert Emerson,
Professor of Government at Harvard University; by my cousin,
Dr. Simon Segal, who suggested the topic of this work and who
helped to sketch its first outline; by my brother, Mr. Jack
Schwebel, and by Miss Sadja Stokowski for their cogent criticism
and research assistance.

The following persons have been kind enough to impart to me,
in interviews which have been as pleasant as they have been in-
formative, the data without which this study could not have
been written:

Mr. David Blickenstaff, Executive Officer of the Office of the
Secretary-General and Chief of Section for General Assembly
Affairs; Dr. Ralph J. Bunche, Director of the United Nations
Department of Trusteeship and Information from Non-Self-
Governing Territories; Sir Alexander Cadogan, former Perma-
nent Representative of the United Kingdom to the United Na-
tions; Mr. Benjamin A. Cohen, Assistant Secretary-General for
Public Information; Mr. Benjamin V. Cohen, former Counselor
of the Department of State and Member of the United States
Delegation to the General Assembly; Mr. Andrew W. Cordier,
Executive Assistant to the Secretary-General; Dr. Clyde Eagle-
ton, Professor of International Law at New York University; Mr.
Archibald Evans, of the International Labor Organization; Mr.
A. H. Feller, General Counsel and Principal Director of the
United Nations Legal Department; Mr. Wilder Foote, Director
of the Bureau of Press and Publications, United Nations Depart-
ment of Public Information; Mr. William R. Frye, Chief of the
United Nations Bureau of the *Christian Science Monitor*; Mr.
Matthew Gordon, head of the Liaison Desk of the Bureau of
Press and Publications, United Nations Department of Public
Information; Mr. Thomas J. Hamilton, Chief of the United Na-
tions Bureau of the *New York Times*; Miss Julia Henderson, Chief
of Section of the Policy Division, United Nations Department of
Administrative and Financial Affairs; Mr. Martin Hill, Deputy
Executive Assistant to the Secretary-General and Director for

Coördination of Specialized Agencies and Economic and Social Matters; Mr. Charles A. Hogan, Deputy Secretary of the Economic and Social Council; Mr. C. Wilfred Jenks, Assistant Director-General of the International Labor Organization; Dr. Juliusz Katz-Suchy, Permanent Representative of Poland to the United Nations; Mr. Alexander Loveday, former Director of the Financial Section and of Economic Intelligence of the League of Nations; Mr. Leo Malania, Special Assistant to the Executive Assistant to the Secretary-General; Dr. Charles Malik, Permanent Representative of Lebanon to the United Nations; Mr. Homer Metz, former Chief of the United Nations Bureau of the *Christian Science Monitor*; M. Pierre de Meulemeester, Assistant Chief of Section for Protocol and Liaison of the Executive Office of the Secretary-General; Mr. Gunnar Myrdal, Executive Secretary of the United Nations Economic Commission for Europe; Mr. Clyde Nichols, Personal Assistant to the Secretary-General; Mr. Walter O'Hearn, Correspondent of the *Montreal Daily Star*; Mr. Clive Parry, former Legal Counselor of the Legal Department of the United Nations and Lecturer in Law at Cambridge University; Mr. Leo Pasvolsky, former Special Assistant to the Secretary of State and Director of International Studies for the Brookings Institution; Mr. Edward J. Phelan, former Director-General of the International Labor Organization; Mr. Byron Price, Assistant Secretary-General for Administrative and Financial Services; Mr. Egon F. Ranshofen-Wertheimer, former Principal Secretary of the United Nations Commission for Korea and Secretary of the United Nations Commission in Eritrea; Mr. Clinton A. Rehling, Information Officer of the Geneva United Nations Information Center; Mr. James Reston, Diplomatic Correspondent of the *New York Times*; Mr. John Rogers, Chief of the United Nations Bureau of the *New York Herald Tribune*; Mr. Mani Sanasen, General Liaison Officer of the Executive Office of the Secretary-General; Dr. Marc Schreiber, Legal Counselor, General Legal Division of the United Nations Legal Department; Mr. Nessim Shalom, Special Assistant for Coördination of the Office of the Director of Coördination of Specialized Agencies and Economic and Social Matters; Mr. Vladimir Sokoline, Soviet Under Secretary-General of the League of Nations; Mr. Arthur Sweetser,

Chief of the Washington Information Office of the United Nations; Mr. Semyon K. Tsarapkin, Minister of the Permanent Delegation of the Union of Soviet Socialist Republics to the United Nations; Mr. Brian Urquhart, Deputy Secretary of the Collective Measures Committee and former Personal Assistant to the Secretary-General; Mr. Gilbert Yates, Secretary of the Economic and Social Council; and Dr. Liang Yuen-li, Director of the Division for the Development and Codification of International Law of the Legal Department of the United Nations.

I further wish to thank Mr. F. L. McDougall, Counselor of the Food and Agriculture Organization of the United Nations; Mrs. Franklin D. Roosevelt; Dr. Alexander W. Rudzinski, former Acting Chief of the Polish Delegation to the United Nations; and Governor Adlai E. Stevenson of Illinois for their kindness in informatively replying to my written inquiries, as did the late Field Marshal Jan Christiaan Smuts.

For their criticism of this study, as it was first prepared as a thesis for Harvard College, I wish to express my appreciation to Mr. McGeorge Bundy, Associate Professor of Government at Harvard; Mr. Byron Dexter, Managing Editor of *Foreign Affairs*; Mr. Clark M. Eichelberger, Director of the American Association for the United Nations; Mr. John A. F. Ennals, Secretary-General of the World Federation of United Nations Associations; Dr. Arthur N. Holcombe, Eaton Professor of Government at Harvard; Dr. Hersch Lauterpacht, Whewell Professor of International Law at Cambridge University; Dr. Alan Burr Overstreet, Associate Professor of Political Science at Smith College; and Dr. Quincy Wright, Professor of International Law at the University of Chicago.

May I further thank Dr. A. C. de Breycha-Vauthier, Librarian of the United Nations Library in Geneva, and the staffs of the United Nations Libraries in Geneva and New York, for their most efficient and courteous assistance. I should also like to thank the Harvard University Press and, in particular, Miss Elizabeth Treeman, for the excellence of their editing and the pleasure of association with them. May I lastly express my warm appreciation to my aunt, Mrs. Miriam Davis, for her careful correcting and typing of the manuscript.

Sources consist of the information and ideas imparted by all of the individuals listed above, the appended bibliography, and less tangible knowledge which I acquired during the instructive three months I worked, during the summer of 1949, as an administrative aide in the Executive Office of the Secretary-General, in association with the United Nations Interne Programme.

S.M.S.

Geneva, Switzerland
August 17, 1951

# CONTENTS

PART 3

**The Future of the Secretaryship General**

# *Introduction*

# INTRODUCTION

## The Legacy of the League

*Clearly the political activities of the Secretary-General, being of the nature I have described, can only have been known to a very few.*
SIR ERIC DRUMMOND

*I was neither a Parliamentarian nor a politician.*
SIR ERIC DRUMMOND

*Sir Eric Drummond was a great administrator. He conceived of his job as that of an administrator.*
MARTIN HILL

*The day that I am reduced to the status of Sir Eric, I will resign.*
ALBERT THOMAS

*It is quite, quite certain that Albert Thomas in my job would have been forced to resign. They wouldn't have stood for it. He would have tried — and failed. The "Chancellor" wouldn't have been successful.*
SIR ERIC DRUMMOND

The Secretary-General of the United Nations is the direct and immediate descendant of the Secretary-General of the League of Nations. Their features bear an evident resemblance, though the former's are more boldly cut. The record of the Secretaries-General of the League is the fixed point from which the developing practice of the Secretary-General of the United Nations may be viewed in perspective. Instructive as the record is, it is not commanding. The present-day international situation presents almost haunting parallels with that of the inter-war era, but the two periods diverge in many respects no less important. The fundamental affinity of the League of Nations and the United

Nations is clear. Their essential similarity gives the experience of the former vital meaning for the latter. But the lessons to be drawn from that experience, in the light of the somewhat differing character and context of the two organizations, are advisory and not absolute.

The authors of the Covenant of the League of Nations initially projected a Secretary-General of the broadest political authority. Lord Cecil's draft, to which the final Covenant clauses concerning the Secretary-General may be traced, spoke not of a Secretary-General but of the more impressively titled Chancellor.[1] "There had been an idea," he later wrote, "of making the office an almost independent institution. . . The eminent Greek statesman, M. [Eleutherios] Venizelos was, I believe, sounded as to his willingness to take the post. He refused, and for that and other reasons the nature of the post was modified and assimilated to that of the Permanent and non-political Under-Secretary of a British Government Office. It could not be quite the same because there was not and could not be a Secretary of State."[2]

"The first idea," Sir Eric Drummond adds, "was to have an important and well-known political statesman. . . He would have wide political powers, even wider than the Secretary-General of the United Nations.[3] . . . The League Secretary-General was supposed to be an international civil servant, the Chancellor an international statesman. It hinged on trying to get Venizelos. When they found they couldn't get the highest caliber man for the job, they had second thoughts about it. . . They decided they didn't want an international 'dictator.'"[4]

That decision was reflected in the Covenant. The clauses which concern the Secretary-General imply only a tenuous political role.[5] The Secretary-General shall "act in that capacity at all meetings of the Assembly and of the Council,"[6] in case of war or threat of war "shall on the request of any Member of the League forthwith summon a meeting of the Council,"[7] and shall "make all necessary arrangements for a full investigation and consideration" of a dispute submitted to the Council which any party to the dispute sees likely to lead to a rupture.[8] The Secretary-General shall be appointed by the Council with the approval of a majority of the Assembly; he in turn shall appoint the staff subject to the Council's approval.[9] He and his officials "shall enjoy diplomatic privileges and immunities." [10]

The Secretary-General, evidently, would have to make his own contribution if his office were to develop into a political force: the way was not defined in the Covenant. The right of the Secretary-General, for example, to "act in that capacity" at Assembly and Council meetings could mean much and it could mean little; the indefinite quality of that "capacity" lent itself to a range of interpretation. Time would show that Sir Eric Drummond, the first Secretary-General of the League, would choose to interpret the Covenant in a conservative manner understandably consonant with his personality and training.

"A very eminent civil servant . . . Sir Eric proposed to introduce into the international field certain of the principles of the British civil service . . . conscious of belonging to the ruling class of his own country, his reflexes were of those of the civil servant, but tempered and modified by the psychology of one who 'belongs.' " [11] "A shy, modest man, terrified of speeches," [12] he "conceived of his job as that of an administrator." [13]

Thus his colleagues describe Sir Eric in the pattern of the British civil servant of the first rank, with the outlook and characteristics of the permanent secretary: the highest standards of administrative efficiency; a passion for anonymity; confidence and competence in his assured, if restricted, sphere; an ability to deliver the most perceptive and balanced advice to his minister but not to be minister. Sir Eric's thirteen-year record of office wholly bears out this description.

Unlike the United Nations Secretary-General, Sir Eric was able to get off to a start relatively unrestricted by the dicta of a Preparatory Commission or by Great Power understandings impinging upon his control of the Secretariat. The first Secretary-General of the League was named in the Annex to the Covenant (the appointive process set forth in Article VI did not apply to the first Secretary-General); in a very real sense, he was his own Preparatory Commission; and the interest of the governments, particularly of the Great Powers, was not so intense that it prompted them to divide the spoils of office before the offices were created.[14] The extreme administrative independence bestowed upon the Secretary-General was reflected in as major a matter as Sir Eric's decision to create a truly international Secretariat, as contrasted with a permanent association of national groupings, and in as secondary a consideration as his setting his salary at a level a good deal higher than that which the Preparatory Commission of the United Nations decided upon for the present Secretary-General.[15]

Compared with the initiative of Sir Eric's internal, administrative activity, the caution of his external, political approach is notable. His political activity was subtle, indirect, inconspicuous — so much so that it not surprisingly gave the false impression of vacuity. In his formal relations with League organs, the Secretary-General was inarticulate in the extreme; in his public role, he was retiring and uninspiring; it was only in his diplomatic, "behind-the-scenes" character that the Secretary-General of the League was a potent political force.

The Secretary-General "never addressed an Assembly of the League at all . . . he had a right to speak in the Council, but he tended to speak in the Council as a Secretary of a committee and not more than that." [16] This was the more notable considering that the Assembly rules of procedure provided that the Secretary-General "may be invited by the President to make verbal communications concerning any question under consideration." [17] His annual report to the Assembly, moreover, rather than being prefaced with an interpretive exposition of international trends and developments, largely contented itself with cataloguing the past year of League activity.

Publicly, the Secretary-General was equally unimaginative. His speeches were infrequent, his appeals to public opinion nonexistent. His Information Section bent over backwards to avoid making propaganda for the League.[18]

The diplomatic story was a different one. That the caliber of Sir Eric's diplomatic activities was high is agreed by those — and they are not many — who were in a position to have knowledge of them. The estimate of a former personal assistant to the Secretary-General is both revealing and typical: "The new international institution," he wrote in 1944, "will be fortunate if it secures the services of one who was as gifted a moderator, as impartial a negotiator, as trusted and well-informed a political confessor . . . as Sir Eric Drummond." [19]

Arthur Sweetser, who for many years was special assistant to the Secretary-General for public-information matters, describes Sir Eric as "shrewd, well-informed, discerning." The delegates, he states, "would approach Drummond for his exposition of all sides of an issue, anxious for his impartial view. After Sir Eric stated the facts and nuances, they would often request his views, and he would give them, cautiously and suggestively." [20] As to the extent of Sir Eric's diplomatic activity, still another former League associate, now high in the Executive Office of the United Nations Secretary-General, characterizes it as "fully comparable" to that of Mr. Lie.[21]

This contrast between his public quiescence, on the one hand, and the energy of his behind-the-scenes diplomatic work, on the other, is best explained by Sir Eric himself. "I don't think people are influenced by public speeches or documents. They are by private talk. The behind-the-scenes work of the Secretary-General is more important." [22] "Behind-the-scenes activities," he adds, "suited my temperament and previous experience. I was neither a Parliamentarian nor a politician and totally unaccustomed to making speeches in public, though I was compelled to make numerous speeches when I went on official tours." [23] Moreover, "owing to the limitations imposed in the Covenant, all my political work had to be done behind the scenes, but I do not think it was any the less effective because of this. To take sides publicly in a political dispute would certainly have lessened my political influence." [24]

Sir Eric goes on to describe a few instances of the type of political activity in which he engaged — illustrations which afford a rare insight into the character of that activity:

An international dispute had arisen. The delegates of each of the Powers concerned had made strongly *ex parti* statements before the Council. The delegate of the Power which we knew to be in the wrong came to see me privately, and acknowledged the guilt of his Government. He asked me if I could not find an honourable way out. I asked the delegate of the other Power to come to see me, and by separate interviews with each of them we gradually worked out a solution which both considered acceptable and which was ultimately approved by the Council.

A further instance was the time when there was tension between Italy and Yugoslavia, and the latter Government was fearful of an Italian attack and was taking military precautions. I was due to make an official visit to Yugoslavia, so I took the opportunity of first going to Italy to see Mussolini and discuss the matter with him. I saw him at Forli and obtained from him a definite assurance that he had not the slightest intention of attacking Yugoslavia. I passed this information to the Yugoslav Government when I went to Belgrade, and they were greatly relieved.[25]

The approach of the only peacetime successor to Sir Eric, Joseph Avenol of France, who was named Secretary-General in 1933, is less easily defined. His distinctive contribution was the initiation of administrative alterations which brought the Secretariat closer to French procedures. In his formal relations with League organs, and in his public role, he appeared no bolder than Sir Eric. His diplomatic influence, if anything, declined with the failing influence of the League. The objects of his political activity were and are controversial. M. Avenol resigned in 1940 under confused circumstances, amidst considerable criticism of his administrative acts and, more, of his political views. The following remarks of M. Avenol — the first of this nature he has made public — are thus of the greatest interest, both for the light they shed upon those views and for their contrast with certain of the concepts of Sir Eric.

"According to the Covenant," M. Avenol suggests, "the Secretary-General was quite a 'personage.' There was nothing which said that he could not take important political initiative. . . I favored an active role for the Secretary-General, like that of the Director of the International Labor Office. My temperament pushed me toward the path of Albert Thomas. But there was the respected example of Sir Eric. He was, you know, very respected. I could not easily change this tradition. . . Once Sir Eric began it in one way, it was difficult to take up another. The texts of the constitutions of the I.L.O. and of the League were alike [with regard to the powers of the Director and the Secretary-General]. But it was the acts which counted and not the writing. Thomas and [Harold] Butler always took a public initiative.

Private work — that was Sir Eric's idea, and he was right to follow it. Sir Eric was a civil servant. And the English civil service was the best in the world. His idea was to do things and not to take the responsibility. . . The role of the Secretary-General depends upon the man. And upon the circumstances. . . My activities were different from Sir Eric's. His was not the time of difficulties. I tried to do more than Sir Eric, but I had no great success."

"I was named Secretary-General," M. Avenol recalls, "just at the time that Hitler came to power. Hitler's rise completely changed the physiognomy. For some months, Hitler was quiet. Then he quit the League. . . Only those who had read his book knew the significance of that. . . I had one hope — [French Foreign Minister Jean Louis] Barthou. He was the only representative who understood Hitler's threat. And he was assassinated. . . I tried to carry through political activity to meet that threat."

The nature and wisdom of the activity upon which the Secretary-General embarked has been in dispute ever since. M. Avenol describes a key episode of his program — an episode which some would view as a sacrifice of the League's principles and others would see as a realistic attempt to quarantine the greater aggressor with the aid of a lesser — in this way:

"I had known Mussolini for years. I knew his defects, and they were considerable. I knew also his qualities. . . He hated the Germans. . . Hitler's march into the Rhineland frightened him. . . I could make an attempt with Mussolini — which was *not* contrary to the Covenant — but I did this only in 1936. I took the occasion of the appointment of an Italian Under Secretary-General to go to Rome. I saw Mussolini and Ciano. . . They were much interested. I pointed out to them that if they did not settle in Ethiopia — what then? I said that the League could not recognize aggression.

"Mussolini received me cordially. He wanted to return to the League. I took this initiative — my own initiative. Mussolini agreed. But when I explained my plans to the Council, there was not a word of encouragement. . . Mussolini and Ciano were furious. They had planned to go to Geneva — they went on to

Berlin. It was the end of Italian collaboration with the League. I thought, I told the others: 'You must take men as they are.' Mussolini wanted to return; he was afraid of Germany. But the Assembly would not do what was necessary. Mussolini only required that the Credentials Committee of the Assembly, the 1936 Assembly, disqualify the Negus. . . This was all he wanted. . . A year later, he was marching with Hitler." [26]

The controversial character and the failure of M. Avenol's efforts notwithstanding, the political importance of the Secretaries-General of the League was, in all, very great and often underestimated. The League Assembly appointed a Committee of Thirteen to look into the functions of the Secretariat, and in 1930 the committee filed a notable report. The majority tended to minimize the political character of those functions, but a minority of two emphasized them in an oft-quoted and oft-criticized statement: "The political influence of the Secretariat, and especially of its principal officers, is, in fact, enormous, and it would be a mistake to close our eyes to this fact." [27]

Sir Eric Drummond's comment upon that statement, had it been publicly made at the time, would have shaken the League to its foundations: "I am afraid," he says, "that the judgment of the minority was entirely right." [28]

That is not to say that the political importance of the League Secretary-General could not have been greater. Unquestionably, he was a distinctly lesser figure than is the Secretary-General of the United Nations. The latter, for one thing, more fully exploits the public and organic [29] potentialities of the position than did the Secretaries-General of the League. More fundamentally, the Charter endows the United Nations Secretary-General with powers which were withheld from his League antecedents. Article 99 authorizes the Secretary-General of the United Nations to bring to the attention of the Security Council any matter which in his opinion may threaten the maintenance of international peace and security. The comparable article of the Covenant, however, merely prescribed that in case of a threat of war the Secretary-General, "on the request of any Member of the League," should summon a meeting of the Council. "The distinction," Sir Eric notes, "is vital. The Secretary-General of the League could only act through and at the request of a Member of the League; the Secretary-General of the United Nations can act on his own initiative. In view of this difference in functioning, the method of approach of the two officers is or was necessarily of a different character." [30]

It may also be said that the Organization of which the United Nations Secretary-General is the chief permanent officer occupies a somewhat more important place on the international scene than did that which the League Secretary-General served. To the extent that this is true, the position of the Secretary-General of the United Nations is the more significant.

If the Secretaries-General of the League are the pale prototype of the United Nations Secretary-General, the Directors of the International Labor Organization are perhaps the vivid archetype. Just how abbreviated was the public and organic impact of the Secretaries-General of the League is the more apparent when contrasted with the full weight of the influence of the Directors of the I.L.O. The relevance of the experience of the I.L.O. Directors to a consideration of the United Nations Secretaryship General, of course, is subject to reservations greater than those taken into account in assessing the record of the League Secretaries-General: Albert Thomas and his successors headed a specialized agency concerned with a sphere of social problems; and the fact that that agency's policy-making organs were (and are) composed of nongovernmental workers' and employers' representatives, as well as governmental delegates, afforded them increased leverage for mediatorial activity. Nonetheless, the extraordinary record of international leadership which the Directors of the I.L.O. built up has the most pertinent contemporary significance. The contrast of the superb, somewhat flamboyant direction of Thomas and those who followed him with the reserved and colorless public activity of the League Secretaries-General is startling. The success of that leadership may be said to be the positive lesson for the future of international administration, as the League experience is in some ways a negative lesson of the past. In the very least, the work of the I.L.O. leaders provides a demonstration of the potentiality of those public and organic functions of the international executive which the Secretaries-General of the League did not or could not exploit.

To compare Thomas, the first Director of the I.L.O., with the first Secretary-General of the League is to contrast the politically creative and responsive minister with the self-effacing civil servant; moreover, it is to contrast the French minister with the British civil servant. The differences in accustomed function, national habits of thought, and, as it happened, personality, were immense.

A man of "overflowing energy and remarkable personal magnetism," [31] Thomas had his own vital ideas about the character of the international leadership the Director of the I.L.O. should exert. He believed that it was upon the Director that "fell of necessity the task of leadership, the task of initiative, the task of taking all those measures which might be necessary to defend the Organization." [32] Not only did he address the I.L.O. Conference, he also placed before it "definite proposals which it might accept, reject or amend, but outside the framework of which it could not stray." [33] His annual report, which surveyed not only the problems before the I.L.O. "but also those which were fermenting in the whole social cosmos," [34] he presented to the conference personally. His relations with the Governing Body were almost dominating.[35] Thomas saw that the organization was represented at all pertinent international gatherings; [36] he set up I.L.O. "embassies" in the principal cities of the world; [37] he personally spoke before the Permanent Court of International Justice in behalf of the organization and in opposition to the contention of a member state.[38]

The Director spent nearly twenty weeks a year traveling, speaking publicly and with great effect wherever he went throughout five continents. Sensitive to public opinion, he went so far as to dictate letters to the press in reply to articles critical of the I.L.O.[39] He made full use of his world-wide acquaintanceship with innumerable public personalities. His operating assumption diplomatically was that "the Governments must be told what they had to do, and told in terms, so far as possible, of their own constitutions and methods . . . he insisted on what he called 'letters of principle' in which the duties of Governments were carefully set out and a method for their performance suggested." [40]

Yet Albert Thomas was no bull in a china shop. Under his leadership, and in his tradition, the I.L.O. has flourished. His record stands as a spectacular example of international leadership, of constructive international statesmanship, sharply contrasting with the publicly cautious approach of the Secretaries-General of the League of Nations.[41] This is not to say that Albert Thomas as Secretary-General could have done what he did as Director of the I.L.O.[42] But it does lend emphasis to the view that the international executive may exert influence in the public and organic spheres as well as in the more important private sphere; and it suggests further that the Secretary-General of the new international organization might well bring to bear elements of strength in his effort to further international order which his predecessors, for reasons both subjective and objective, were unable to exploit.

# PART 1

# The Framework of the Secretary-General's Powers

# CHAPTER 1

## San Francisco, the Charter, and the Preparatory Commission

*I wish Article 99 had been at my disposal.*
SIR ERIC DRUMMOND

A root concept of the United Nations is that the Secretary-General is an international statesman. As far back as the days of the unpublished memoranda of the State Department's years of study and consultation in preparation for the Dumbarton Oaks conversations, the most influential of the Powers sponsoring the creation of the United Nations had agreed that a permanent officer of the postwar international security organization should be endowed with specific political prerogatives. So firmly was this principle held that the Department's planning group at one time envisaged its application by an officer whose functions would be wholly political. The future international organization would have two permanent officers: the President, who would deal with political and executive matters of concern to the world organization; and the Secretary-General, who would manage the internal administration of the Secretariat. The plan was "seriously considered" by Washington, according to Dr. Leo Pasvolsky, who directed the Department's studies preparatory to Dumbarton Oaks.[1] But before the opening of the conversations with the United Kingdom, the U.S.S.R., and China, which were held from August through October of 1944, the Department decided in favor of a single permanent officer combining the external, political prerogative of the President with the administrative responsibility of the Secretary-General. The plan's consideration nevertheless accents the view early accepted in governmental circles that the Secretary-General would be a good deal more than the world organization's highest administrative functionary.[2]

It has been said that President Roosevelt considered the possibility of himself becoming Secretary-General.[3] If true, this would furnish dramatic substance for the impression that the United States government viewed the office as most important. Mrs. Eleanor Roosevelt, however, states, "I never heard my husband mention any possibility that he might become the Secretary-General of the United Nations," although "he thought that office a most important one."[4]

How important is indicated by the fact that Mr. Roosevelt would not have named the chief permanent officer of the United Nations the "Secretary-General"; it was too modest a title. "He thought the phrase 'Secretary-General' was not sufficiently significant for a position which in his opinion should be regarded as one of the most important in the world. He said that if a man such as General Smuts had been appointed the first man of the old League in, say 1919, the powers and significance of the post might have been much more widely recognized with results that might have led to the avoidance of World War II. The President, no doubt speaking quite casually, suggested the term, the 'World's Moderator.'"[5]

The Dumbarton Oaks negotiations regarding the Secretaryship General were in accord with the spirit of the United States draft. There was a "general desire" to create a chief permanent officer who would be "effective"[6] administratively and politically. The end product of the tentative recommendations emerging from the two series of three-Power talks, which were to be used as the bases of the San Francisco drafting, largely contained what later came to be Chapter XV of the Charter. These recommendations, particularly that for Article 99, closely followed the American proposals and were agreed upon without conspicuous difficulty.

The role of the Secretary-General was not a central issue at San Francisco. The late Field Marshal Smuts noted that it was agreed that the "position . . . should . . . be of the highest importance, and for this reason a large measure of initiative was expressly conferred." [7] The relative ease of reaching such agreement is indicated by the fact that the fundamentals of the crucial Article 99 were hardly debated at all, although its great significance was of course recognized. The four sponsoring Powers offered several amendments regarding mode of appointment, tenure, and deputy Secretaries-General on the whole restrictive of the Secretary-General's power; these were largely rebuffed by a Small Power "revolt." There was some sentiment among the smaller states for augmenting the Secretary-General's political power; here, too, however, the Dumbarton Oaks suggestions emerged more or less intact. All in all, the five articles of Chapter XV, "The Secretariat," were produced with but moderate wear and tear and voted through with heavy majority backing.[8]

### Article 99

*The Secretary-General may bring to the attention of the Security Council any matter which in his opinion may threaten the maintenance of international peace and security.*

If there is any doubt about the reality of the political prerogative of the Secretary-General, it is resolved by Article 99. It demands, in the words of the Preparatory Commission of the United Nations, his "exercise of the highest qualities of political judgment." [9] It supplies the legal basis for a significant range of political activity. It may be said to be the formal recognition of the vitality of that international synthesis of outlook which is more than the sum of the national parts, a synthesis of which the Secretary-General, who "more than anyone else . . . stand[s] for the United Nations as a whole," [10] is made the voice. Article 99 conclusively demonstrates that, as Dr. Herbert V. Evatt puts it, "the Secretary-General is intended to be far more than an administrative officer." [11] To do justice to its terms and implications, he must be an international statesman.

Debate at San Francisco over Article 99 was concerned with three issues: whether its invocation should be a matter of the Secretary-General's right or a prescription of duty; whether its application would extend to the General Assembly or be restricted to the Security Council; and whether, additional to matters threatening international peace and security, the Secretary-General should be empowered to draw the Organization's attention to "any matters which constitute an infringement or violation of the principles of the Charter." [12]

There was some sentiment for imposing as a duty the authority of Article 99; and a motion was offered which would have changed the article to read, "The Secretary-General shall bring to the attention of the Security Council," instead of "may bring." The majority, however, appeared to lean in the direction of the exercise of Article 99 as a matter of the Secretary-General's discretion, and the motion was withdrawn. [13]

Venezuela proposed that the Secretary-General have the right to bring matters which might threaten international peace and security before the Security Council "and/or before the General Assembly." [14] It advanced its amendment on the grounds that it could serve to keep the Assembly informed of certain situations which states might not bring to its attention, and that it would reiterate the competence of the Assembly in matters of peace and security. The amendment was voted down in committee because the majority felt that the Secretary-General's having to decide between the Assembly and the Council might place him in a difficult position [15] and would impinge upon the Security Council's primary responsibility for the maintenance of peace and security; [16] further, the provisions of Article 98 for an annual report were seen as sufficient base for the Secretary-General's relations with the Assembly. [17]

Uruguay suggested that Article 99 be broadened to include within the Secretary-General's discretion matters which would not necessarily threaten the peace, but which would constitute violations of the principles of the Charter. Iran and Egypt were prominent in backing the Uruguayan amendment, which viewed the Secretary-General as the agent who would bring to the Organization's attention domestic infringements of the Charter's principles. The United Kingdom, Canada, and New Zealand led the majority opposition to the Uruguayan amendment: it would, they held, give to the Secretary-General wider authority than had been given to the members in this respect, and, the more so in view of the "very heavy burdens" already placed upon him,

would put the Secretary-General in a "very difficult position." [18]
The Uruguayan amendment lost by three votes; [19] its serious bid
constitutes renewed demonstration of the desire widespread at
San Francisco to invest the Secretary-General with substantial
political authority.

Article 99 emerged from San Francisco as put forth at Dumbarton Oaks, potent enough to justify fully the expression of the
delegates that it "manifests our deep trust in the Secretary-
General to perform his tasks impartially and in the interests of the
world at large." [20]

The Preparatory Commission moderately expanded the body of
official interpretation of Article 99. It was pointed out, in its
Executive Committee discussions, that, as regards political disputes, the cases in which the Secretary-General would find it
necessary to exercise the functions in point might well be rare.
Normally, some state could be expected to raise a situation threatening the peace before the Security Council.[21] Article 99 was
seen of "very great political importance from a broader point of
view. The Secretary-General's function encompassed the reporting of *any* developments — for example, in the economic and
social field — which in his view could have serious political implications remediable only by political action. In holding this responsibility, the Secretary-General formed a vital link between
the various units of the Organization." [22] And in its Report, the
Commission notes that Article 99 endows the Secretary-General
with "a quite special right which goes beyond any power previously accorded to the head of an international organization." [23]

A last source of governmental commentary upon the article are
the summary records of the remarkably interesting meetings of
the Committee of Experts of the Security Council, held in May
1946, in which the Council's rules of procedure were revised.
(The Committee of Experts is composed of the representatives
of the members of the Security Council; as a rule, of the chief
legal officers attached to each of the eleven delegations.) The
central issue was the character of the rights of intervention in
the Security Council's proceedings which the Secretary-General

should enjoy. There were, however, a number of comments on Article 99 of the most important substance and, at first glance, of the most surprising authorship.

Professor Boris Stein, of the Soviet Union, in proposing an unrestricted right of intervention by the Secretary-General, "pointed out the difference in the conception of the powers accorded the Secretary-General of the United Nations as opposed to those accorded the Secretary-General of the League of Nations. Specifically, he noted the additional powers given the Secretary-General under Article 99." [24] His Polish colleague, Dr. Alexander Rudzinski (who since has received asylum in the United States), went on to say in substance that "when the Secretary-General considered that there was a threat to international peace and security, Article 99 of the Charter conferred special powers upon him which put him in the same position as a sovereign state. . . Furthermore, under Article 99 . . . the Secretary-General had the power to submit [to the Security Council] proposals and draft resolutions." [25]

In reply, the representative of the United States, Professor Joseph E. Johnson, doubted "whether the Secretary-General had the right to draft specific resolutions and proposals under Article 99." But he emphasized his "Government's interest in building up the strength of the Secretary-General within the provisions of Article 98" [26] (which speaks of the "capacity" in which the Secretary-General shall act in his relations with the Security Council). Professor Johnson's suggestion that the committee's discussions did no more than establish "the minimum rules on the basis of which the Secretary-General's role could be developed in practice" and did not constitute a "definitive definition" of his rights under Article 99 was agreed to without difficulty.

The discussion was in fact hardly definitive with respect to Article 99. The breadth of initiative attributed to the Secretary-General by the representative of Poland is nonetheless provocative. It would raise absorbing questions regarding the meaning of the ardency of Warsaw's pro-Secretary-General feeling, if Dr. Rudzinski had not stated later that "my view concerning the rights of the Secretary-General under Article 99 was entirely my own." Dr. Rudzinski adds that he acted in the committee "almost without instructions," but that his delegation chief, Ambassador Oscar Lange, who gave him Poland's broad policy concerning the role of the Secretary-General "on the spot, without asking Warsaw," seemed to regard Mr. Lie as a man "who may be trusted to make the best use of his powers." Dr. Lange "consented gladly to my doing my best to strengthen his [Mr. Lie's] position." Dr. Lange's attitude toward Mr. Lie, Dr. Rudzinski suggests, was perhaps "determined by a kind of good will of a Socialist towards another Socialist."

The substance of Dr. Rudzinski's views, their author notes, met with "little enthusiasm." Even Professor Stein, who in these meetings pressed for a generous construction of the Secretary-General's rights, "was a little startled and taken aback." [27] Dr. Rudzinski, however, in the light of the development of the Secretary-General's role in practice, appears as no extremist, for Mr. Lie has in considerable measure realized his views.

In summary, seven interlocking powers flowing from Article 99 and its official exposition may be reasonably distinguished:

1. The evident authority of the Secretary-General to bring to the attention of the Security Council any matter which in his opinion may threaten the maintenance of international peace and security. In this, when taken together with Article 98, the position of the Secretary-General may be said to approximate that of a twelfth member of the Security Council, without veto or vote. Or his situation may be likened to that of a member state under Article 35,[28] which may similarly have placed upon the provisional agenda of the Security Council any dispute or situation it sees endangering the peace.

The Secretary-General's prerogative here extends further, in fact, for he may place "any matter" on the provisional agenda, not just any dispute or situation. And, though the Secretary-General, like a state, can place a question on the Council's provisional agenda only — the Council always remaining master of its working agenda — it seems highly improbable that the Council would refuse to take up an item submitted by the Secretary-General under Article 99. But the Council has been known to reject items placed on its provisional agenda by a member state.

More impressive still, the Secretary-General may be compared to the whole of the General Assembly, which likewise "may call the attention of the Security Council to situations which are likely to endanger international peace and security." [29]

It does not demand searching analysis, however, to demonstrate that, narrowly viewed, the Secretary-General's rights in this respect, while an important part of his powers, are not actually of great moment on the international scene. Normally, as the Preparatory Commission pointed out, a state may be expected to raise before the Council a situation or dispute which may threaten the peace. The occasions upon which the Secretary-General will be impelled to exercise formally his powers under Article 99, as the circumstances of the situation and the record of the Organization combine to demonstrate, will be rare — so far, Article 99 has been expressly invoked but once. And in this case (Korea) it was more the United States than the Secretary-General that initially drew the crisis to the Council's attention.

Moreover, the influence the Secretary-General would be likely to exert by invoking the article evidently would be severely limited by the facts of present-day international life. Such influence would not be inconsequential; it could have notable moral impact; but it would not have, of itself, more than moral force behind it.

2. Article 99 is more important as the prime and unmistakable affirmation of the political character of the Secretary-General. The power it confers, taken together with his strategic world position as the chief permanent officer of the United Nations and as the individual who "more than anyone else . . . stand[s] for the United Nations as a whole," constitutes, particularly when blended with Article 98, the broad legal base for the Secretary-General's political personality.

3. The fact that his authority under Article 99 extends to "the reporting of *any* developments — for example, in the economic or social field — which in his view could have serious political implications remediable only by political action" gives the Secretary-General the character of a "vital link" between the Security Council and the other organs of the Organization.[30]

4. Evidently, the Secretary-General would choose to exercise

his powers under Article 99 only upon the basis of full and impartial data concerning the matter in point. From this assumption it reasonably follows that the Secretary-General has the right to make such inquiries and investigations as he may think necessary in order to determine whether or not to invoke his powers; in fact, his assertion of this right in the course of Security Council proceedings went unchallenged and was even acknowledged.[31] The intriguing possibilities of such investigations are obvious.[32]

5. Furthermore, there can be said to flow from the discretionary nature of the Secretary-General's power under Article 99 his right to choose the most appropriate means of implementing the article. As a matter of strategy, he may exert his influence so that it will not be necessary for him formally to bring the matter in question to the attention of the Security Council. Article 99, in other words, may be interpreted as providing a specific legal justification for that extensive, informal, behind-the-scenes political activity of the Secretary-General for which the essential character of his office, and the precedent of the League, provide a more general basis. The option of attributing certain of that activity more or less directly to the Charter's text could well prove valuable to a Secretary-General under fire.

6. Article 99, moreover, could be called into play as the authorizing clause of declarations, proposals, and draft resolutions which the Secretary-General may wish to offer in connection with the Security Council's work. The Secretary-General has formally submitted several proposals, a draft resolution, and amendments to another resolution, in the course of the Security Council's proceedings. The amendments, and the proposal implied in his statement to the Council of June 25, 1950, concerning the invasion of South Korea, can be viewed as well within the ambit of Article 99. The express citation of Article 99 as the basis of the more boldly political participation of the Secretary-General in the work of the Security Council, with regard to his suggesting draft resolutions and making proposals, is largely a virgin field of influence which the Secretary-General might, if the need arises, find himself capable of exploiting.

7. Finally, Article 99 supplies the Secretary-General with a Security Council springboard for a dramatic appeal to world

public opinion fully comparable to that provided in the case of the General Assembly by the annual-report provision of Article 98. An appeal under Article 99 would, indeed, tend to be of greater intensity, though of lesser breadth and diversity, than that contained in the introduction to the annual report. The Secretary-General of the United Nations calling upon the Security Council, in the full blaze of world publicity, to meet what he, as the servant of all the nations, sees as a threat to the peace, has qualities of high drama which could considerably influence international popular feeling in the direction the Secretary-General considers desirable. Were such an appeal well chosen, well timed, and colorfully staged, Article 99 might after all prove itself as a weapon to which even the colossi of the cold war would find it advantageous to adjust their policies.

### Article 98

*The Secretary-General shall act in that capacity in all meetings of the General Assembly, of the Security Council, of the Economic and Social Council, and of the Trusteeship Council, and shall perform such other functions as are entrusted to him by these organs. The Secretary-General shall make an annual report to the General Assembly on the work of the Organization.*

Discussion of Article 98 at San Francisco was minimal. It was unanimously agreed that the Secretary-General could deputize his functions under the article so that his assistants might act for him in his capacity at the Assembly and Councils. More important was the feeling of the Conference that Article 98 should be kept sufficiently broad [33] "to cover all functions" of the Secretary-General.[34] Article 98 is indeed broad, the vagueness of its first sentence leading to a variety of interpretations.

The provision that "the Secretary-General shall act in that capacity in all meetings of the General Assembly, of the Security Council, of the Economic and Social Council, and of the Trusteeship Council" is precise insofar as it specifies "all" meetings: a precaution of demonstrated foresight in view of the difficulties of Mr. Lie in acting in any capacity at all at the meetings of the Security Council's Military Staff Committee. Article 98 is further "unambiguous in protecting him [the Secretary-General] against the rise of rival Secretaries-General attached to the several councils . . . [it confirms] the fact of his single leadership and of the unity of the Secretariat's functions under his direction." [35] But what is less clear is what capacity is "that capacity" in which the Secretary-General shall act. Literally, the phrase would seem to depend upon the sentence which immediately precedes it in the Charter: the Secretary-General shall be "the chief administrative officer of the Organization." The Secretary-General, however, by the terms of Article 99, clearly is more than the chief administrative officer.

A partial definition of the actual nature of the Secretary-General's capacity may be had by considering the rules of procedure of the organs in question — a definition which will be filled out later with a consideration of the active precedent developed by the Secretary-General in his relations with these organs. The provisional rules were drafted by the Preparatory Commission, while the permanent rules were hammered out by the organs themselves. The latter process constituted an important phase of the pragmatic development of the Secretary-General's powers, both because of the broadened view of his capacity which the permanent rules set forth and because of the initiative of the Secretary-General in promoting that broadened view.

The rules of procedure, provisional and permanent, may, with respect to the Secretary-General, be seen as falling into two categories: those specifying routine duties of a nondiscretionary nature, such as the provision and direction of the necessary staff, the custody of documents, and the like, and those involving an element of political discretion. The Preparatory Commission discussions concerning the latter evolved differing privileges for the various organs.

The provisional rules of the General Assembly provided that "the Secretary-General may at any time, upon the invitation of the President, make to the General Assembly either oral or written statements concerning any question which is being considered by the General Assembly," and that among the items of the Assembly's provisional agenda shall be "all items which the Secretary-General deems it necessary to put before the General

Assembly." [36] The importance of defining the Secretary-General's Assembly capacity so as to include the right of making oral or written statements on any question considered is evident. His right to place items on its provisional agenda also awards valuable leverage: it constitutes, in fact, something of a counterpart to his Security Council privileges under Article 99 (for the rules do not specify that the questions submitted by the Secretary-General must be nonpolitical).

One point of interest raised in the Preparatory Commission's drafting of the provisional rules was the suggestion of the Commission's secretariat that the Secretary-General should preside at the opening of each session of the Assembly. The delegates viewed the proposal as "in line with parliamentary practice and in conformity with the special position accorded the Secretary-General under the Charter." [37] But consideration of the duties which the holding of the temporary Assembly Presidency would impose upon the Secretary-General, such as proposing the names of the delegates for the Credentials and Nominating Committees, impelled the Commission to take up unanimously the suggestion of the French delegate that the Assembly be opened by the chairman of that delegation from which the President of the previous session had been selected. [38]

The draft rules which the Preparatory Commission prepared for the Security Council reiterate Article 99 [39] and provide that "the provisional agenda for each meeting shall be drawn up by the Secretary-General and approved by the President of the Council." [40] Taken together, these provisions most certainly assure the Secretary-General the right of submitting items for the Council's agenda; moreover, his drawing up the provisional agenda affords the Secretary-General a modicum of discretion in influencing the Council's priority of consideration. [41] The authority of the Secretary-General to participate orally and by written communication in the Council's proceedings was not set forth in the draft rules but was won under circumstances fully described later. [42]

The provisional rules of procedure of the Economic and Social Council prescribe that the "provisional agenda . . . shall be drawn up by the Secretary-General in consultation with the President" [43] and that among its points shall be "all items and reports which . . . the Secretary-General deems necessary to put before the Council." [44] The Secretary-General may also make oral or written statements, upon the invitation of the presiding officer, to the Council or its subsidiaries concerning any question under consideration. [45] The provisional rules drafted by the Preparatory Commission for the Trusteeship Council, with respect to the Secretary-General, are virtually the same as those of the Economic and Social Council. [46]

The last clause of the first sentence of Article 98 adds that, in addition to acting in his capacity in the Assembly and the Councils, the Secretary-General "shall perform such other functions as are entrusted to him by these organs." The sense of this is clear; and, indeed, other functions have been bestowed upon the Secretary-General. He has, for example, been designated as potential rapporteur, that is to say, mediator, by the Security Council.

The clause could prove meaningful in a subtler respect, however. If the Secretary-General is to perform such other functions as are entrusted to him, it could be held that he is *not* to assume any functions relating to the activities of these organs *not* so entrusted to him. This restrictive interpretation of the Secretary-General's authority has not been formally affirmed by any member, but it has been bruited about informally [47] and might be called forth more determinedly in the future. (That is not to say that this absence of challenge is in deference to the powers specifically conferred upon the Secretary-General by Article 98; it rather flows from a liberal interpretation of the general powers conferred by Article 97.)

The Charter, it may be noted, offers further possibilities for those who would restrict the development of the authority of the Secretary-General. The Charter's basic characterization of the Secretary-General merely as "the chief administrative officer of the Organization" (Article 97) may be so interpreted as to pare down considerably the political prerogative afforded by Articles 99 and 98. And a subtler weapon with which to oppose the growth of the international executive is provided by the provision of Article 2 that "the Organization is based on the principle of the sovereign equality of all its Members." But these restrictive possibilities are easily overstressed. The Secretary-General's range of political activity is delimited far more by the facts and biases of the international situation than by such legal inhibitions.

"The Secretary-General," concludes Article 98, "shall make an annual report to the General Assembly on the work of the Organization." [48] The importance of the annual report has already been touched upon in evaluating the experience of the Secretaries-General of the League and the Directors of the I.L.O. At the very least, it provides the immediate setting for the Assembly's deliberations; at most, it can give those deliberations direction. Whether the annual report will do one or both of these things largely depends upon the Secretary-General's concept of his role in "the work of the Organization." As will be shown, Mr. Lie's concept involves offering critical appraisal and vigorous suggestion. In his hands, the annual report has become a vital document.

## Article 97

*The Secretariat shall comprise a Secretary-General and such staff as the Organization may require. The Secretary-General shall be appointed by the General Assembly upon the recommendation of the Security Council. He shall be the chief administrative officer of the Organization.*

That "the Secretariat shall comprise a Secretary-General and such staff as the Organization may require" of itself bears little comment. It is the assertion of the existence of the Secretary-General; more than that, it is of interest in its distinguishing among the whole of the Secretariat the Secretary-General alone.[49] The direct affirmation of his administrative preëminence with which Article 97 concludes is here suggested by the singling out of the Secretary-General.

His uniqueness in this respect was not taken for granted at San Francisco. The four sponsoring governments — China, the United Kingdom, the United States, and the Soviet Union — introduced an amendment to the relevant Dumbarton Oaks draft.[50] The amendment provided for four deputies, to be elected, together with the Secretary-General, by the General Assembly on the Security Council's recommendation, for three-year terms. The

Secretary-General would be eligible for reëlection; the Deputy
Secretaries-General would not.

When this amendment ran into strong opposition, the sponsoring Powers modified their proposal so as to increase the number of proposed Deputy Secretaries to five and to make them
eligible for reëlection.[51] The U.S.S.R., apparently desirous of
assuring that one of these posts be allotted to a Soviet national,
took the lead in pressing for provision for five, rather than four,
deputies.

The Great Powers pointed out, in advancing their amendments,
that the need of deputies is evident, that the number suggested
would aptly cover the four principal organs and leave a fifth
deputy as the Secretary-General's alternate, and that their mode
of election would give the deputies considerable prestige while
protecting the international character of the Secretariat.[52] Im-
plicit in their reasoning was the recognition of the importance of
the higher Secretariat posts and the corresponding desire to
secure, through the elective process, political control of those
posts.

The Small and Middle Powers downed the amendments of the
Great with a barrage of more convincing argument. They did not
dispute the necessity of deputies, but concentrated their fire upon
specifying their number and upon the mode of selection. It was
impossible, they held, to foresee the number needed, which
would depend upon the evolution of the Secretariat.[53] (As it
turned out, eight Assistant Secretaries-General were appointed,
in accordance with the recommendation of the Preparatory
Commission; and a ninth Assistant Secretaryship General was
created by Mr. Lie in 1948, on an experimental basis, and abolished later that year.) Moreover, charged the delegate of New
Zealand, the fact that four deputies and a Secretary-General were
called for "would almost certainly mean that these officials would
be nationals of the permanent members of the Security Council
— which would produce a crisis in the Secretariat at the beginning of its work." [54] The election of the deputies rather than their
appointment by the Secretary-General would tend to inhibit relations between the latter and subordinates enjoying political
endorsement equal to his own; [55] the Secretary-General's effecting

of his duties could be hampered if, as feared, decisions on important administrative matters would have to be taken by a committee of five. If the deputies would not be eligible for reëlection, their turnover would introduce marked instability in the long-term functioning of the Secretariat. And far from insuring the Secretariat's international character, the political aspects of the election of the deputies would corrode it.[56]

The amendments were defeated; and the first thoughts of the sponsoring Powers on the question, as revealed in their Dumbarton Oaks draft, were ratified by the San Francisco majority over their protest. It may well be that the unhappy experience of the League with Under Secretaries-General of political background was a factor in the vigor of the Small Power revolt. But, in a sense, the Great Powers snatched some elements of victory from defeat when they later apportioned five of the Assistant Secretary-General posts among themselves.

The provision that the "Secretary-General shall be appointed by the General Assembly upon the recommendation of the Security Council" is the end product of a second lively San Francisco debate, which concerned itself with two interlocking issues: the term of office of the Secretary-General and his mode of selection. The former was purposefully not resolved and was left to the ingenuity of the Preparatory Commission. The procedure of choosing the Secretary-General was for the most part decided upon after something of a struggle — the Great Powers, with certain rational as well as political strength on their side this time, prevailing.

The sponsoring governments proposed that the term of the Secretary-General be three years and that he be eligible for re-election. There was a countercurrent of considerable strength in the direction of either a five-year term or no Charter definition of term at all. Supporters of the latter view argued that the Organization should not be bound by the Charter in this respect, but, like the League of Nations, be free to determine the length of office as conditions might warrant. The three-year suggestion with provision of eligibility for reëlection was initially approved in committee, however, the majority feeling being that it pro-

vided an "adequate method of attracting outstanding candidates
. . . and at the same time protecting the Organization from the
lengthy tenure of an unsuitable Secretary-General." [57]

Approval was won in the knowledge that a second committee
had voted that the veto would not apply to the recommendation
of the Security Council upon which the Assembly's appointment
of the Secretary-General would be based. That vote was over-
turned on the initiative of the Great Powers. It was decided that
all five of the permanent members would have to be among the
recommending majority. "The new ruling," the delegate of the
Netherlands thereupon warned, "would compel the permanent
members to reach a compromise, and this might result in the
appointment of the 'lowest common denominator.' Furthermore,
the Secretary-General would work in the knowledge that his
chances of re-election would be small if he were to incur the dis-
pleasure of one of the permanent members." [58] The necessity of
the unanimous agreement of the permanent members for the re-
election of the Secretary-General every three years would either
deprive him of his independence or force him to leave office at a
time when his experience would be most useful to the Organization.[59] The Netherlands delegate therefore moved the rescinding
of the earlier decisions, the Charter to prescribe no term, and his
motion passed with ease.[60]

Before the vote was taken, the delegate of New Zealand pointed
out that, if the Dutch motion were carried, the terms of the Secretary-General's appointment would be worked out by agreement
between the Security Council and the General Assembly. The
delegate of the United States was assured, moreover, that when
these terms came up for settlement, the principle of unanimity
among the permanent members of the Council would be observed.

The fears expressed by the Dutch delegate were anticipated in
the debate over whether the veto would after all apply to the
Security Council's recommendation. All sorts of suggestions were
put forth alternative to the plan of the Assembly's passing on the
Council's vetoable nomination,[61] and the pernicious possibilities
of the unanimity rule were colorfully and repeatedly set forth.
But the Great Powers successfully responded by maintaining that
the value of a Secretary-General who did not enjoy the confidence

of the permanent members of the Security Council would be distinctly limited.

The consideration at San Francisco of Article 97, finally, concluded, first, with a move to define the Assembly's election of the Secretary-General as a question requiring a two-thirds vote. The election was not included in Article 18's listing of questions demanding a two-thirds vote, however, and later the Assembly specified that a simple majority of its members present and voting would suffice.[62] And secondly, on the motion of the Netherlands, the phrase, "The Secretary-General shall be elected," as the Dumbarton Oaks draft put it, was altered to read "The Secretary-General shall be appointed" in order "to emphasize the administrative nature" of the office.[63]

It was left to the Preparatory Commission to work out the length and terms of the Secretary-General's appointment, its salient recommendations then being adopted by the First Session of the General Assembly.[64] The Commission recommended, unanimously, though without enthusiasm — after lengthily debating the merits of three-, five-, seven-, and ten-year terms — that "the first Secretary-General should be appointed for five years, the appointment being open for renewal at the end of that period for a further five-year term." The same rules that governed the original appointment were to apply to a renewal of appointment. It was agreed that "it would be preferable that the Secretary-General's appointment should be renewed only once on the general ground that from time to time a change in the personality, and a rotation in the nationality, of the Secretary-General would be desirable." [65] "There being no stipulation on the subject in the Charter," the Commission added, "the General Assembly and the Security Council [66] are free to modify the term of office of future Secretaries-General in the light of experience." Moreover, "it would be desirable for the Security Council to proffer one candidate only for the consideration of the General Assembly, and for debate on the nomination . . . to be avoided." [67] Discussion should be in private and voting in secret (an injunction honored in the breach when the Assembly appointed Mr. Lie at a public meeting).

The Commission further suggested that since "the Secretary-General is a confidant of many governments . . . no Member should offer him, at any rate immediately on retirement, any governmental position in which his confidential information might be a source of embarrassment to other Members, and on his part a Secretary-General should refrain from accepting any such position." Presumably to relieve the Secretary-General of any financial strain he might incur in carrying out this recommendation — and there might well be such a strain, considering that the Secretary-General's training and experience would in all likelihood be governmental — it was subsequently decided, at the Assembly's London Session, that the Secretary-General would be granted, upon retirement, a life pension of half his salary. The Assembly doubtless found the League experience instructive in this regard: it is said that Sir Eric Drummond accepted the post of Ambassador of the United Kingdom at Rome, after he had retired as Secretary-General, in response, in some measure at least, to financial pressure. Sir Eric's decision did not of course enhance the usefulness or prestige of the Secretaryship General; [68] and it seems to have embarrassed the League's Ethiopian effort.

Finally, it was recommended that the conditions of appointment of the Secretary-General should "be such as to enable a man of eminence and high attainment to accept and maintain the position." To this end, the Preparatory Commission suggested that the Secretary-General receive a net salary of $20,000 per year, an expense allowance of the same amount,[69] and a furnished residence provided by the Organization.

How the $20,000 figure was arrived at is an interesting, if minor, point. "It was suggested," the pertinent report relates, "that the Secretary-General should be paid rather more than the top officials in the most highly paid national service, but not necessarily as much as the Ambassador of an important country. It was important not to give public opinion the impression that the officials of the Organization were overpaid. At the same time, it was difficult to give the Secretary-General a salary lower than that which had already been laid down for the head of a Specialized Agency, and above all the salary must be such that a man of great eminence could afford to accept the post. . . It was agreed to take the figure of 20,000 United States Dollars as a starting point." [70]

The election of the Secretary-General by the Assembly upon the "qualified" recommendation of the Security Council is probably about as good a compromise between the desiderata of securing a world-wide endorsement and of insuring unanimous Great Power sponsorship as could be devised — provided that the permanent members can achieve unanimity. Moreover, the nomination by the Security Council of but a single candidate, in effect selected by negotiation, in closed meeting, enables the Secretary-General to assume office unembarrassed by the inevitable casualties that would result from a public election campaign. [71]

The Charter's specifying no term of office is all to the good, since it enables the Organization to fit the Secretary-General's tenure to its needs and experience. [72] However, some definition of tenure is necessary to establish his independence of the policies of the member states, particularly if the Secretary-General is to undertake a measure of political activity. As a study of the Carnegie Endowment for International Peace aptly puts it, "To have provided that [the Secretary-General] serve at the will of the Assembly would have placed him in sharp dependence upon a fluctuating majority among the national delegations, and would have made almost every vote upon an issue in which he had taken the initiative or otherwise exerted his leadership as a vote of confidence directly affecting his role as chief executive." [73] The five-year term proposed by the Preparatory Commission and adopted by the Assembly provided the necessary definition of tenure. It does so, moreover, with a term long enough for the Secretary-General to "take hold" and yet not so long that he will not be kept sensitively in touch with the political realities which must constitute the material of his work.

The study just cited goes on to point out perceptively in this latter regard that "to have followed League precedent by providing for a ten-year term would not, as might at first be supposed, have added to [the Secretary-General's] strength. Instead, this almost permanent appointment (considering the most likely age for appointment) would have served to minimize his political role. The requirement that the Secretary-General receive a new franchise for the continued exercise of his leadership after five years seems entirely consistent with the premise that he should be a strong chief executive and that he should be more than a neutral and impartial civil servant." [74]

There is, of course, a less subtle position on the question of reëlection, not without cogency. That is, that the Secretary-General's freedom of action will be understandably modified by the necessity (and this applies only to his first term) of considering that to antagonize deeply one of the permanent members would be to jeopardize or even eliminate his chances of reëlection. That the first Secretary-General was not deterred from doing his duty as he saw it either by the explicit threat to block his reappointment made by Nationalist China on June 22, 1950,[75] or by the assaults of Soviet Russia which began three days later,[76] is both a tribute to Mr. Lie and an expression of the peculiar circumstances surrounding his continuance in office. The Soviet exercise of the veto in October of that year did in fact preclude the reëlection of the Secretary-General, the Assembly falling back, in the absence of a qualified Security Council recommendation, upon the lame device of extending his term of office.

The terms of appointment are open to criticism on grounds of two possible errors of omission. There is no provision for removal of a Secretary-General who might prove unfaithful to his oath, incompetent, or insane. Nor, should the permanent members of the Security Council prove unable to agree upon a nominee for the Secretaryship General, is there provision for resolving or even temporarily overcoming the deadlock.

With regard to the lesser of these two evils, the lack of a removal clause, the British, with characteristic caution and, more, with a recollection of their differences with M. Avenol in 1940, raised the issue when the Executive Committee of the Preparatory Commission was sitting in London. They proposed that the Security Council be empowered to suspend the Secretary-General, should the need arise, as an emergency measure, subject to veto; and that the General Assembly have the right to dismiss the Secretary-General by a two-thirds vote.[77] But in the face of the majority feeling that no removal clause was necessary since "there was little real danger of the Secretary-General remaining in office if a serious rift developed between himself and the Member states," [78] the United Kingdom withdrew its suggestion (with the effect, Leo Pasvolsky reports, of influencing the delegates in favor of a five-year term rather than a longer period of office [79]). Undoubtedly, there is "little real danger"; and a removal proviso could even prove pernicious if there were the chance of its being interpreted as a weapon of recall rather than as an emergency means of removal "for cause." [80]

More serious is the absence, from both the Charter and the terms of appointment, of any method of overcoming the failure of the Security Council to recommend a candidate for appointment.[81] Veto of proposals commanding majority support, or the inability of proposals even to muster majority support, are not unknown in the proceedings of the Council. The General Assembly was confronted with both of these eventualities, and accordingly no recommendation, when the impending expiration of the term of office of the first Secretary-General absorbed its attention in October 1950.

Several avenues of escape are open. First of all, assuming the incumbent Secretary-General to be willing to continue to serve, the Assembly may extend (not renew) his term. This is the most inviting way out, and the one that the Assembly followed in 1950. This avenue, however, has two forks, and the Assembly would seem to have chosen the one more exposed to legal attack.

The Assembly, which modified and accepted the Preparatory Commission's recommendations regarding the length of the Secretary-General's term of office, might well have modified them again. It might simply have altered the incumbent's term from five years to seven or eight or whatever number of years it pleased. Since the only basis of the five-year term is the Assembly's resolution adopting the Preparatory Commission's recommendations, and since it is indisputably within the province of the Assembly to amend its own resolution, it could legally have extended the Secretary-General's term of office for, say, three years by resolving that the length of that term shall be not five years but eight.[82]

This, however, the Assembly did not do. Rather, it employed a method of extension more frank, if legally less sound. It noted the

Security Council's inability to agree upon a nominee; considered "the necessity to ensure the uninterrupted exercise of the functions vested by the Charter in the office of the Secretary-General"; further noted Mr. Lie's initial appointment upon the recommendation of the Council; and decided "that the present Secretary-General shall be continued in office for a period of three years." [83]

The Assembly apparently did not alter its earlier resolution setting the Secretary-General's term at five years. Rather, it extended the term of "the present Secretary-General." It concerned itself not with the office, but with the man. It legislated not with general regard to the Secretaryship General, but with particular regard to Mr. Lie.

Legally speaking, it is one thing to lengthen the term of an office and another to prescribe that the present occupant of an office shall continue to hold it after his term expires, without changing the length of the office's term except, by implication, with respect to that present occupant. It is difficult to see how this latter course, as here followed by the General Assembly, much differed from the Assembly's arrogating to itself the right to appoint Mr. Lie to an additional three-year term. Yet nowhere was it claimed that the Assembly could appoint or reappoint the Secretary-General in the absence of a recommendation from the Security Council.

Those delegations which supported the resolution to continue Mr. Lie in office advanced a variety of political and legal arguments in its favor. The political arguments were much the stronger and are considered in Chapter 8. As to the legalities of extending the Secretary-General's term in the fashion followed by the Assembly, three prime points were made by the resolution's proponents:

1. The Charter must be interpreted so as to make it effective. The principle of the effectiveness of treaties in this instance requires the uninterrupted exercise of the functions of the Secretary-General. Since the appointment of a Secretary-General is blocked by the absence of a Security Council recommendation, emergency measures must be taken.[84]

2. The Assembly is the organ which may properly take these measures. It determines the length of the Secretary-General's

term — the fact that the existing term of office was set by it indicates that. And it is both the most representative organ and the organ of residuary powers. Article 10 of the Charter authorizes it to make recommendations [85] "relating to the powers and functions of any organs," of which, of course, the Secretary-General is one.[86]

3. The Charter does not prohibit continuing the Secretary-General in office. "There is no use pretending that it is provided for in the Charter, but there is nothing in the Charter to forbid it." [87]

The opposition to the resolution, led by Mr. Vishinsky, concentrated its fire on the fragility of the conception of extension. It argued, on the one hand, that the concept of extension was nowhere to be found in the Charter, and, on the other, that extension equated with reappointment. Thus, the Assembly's very consideration of the question was illegal in the absence of a recommendation from the Security Council; it was a matter of reappointment, and it therefore had to wait upon the Council's prior positive action.[88] The Charter must be so interpreted that it would be not merely effective, but legally effective; the role of the Security Council in the reappointment of the Secretary-General could not be legally evaded by calling that reappointment an extension; and it cannot be assumed that all that is not forbidden by the Charter is permissible.[89] "It is true," suggested the delegate of Syria, "that the Charter neither allows nor prohibits such an extension. But there is a procedure set forth in the Charter for the appointment of a Secretary-General. It is therefore the legal procedure, and any other is out of order." [90]

To attempt to pass definitive judgment upon the precise legality of the Assembly's action, in view of the 46 votes cast in its favor, would be an exercise more academic than the Assembly debate itself (for the extension of Mr. Lie's term was by that stage never in doubt). On the evidence presented, perhaps the majority made out the better legal case in an episode which in reality turned on questions of high politics and not of fine law. But no one could censure the delegation of Australia for having had "genuine doubts." [91]

Such doubts might have been more widespread had the opponents of the Secretary-General's continuance in office been more diligent in examining the records of the San Francisco Conference which relate to the drafting of Article 97.[92] Mr. Vishinsky might have quoted with effect the following comment of an American Secretary of State upon the intent of that drafting: "It was agreed that no provision be made in the Charter concerning the term of office. It was understood by the Committee that in the absence of any mention of the term of the Secretary-General this matter would be subject to agreement between the Security Council and the General Assembly. It was also understood that the concurring votes of the permanent members of the Security Council would be required in any decision on this question." [93]

At first glance, these embarrassing words of the chief American delegate to the San Francisco Conference would seem to brand as out of order the unilateral action taken five years later by the General Assembly in altering the tenure of the present Secretary-General — an action of which the United States was the prime mover. However, while the intention of the San Francisco delegates regarding the meaning of Article 97 obviously conflicts with the Assembly's extension of Mr. Lie's term, that intention, being expressed not in the Charter but only in its preparatory work, would not necessarily be given overriding legal force by a judicial body which might be called upon to adjudge the legality of the Secretary-General's continued tenure.[94] The Secretary-General's supporters, moreover, could point to the precedent of the Assembly's initially having set the term of the Secretary-General without consulting the Security Council — a procedure to which the Security Council took no exception. If the Assembly's unilateral action of 1950 in altering the tenure of the Secretary-General was illegal because of the lack of formal agreement with the Security Council, then equally illegal was its action in 1946 which set the Secretary-General's term at five years. But no member or organ of the Organization suggested during the years 1946–1950 that the Secretary-General held office illegally.

It might indeed be argued that the Secretary-General's tenure was the subject of an implied agreement between the Security Council and the General Assembly, in that the former made no objection to either the lack of an express agreement or to the term which the General Assembly adopted. Moreover, in 1950, when the Security Council voted upon a proposal to reappoint Mr. Lie, there was no mention of the term of the proposed reappointment. Apparently that was left to be settled by a resolution of the General Assembly, as it had been settled on the previous occasion in 1946.

In the course of the debate, Egypt and Syria suggested an interesting alternative to the extension of the incumbent's term. Egypt first posited that the Security Council, once it conceded failure to agree upon a recommendation, "exhausted its competence." The Council abandoned its competence in favor of the Assembly, passing it, "entire and intact," into the Assembly's hands.[95] The Assembly's competence was then not limited to a certain proposal or a certain candidate (that is, to the extension of the incumbent's term). To so limit the Assembly might give rise to a situation where, in the continued absence of Security Council agreement, the only course open would be the perpetuating of the term of the present Secretary-General.[96] The unfettered competence of the Assembly being thus established, it could consider a number of candidates. "Is it necessary," demanded Faris el-Khouri Bey, "for the Security Council to recommend . . . one candidate only?" The Council, he suggested, should pass on to the Assembly the names of all the candidates who enjoyed substantial support among its membership — the permanent members in this instance refraining from exercising the veto. The candidate receiving a majority of the Assembly's votes would then be appointed.[97]

There is nothing legally amiss with this latter proposal. To be sure, the original Assembly resolution governing the terms of appointment of the Secretary-General notes that "it would be desirable for the Security Council to proffer one candidate only for the consideration of the General Assembly," [98] but the Assembly may alter that resolution. The difficulty is not legal but political. It is unlikely that the permanent members of the Council would so consent to surrendering the greater part of their power in the choice of the Secretary-General. Any permanent member could block such a surrender at will by the exercise of its veto.

Of course, if one carries to its logical conclusion the debatable Egyptian theory that the Security Council, in throwing up its hands, abandons its competence in the Assembly's favor, then the Assembly might proceed to appoint whom it chooses, unhindered by the lack of any Security Council recommendation.

There are still other possibilities. Theoretically speaking, there might be an *ad hoc* agreement among the Great Powers, perhaps ratified by an Assembly vote, that the incumbent serve until the deadlock is broken. Or the Assembly alone might simply resolve that "the present Secretary-General shall be continued in office until the Security Council is able to agree on a recommendation to the General Assembly" — a proposal in fact made by the representative of Nationalist China.[99] In the last resort, in the absence of any sort of decision, it might be that the Secretary-General would continue in office pending action by the Council or the Assembly or both. The psychological and administrative weakness of these last possibilities is obvious.

All these improvisations, including extension of the incumbent's term of office, disappear, however, if the Secretary-General's service is cut short by death or incapacity.[100] The desirability of an advance provision for overriding a stalemate among the permanent members is evident: perhaps some ingeniously balanced political solution involving an Assembly vote; or the referral of the issue to the resolution of a "detached" body such as the International Court of Justice; or, at least, prescription that the Assistant Secretaries-General rotate in office pending agreement among the permanent members.[101]

The Secretary-General, concludes Article 97, "shall be the chief administrative officer of the Organization." The administrative supremacy foreshadowed by the first sentence of Article 97, and elaborated in Articles 98 and 101, is thus affirmed. This supreme administrative position of itself carries a modest political potency. The normal work of the Secretariat, under the Secretary-General's ultimate direction, for example, in preparing the documentation, the draft reports, the summaries, and the working papers, which constitute much of the frame of reference within which the delegations take decisions, inevitably exercises an indirect influence upon those decisions. As the Report of the Preparatory Commission puts it: "While the responsibility for the framing and adoption of agreed international policies rests with the organs representative of the Members . . . the essential tasks of preparing the ground for those decisions and of executing them in coöperation with the Members will devolve largely upon the Secretariat. The manner in which the Secretariat performs these tasks will largely determine the degree in which the objectives of the Charter will be realized." [102] Similar examples of the political side of the Secretary-General's administrative personality can be cited almost without number.

Nevertheless, Article 97's generalized description of what the Secretary-General shall be says nothing of his political character, which is left to the interpretation of Article 98 and the terms and implications of Article 99. The description is totally and inescapably administrative. It serves to emphasize the view of the authors of the Charter that, while the Secretary-General is to be more than the Organization's first functionary, he is also to be that functionary. Its stress of the Secretary-General's administrative responsibility tends to put his political authority in more subdued perspective.

### Article 101

*1. The staff shall be appointed by the Secretary-General under regulations established by the General Assembly.*

*2. Appropriate staffs shall be permanently assigned to the Economic and Social Council, the Trusteeship Council, and, as required, to other organs of the United Nations. These staffs shall form a part of the Secretariat.*

*3. The paramount consideration in the employment of the staff and in the determination of the conditions of service shall be the necessity of securing the highest standards of efficiency, competence, and integrity. Due regard shall be paid to the importance of recruiting the staff on as wide a geographical basis as possible.*

The selection of Secretariat personnel might be thought to be not so much a source of the political influence of the Secretary-General upon the members as a wellspring of the influence of the members upon the Secretary-General. This is perhaps the case in very minor degree. Certain members do attempt to inspire the

Secretary-General's choice of staff — a practice which met with more success in League days than at present.[103]

Actually, the appointment of the Secretariat is more a source of the Secretary-General's influence, if an indirect one. The Preparatory Commission's Report stated that the Secretary-General "alone is responsible to the other principal organs for the Secretariat's work; his choice of staff — more particularly of the higher staff — and his leadership will largely determine the character and efficiency of the Secretariat as a whole." [104] And, continued the Commission, that character and efficiency in turn "will largely determine the degree in which the objectives of the Charter will be realized." [105]

The Secretary-General of course does not consciously endeavor to select the staff [106] so as to infuse it with a political bias — any bias, that is, other than "a broad international outlook and a detachment from national prejudices and narrow national interests." [107] But his care in the selection of his associates for their integrity of approach and capability of performance will evidently affect the character and range of the influence the Secretary-General may exert.

His initiative in the exercise of such care is facilitated by giving him the appointive power, subject to regulations, to be sure, established by the General Assembly,[108] but not subject to the officious scrutiny of a second Supervisory Commission, like that of the League of Nations.[109] That the "paramount consideration" in the employment of staff shall be the necessity of "efficiency, competence, and integrity" further broadens the Secretary-General's appointive discretion and strengthens his ability to resist political pressure (an ability somewhat lowered by his obligation to pay "due regard" in recruiting to geographical distribution). An additional source of administrative strength is the provision that the "appropriate staffs" which shall be assigned to the Councils shall form part of the Secretariat. Without this provision, the insurance of Article 98 against the rise of rival Secretaries-General based on the Councils would be perhaps diluted.

*Article 100*

*1. In the performance of their duties the Secretary-General and the staff shall not seek or receive instructions from any government or from any other authority external to the Organization. They shall refrain from any action which might reflect on their position as international officials responsible only to the Organization.*

*2. Each Member of the United Nations undertakes to respect the exclusively international character of the responsibilities of the Secretary-General and the staff, and not to seek to influence them in the discharge of their responsibilities.*

Article 100, as an explicit statement of the exclusively international character of the Secretary-General and the staff, and of the responsibilities of both Secretariat and members imposed by that international character, is unmixed virtue. The League experiment demonstrated that loyalty and effective service to the world community are possible and practical on a considerable scale. It unfortunately also demonstrated, in the behavior of the Italian and German Under Secretaries-General, particularly, the dangers inherent in any corruption of that loyalty by governments. Article 100 does as much as any "loyalty oath" can do toward preventing the subversion of the Secretariat's proper spirit. As such, it can only strengthen the Secretary-General's hand.

*Article 7*

*1. There are established as the principal organs of the United Nations: A General Assembly, a Security Council, an Economic and Social Council, a Trusteeship Council, an International Court of Justice, and a Secretariat.*

*2. Such subsidiary organs as may be found necessary may be established in accordance with the present Charter.*

The fact that the Secretary-General is a principal organ of the Organization — and, as Professor Kelsen points out, it is the Secretary-General and not the Secretariat that is truly a principal organ [110] — is important both for considerations of prestige and of power. To so place the Secretary-General on the plane of the prime governmental and judicial organs of the United Nations evidently heightens his standing. Again, the contrast with the stature of the Secretary-General of the League is instructive. The comparable article of the Covenant spoke of "an Assembly and of a Council, with a permanent Secretariat." [111] But the earlier drafts of the Covenant, which envisaged a more independent and political Secretariat, contained the word "and" in place of "with." [112]

The Secretary-General enjoys specific powers which flow from his status as a principal organ. For example, the Statute of the International Law Commission provides: "The Commission shall . . . consider proposals and draft multilateral conventions submitted by . . . the principal organs of the United Nations." [113] Since the Secretary-General has at his command a Division for the Progressive Development and Codification of International Law, and since a body composed of part-time professors, as is the Commission, is in any case largely dependent upon the preparatory work of the Secretariat, his powers in this regard could prove significant. Their potential is demonstrated by the fact that the Genocide Convention is in large measure the end product of a draft submitted by the Secretary-General to an Assembly committee which antedated the creation of the International Law Commission.[114]

In summary, it is clear that the Charter, the Preparatory Commission, and the General Assembly join to construct a framework for the development of the authority of the Secretary-General which is at once resilient and solid. He is the chief permanent officer; his political personality is unmistakably affirmed; his administrative strength is unquestioned; and there is, moreover, a lack of confining detail in the Charter which of itself is an invitation. It is, however, a framework and not a rubber band. There are limits to the elasticity of the Secretary-General's initiative — textual limits and, far more important, limits imposed by the essential nature and dominating emotions of present-day international life. The Secretary-General controls no extensive territory, no large and skilled population, no industrial plant, no army, no hydrogen bomb. He is "the most highly qualified representative of the international spirit," [115] and this is a great deal. But in a world in which that spirit is depressed, he must proceed with caution. He must strike a sensitive balance between the ideal with which he is charged and the reality with which he is confronted. The ideal could not be higher, nor the reality much harsher.

CHAPTER **2**

## Trygve Lie, and How He
## Came to Be Secretary-General

*From [our] conversations . . . it was clear that
the President's wish was that the post should be
filled by a leader of the first rank, whose personal
status would itself add to the distinction and
authority of the post and of the United Nations
Organisation itself.*     FIELD MARSHAL SMUTS

*Clearly the Secretary-General should be elected
upon personal qualifications.*   HERBERT V. EVATT

*In fact, it is not too much to say that to a large
extent the fate of the United Nations Organization is likely to be determined by the wisdom and
character of its Secretary General.*
                    THE NEW YORK TIMES

The selection of the first Secretary-General of the United Nations
was made by the United States, the Soviet Union, the United
Kingdom, and circumstance.

Trygve Lie was not at the head of the list of candidates for
Secretary-General of any of the Big Three. He was the first choice
of both the United States and the U.S.S.R. for President of the
General Assembly, the United States having first put forth his
name for the presidency. With regard to the Secretaryship General, Mr. Lie held second place in Washington's favor; third place,
to all appearances, in Moscow's; and, so far as can be learned, no
place at all in the plans of the United Kingdom.

The United States delegation came to London in January 1946

with the following candidates for Secretary-General in mind, listed in descending order of desirability: (1) Lester Pearson of Canada, today that country's Minister of External Affairs; (2) Trygve Lie; (3) N. J. H. van Royen of the Netherlands, who subsequently was to argue his government's case against United Nations "interference" in Indonesia before the Security Council, and who is presently Ambassador to Washington; (4) C. Parra Peréz of Venezuela, a Senator who had played an active role at San Francisco.

The decisions of the Kremlin on the question cannot, of course, be likewise categorically asserted. By combining press accounts and the course of events, however, one arrives at the following likely estimate of the Soviet preferences regarding candidates: (1) Stanoje Simitch, then Yugoslav Ambassador to Washington; (2) Wincenty Rzymowski, a leftist journalist, then Foreign Minister of Poland, who died early in 1950; (3) Trygve Lie.

The United Kingdom, it seems, inclined toward Sir Gladwyn Jebb, the able Executive Secretary of the Preparatory Commission, who is now Permanent British Representative to the United Nations. It also cast a not unfriendly, and more than half-serious, eye upon General Dwight D. Eisenhower, who was being boomed by the Beaverbrook press.[1]

Mr. Lie, it turned out, would find victory in defeat. He was the candidate of the bigger two of the Big Three for President of the Assembly's First Session. The British, however, were strong for Belgium's Paul-Henri Spaak. The fact that the Russians opposed M. Spaak would not, perhaps, have been of itself enough to assure his election — after all, the Americans also preferred another — had not the Soviet delegation gone so far as to make a nominating speech on behalf of his opponent, the Foreign Minister of Norway. It was the only nominating speech which any delegation made for either candidate — it is interesting to note that the Assembly subsequently amended its rules of procedure so as to prohibit nominating speeches for the presidency — and, it seems, decided things in favor of M. Spaak. (It may be that that speech is a source of the nonsensical canard once current that Mr. Lie is "Moscow's man.") Had Mr. Lie been elected President — an office that changes with each Assembly session — he would, of

course, have been removed as a candidate for the Secretaryship
General.

When the permanent members of the Security Council as-
sembled in Church House to select the nominee whom the
Council would propose (there was little point in a meeting of the
full membership of the Council at this stage, since unanimous
agreement among the permanent members was a prerequisite of
the Council's recommendation), the man with the most prospec-
tive votes was the undeniably qualified Canadian, Mr. Pearson.
The Soviet delegation, it is reported, did not doubt his capabilities; they opposed him, and put forth the candidacy of Mr.
Simitch, on more general grounds. (One may assume that Moscow
is not unhappy nowadays about the fact that the Secretary-
General is not a Yugoslav!) The Russians maintained that the
Secretary-General should not be a North American in view of the
fact that the permanent headquarters were to be located in North
America (and in this they received considerable support, particularly from the French); he should not be French or British,
since those nationalities would doubtless be heavily represented
in the Secretariat; and, moreover, the post should rightfully go to
a national of a European country overrun by the Germans during
the war.

This emphasis upon Europe, the center of the recent global
war and traditionally the center of world diplomacy, again was
not peculiar to the Russians. There was a considerable feeling in
favor of selecting a citizen of a European state that had suffered
the onslaught of Hitler. There was, additionally, a general predisposition in favor of a national of a small state: the Great
Powers had their veto, and this, at least felt the smaller states,
was quite enough. A Russian could not get elected, of course;
there was the usual disposition to overlook Asia; South America's
war record was inadequate and her dearth of candidates notable;
and the Soviet Union put forth the aforestated objections to the
candidature of an American, Briton, or Frenchman.[2] That
the Soviet Union may have had unstated motives of a less abstract kind than these for blocking the nomination of Mr. Pearson
goes without saying.

Mr. Simitch was not, of course, a serious contender. The Soviet

Union was well aware that it would have to do better than that. Without formally putting forth his name in the course of the exploratory discussions among the permanent members, the Soviet delegation let it be known that their government would not be averse to the election of the man whom they had too vigorously backed for Assembly President.

The inevitable thesis has of course been raised that "the Russians planned it that way" — that they knowingly torpedoed Mr. Lie's presidential chances with a warm and public endorsement in order to insinuate him later into the Secretaryship General. Few can do more than guess at the Kremlin's mental processes, and there may conceivably be something to this theory. But it hardly seems likely.

Why the Soviet Union was friendly to Mr. Lie's candidacy is a fascinating question, the answers to which may again only be guessed at. Probably the most compelling reason was that they had to be friendly to someone whom the West could reasonably be expected to accept, and Mr. Lie was the likeliest, from their point of view, in this category. As a man who all his life had been an advocate of the working classes and who had been closely associated with the Norwegian Labor Party (which, in earlier years, had played hot and cold with the Communists), as one who had been prominent in opposing fascism and nazism, and as a citizen of a state evidently more sensitive than Canada to the views of its huge Soviet neighbor, Trygve Lie would understandably be preferred by the Russians to the dynamic Canadian professor-diplomat. All this is hazarded without the slightest imputation that Mr. Lie was or is in fact in any sense responsible to Moscow. Whether the Russians may or may not have had "hopes" it is impossible to divine.[3] Indeed, with the same facts, one can build a contrary thesis. Mr. Lie is a socialist and an ardent anti-fascist; but so was Léon Blum, whose relations with the Kremlin were not celebrated for their cordiality.

It is easier to suggest the reasoning behind the American support of Mr. Lie both for President and for Secretary-General. Here was the Foreign Minister of one of America's most intrepid wartime allies; a man who had a fine war record and who had rendered conspicuous service to the cause of the Grand Alliance;

whose political background was consonant with the then ascendant socialist forces of the European world with which the United States was and is allied (which is not to say that the United States was interested in promoting socialism; it may be assumed, however, that a candidate who would tend to win socialist support in competition with socialists not on the list of American possibilities, such, for example, as M. Spaak, was in American eyes that much more valuable). Mr. Lie had performed well at San Francisco, demonstrating, as in the London war years, marked ability. Moreover, as a man on good terms with Moscow, and an obvious Westerner withal, he occupied a mediate position obviously desirable for the Secretary-General of the United Nations.

The negotiations finally came to a head when Mr. Gromyko informed Secretary of State Stettinius that fresh instructions from home precluded the election of Mr. Pearson. Mr. Stettinius, with the first name on his list thus blacked out, understandably turned to the second. He promptly requested a meeting of permanent members, to whom he proposed the designation of Trygve Lie. The United Kingdom, France, and China were agreeable; the Soviet Union, as Mr. Stettinius was no doubt led to expect by its attitude publicly demonstrated at the time of the Assembly election and privately indicated since, was receptive. Unanimity was thus achieved; the Security Council met in private plenary session the next day and "decided" to nominate Trygve Lie. The General Assembly proceeded on February 1, by a vote of 46 to 3, to appoint him Secretary-General.[4]

Thus the manner of choice of the first Secretary-General was as naturally and eminently political as the office itself.

Lie, Trygve Halvdan; *b.* July 16, 1896, Oslo, Norway, son of Martin and Hulda Arussen Lie. Educated Oslo Univ., law degree, 1919. Married Hjordis Joergensen, Nov. 8, 1921; three daughters. Became member Norwegian Trade Union Youth Organization 1911; assistant to Secretary of Norwegian Labor Party 1919–22; Legal Adviser to Trade Union Federation, 1922–35; National Executive Secretary, Labor Party, 1926. Minister of Justice, Labor Party Gov't., 1935–39; Member of Parliament, 1935; re-elected, 1945; Minister of Trade, Industry, Shipping and Fishing, 1939–40. Acting Foreign Minister, 1940; Foreign Minister, 1941; evolved provisional measures that saved

Norwegian fleet for Allies. Chairman, Norwegian Delegation to United Nations Conference on International Organization, San Francisco, 1945 (Chrm., Committee III, for drafting Security Council Articles). Resigned as Foreign Minister, June, 1945; appointed Acting Foreign Minister, interim coalition government, June, 1945; Foreign Minister, October, 1945; Chrm., Norwegian Delegation, U.N. General Assembly, London, Jan., 1946. Elected Secretary-General of the U.N., Feb. 1946. Clubs: Norwegian Sports Ass'n. (active until 1940). Publications: "The Anti-Labor Laws and the Battle Against Them"; "The New Labor Arbitration Law."[5]

A page or two can hardly suffice to describe a man who merits a biography. Some sketch of the Secretary-General's personality and approach is nonetheless a *sine qua non*. For the Secretaryship General is largely uncharted territory, and Mr. Lie is the first to explore it. The personality of the man who occupies even a well-defined and precedent-illuminated office gives a special character to that office as long as he holds it and perhaps for some time afterward. This applies with the more force to a position defined only in general terms and for which precedent exists only by analogy.

Trygve Lie, as a very human being, is large, squarish, substantial looking. His features are rounded and agreeable, his hair black and thinning, his dress subdued. He walks with a heavy vigor, and when he stands still, he has a habit of pushing away at the wall with his fist, cautiously and repeatedly, like a boxer in slow motion. His deep-voiced English is heaved forth, sometimes haltingly, with a thick Norwegian accent endearingly comic in its appeal to American ears. He is warm in his personal relationships and immersed in his family relationships. He is at once shrewd and sincere, hardheaded and softhearted. His personality is animated, even emotional; it gives the impression of turbulence, of worry, brightened by a certain unmistakable boyishness. "For six days a week, I think Trygve is a genius," a colleague of the days when Mr. Lie was Minister of Justice has remarked, in a somewhat different reaction to perhaps the same youthful characteristic; "on the seventh he is just a child."[6]

Trygve Lie, as a public figure, has for the greater part of his life been a lawyer and a labor man. He joined the Norwegian Trade Union Youth Organization at fifteen, became the Labor

Party's National Executive Secretary at thirty. He was legal adviser to the Trade Union Federation for thirteen years, acquiring
a training and facility in conciliation and mediation that was to
stand him in good stead in a wider sphere. His politics may be
compared to those of a British Labourite, convinced of social
democracy and the possibilities of peaceful progress. At home, he
has demonstrated that indispensable attribute of the successful
politician, the capacity to get elected. He has also demonstrated
a not necessarily integral quality for political success — competence in office. The caliber of his diplomatic career before 1946 is
evidenced by his candidacy for President of the General Assembly
and by his election as Secretary-General.

Mr. Lie's record as Secretary-General may better be assessed
after that record has been presented. His approach to the position
has an immediate pertinence, however, and in this he speaks for
himself as follows: [7]

"I can tell you the views on the subject [of the Secretary-
General and his political role] . . . There are two.

"First, there is the X-ist [8] view; they've told me it several times.
The Secretary-General is purely the administrative chief . . .
this is the X-ist ideal. And there are several governments of the
same opinion. . .

"Second, there is the Charter view. The Secretary-General is
charged with heavy political responsibilities. Under Article 99
. . . I can use the big gun, the biggest gun in the world, to tell
the world, before the most important security body, that the
peace is in danger. . .

"There is a third view, not expressed by any Government. I
should be the leader, over governments . . . and lead the way,
tell them what they should do — you have to do that and that and
that. I should be a kind of 'first citizen of the world,' 'world citizen number one.' Such an opinion has no roots in the Charter. . .

"I have to use my rights in a very discreet way, if I want to do
good. I could blow up this Organization very soon if I wanted
to be a world leader. . .

"The Secretary-General isn't that world leader. He has no government, no press of his own to appeal to. . .

"What weapons has the Secretary-General? Only his own intelligence, tact, and tactics. . . They haven't given the Secretary-General the means in the Charter to be a world leader. . .

"So I am in between. I've chosen the middle road, myself. . .

"The Secretary-General must be a diplomat, a . . . politically minded man, and he must understand his duty to keep the Organization together. . . He must be ready to compromise, and at the same time he must never lose sight of the Charter's ideals. . .

"It is not an easy job."

Politicking in London was not confined to the properly political post of Secretary-General. The long arms of the Big Three reached down to the level of the Assistant Secretaries-General and apportioned out the offices and, less thoroughly, the personalities who could occupy those offices, as seemed desirable. The U.S.S.R. preëmpted the Assistant Secretaryship General for Security Council Affairs; the United States, that for Administrative and Financial Services; Great Britain was assured, by the terms of the Big Five agreement, of the "portfolio" for Economic Affairs; and the Assistant Secretaryships General for Social Affairs and Trusteeship were left to the French and Chinese, respectively. The remaining posts went to a Czech (Legal Affairs), a Hollander (Conferences and General Services), and a Chilean (Public Information).

Five of the eight Assistant Secretaries-General were thus European, as is, of course, Mr. Lie — an indication of how "Europe-centered" was the London Assembly, particularly as contrasted with the prominent role the Latin-American bloc, the Middle Eastern states, and certain Asiatic nations were later to assume. Mr. Lie, in an effort to right the balance, appointed an Indian to succeed Adrian Pelt of the Netherlands, upon the latter's election as United Nations Commissioner for Libya.

Why Washington insisted upon the Department of Administrative and Financial Services seems beyond the comprehension of Secretariat and delegates alike. Questions in this regard evoke a response most charitably interpreted as naïveté on the part of the United States. A high-ranking member of the Secretariat hazards that the Americans thought "the administrative tail would wag the dog"; other opinion suggests that Washington, knowing it would bear the greater percentage of the bill, hoped that United Nations costs would be kept as low as possible by an American executive.

The U.S.S.R.'s choice is more understandable; and it is one that since has been lamented increasingly in non-Soviet circles, as Soviet obstruction of United Nations security efforts has grown. There is much to be said against a national of any Great Power holding a top Secretariat post directly concerned with keeping the peace, when a major threat to the peace may be offered only by a Great Power. The undesirability of having a Soviet citizen, in particular, in that crucial post has been dramatically illustrated by the situation of Constantin Zinchenko, who, as Assistant Secretary-General for Security Council Affairs, has been in the peculiar plight of reading aloud to the Council condemnation of aggression in Korea cabled by the United Nations Commission there. That Mr. Zinchenko's position may be more than just peculiar is perhaps indicated by his not having been asked to serve on the Secretary-General's special Korean coördinating committee, established to carry out the Security Council's resolution authorizing the use of armed force to repel the North Koreans. His key position may also have had something to do with Mr. Lie's requesting members to inform him in "general terms" only of the military aid they would render United Nations forces in Korea, reserving details for American ears. It may in fact be that the pernicious effects of a Soviet subject at the head of the Department of Security Council Affairs extend well beyond so clear-cut an action as the Korean. The capacity of the Secretary-General for political accomplishment, it has been suggested, has been significantly impaired by the Department's failure to produce the balanced, supremely informed analyses of political problems which should form much of the material from which the Secretary-General fashions his political judgments. With a few exceptions — particularly that of the Department's Political Division in preparing working papers for the Interim Committee — the Department has contributed little to the Secretary-General's political perception. This lack of productivity may be traced directly to the character of the Department's high direction.

The interest of the Great Powers in having their nationals

head key departments was unfortunately not followed up with a comparable enthusiasm for submitting for the posts, in all cases, nominees representative of the best their vast civil services could offer. It is the Secretary-General's prerogative to name whom he chooses as Assistant Secretaries-General. Legally, he is absolutely sovereign in the disposition of the Assistant Secretaryships General, both with respect to their nationality and personality. This right was, in fact, the point of the San Francisco Deputies' decision, a decision with which the London understanding of the Big Five is not altogether consonant. Practically speaking, however, Mr. Lie has considered himself bound by the agreement of the permanent members (though it may be that the Great Powers, with the probable exception of the U.S.S.R., would not obdurately urge compliance with their understanding upon the present or a future Secretary-General).[9] Moreover, as a normal procedure of politic relations, Mr. Lie has asked the government whose subject is to be appointed an Assistant Secretary-General for suggestions for the post. This is all very well when more than one suggestion is forthcoming. At London, however, nominations were single or few. The United States, for example, submitted a single nominee, John G. Hutson; later, in the appointment of his successor, the United States gave the Secretary-General a wider choice. Mr. Lie selected the highly regarded Byron Price.

Nor were nominations at London of a uniformly high standard. The Soviet Union, less able than some other governments to spare a high-caliber administrator, made available the competent Arkady Sobolev, since replaced by Mr. Zinchenko. ("Sobolev was an absolutely first-class administrator," runs a representative assessment by a well-informed source, "but not working for this Organization.") Nominations by other governments were not up to the Soviet level, and one of the Big Five even seemed unconcerned about making a nomination at all.

Mr. Lie, fresh in office, was in a difficult position, and many of the difficulties the Secretariat has suffered since may be attributed to the attitude of various governments in respect to these nominations. Mr. Lie has been criticized in responsible nongovernmental quarters for failing to make an issue over "the Governments making available to him a cabinet the equal of any in the world." Whether Mr. Lie should have made an issue amid issues enough, uncertain of success if he had, at a stage when failure would have particularly impaired his prestige, is debatable. At any rate, the worst imposition has since been overcome, with considerable effort on the Secretary-General's part, and with noticeably healthy results.

# PART 2

# The Exercise and Development of the Secretary-General's Powers

# CHAPTER 3

## Relations with the General Assembly

The Secretary-General is probably in more intimate touch with the General Assembly than with any other of the United Nations organs. The Assembly's inclusive membership and inclusive agenda, its position as the "parent body," afford the Secretary-General "area" within which to operate. Its yearly budget authorization and concomitant review of the Secretariat's work constitute a permanent core of common concern. The Secretary-General, moreover, is assured of prominent entree by the provision of Article 98 that he "shall make an annual report to the General Assembly on the work of the Organization."

### Annual Report

The annual report,[1] as the official Secretariat review of the year's United Nations activity, provides the setting for the Assembly's annual review of international ills.[2] For the most part, the report, a succinct document of about 150 large pages, is unvarnished summation of the answers the United Nations has attempted to supply to political and security questions, economic and social questions, and the like. The treatment is factual and not forensic. The report as a whole, however, is prefaced with the Secretary-General's introduction, a section of about ten thousand words, the structural conciseness of which contrasts with its profound sweep of substance.

The introduction is as interpretive as the body of the report is narrative. The introductions to the third (1948), fourth (1949), and fifth (1950) reports assess the world's situation in the broadest terms; examine current crises in their historical context; survey the year's record of United Nations progress and lack of progress; approve, criticize, and recommend. They are at once evaluative and programmatic, adjudging the policies of the member states, if not explicitly, at least by implication, and putting forth the Secretary-General's suggestions for the improvement of those policies. Both in its imaginative concept and forthright content, the Secretary-General's introduction to his annual report is of the most crucial consequence to his position and to the work of the Organization.

The introductions to the first (1946) and second (1947) annual reports were cautious. With the third report, the Secretary-General advanced from a level of worried assessment and general exhortation to that of courageous criticism and positive suggestion. In the fourth and fifth, he maintained his critical, and improved upon his constructive, standards.

The following quotation is an illustration of the expanse of the introductions:

> It would be a grave mistake to believe that most of the world has any intention of accepting any single economic system, whether based on the communist doctrine of classless society, or the most extreme American capitalist version of a free enterprise system. . . domination by any single ideology, whether it be religious, or political or economic, is unthinkable and impossible. It is equally unthinkable that any one nation or group of nations could establish and maintain in such a world a new empire resting on either economic power or military might. [3]

Another similar example, no less spacious in its extent (and decidedly "right-deviationist" in its view of history for "Moscow's man"):

> I believe the rise of the dependent peoples and the human rights movement will, in the long run, have far more significance and give rise to greater events in the second half of the twentieth century than will the present ideological struggle. . . The establishment of the State of Israel . . . one of the epic events of history, coming at the end not merely of thirty years, but of 2,000 years of accumulated sorrows, bitterness and conflict . . . symbolizes historic forces beside which the present ideological conflict appears to be a transitory phenomenon. [4]

An illustration of the Secretary-General's critical boldness:

It is impossible to obtain lasting security from war by any arrangement that leaves out any of the Great Powers. While regional security arrangements may sometimes redress the balance of power in the world, collective security can be achieved only by working out means by which all the Great Powers may live peacefully together under the Charter, however long this process may take.[5]

The communist world press chose to regard the last-quoted lines as Mr. Lie's indictment of the Atlantic Pact, and in this they may have been right. Yakob Viktorov, noted *Pravda* commentator, in a broadcast over the Moscow radio of August 16, 1949, asserted that Mr. Lie "went so far as to speak the truth on a number of points . . . though in guarded terms and indirectly, to censure the North Atlantic Pact, that gospel of the warmongers." *Le Drapeau Rouge* (Brussels, August 9, 1949) saw the report as "unqualified condemnation of the Atlantic Pact." The *London Daily Worker*, the same day, apparently got the signals mixed, finding Mr. Lie "strangely silent" on the Atlantic Pact; but the Czech press took no chances, printing a Tass dispatch headlined "Trygve Lie Criticizes the Atlantic Pact" (*Obrana Lidu*, August 10, 1949).

Mr. Lie's commendation has been as bold as his criticism. "The European Recovery Program," he wrote in his third annual report, ". . . holds great promise for the restoration of Western Europe to economic and political stability, but it can have lasting results only if present political divisions are not permitted to block co-ordinated action within Europe as a whole and an increase of trade between East and West Europe."

Mr. Viktorov, in a sensationally vitriolic attack upon Mr. Lie in a review of the third annual report entitled, "The Distorted Mirror in the Form of a Report," [6] was not equally pleased with this example of Mr. Lie's critical faculties. "The crown of Trygve Lie's departure from the purposes and principles of the United Nations is his position in regard to the 'Marshall Plan' . . . Members of the U.N. would be entitled to expect that the Secretary-General, in his appraisal of the 'Marshall Plan' would at least observe impartiality and not praise actions which bypass the U.N. and are contrary to its basic purposes. . . It appears that the Secretary-General . . . is acting as an obedient medium for carrying out the line of the Anglo-American bloc aimed at undermining the United Nations."

Whatever else may be said about the above quotations, they illustrate the care with which the introductions to the annual reports are scrutinized. Mr. Viktorov's watchfulness is duplicated in other countries.

Finally, a few examples may be given of Mr. Lie's use of the annual reports to place before the member states and the world his views on proper United Nations policy and program:

> If there is the slightest prospect that progress can be made I would urge a resumption of negotiations . . . on the future of Germany. . . Pending a break in the present deadlock between the majority and the minority over methods of control of atomic energy, it might be fruitful to begin a study of some of the problems involved in the control of bacteriological and lethal chemical weapons.[7]

> It is essential for the Great Powers . . . to seriously negotiate. . . To refuse such consultations as futile is to deny the whole concept of the United Nations. . . The good offices of the Secretary-General are always available to facilitate such consultations. . . The best solution of the problem [of the disposition of the former Italian colonies], in my opinion, would be a direct United Nations trusteeship with an administrator responsible solely to the Trusteeship Council. It is, of course, for the Member States to decide, but I feel sure that such a bold forward step would help the people of the territories concerned to follow the peaceful path towards self-government or independence. . . Member Governments are familiar with my views on the desirability of moving as rapidly as possible towards universality of Membership. . . The applicants . . . can reasonably be considered as meeting the requirements of Membership. Whatever may be said regarding the Governments of the Countries concerned, their peoples, and the world as a whole, would certainly benefit if all the applicants were to be admitted to the Organization.[8]

Phrases such as "Member Governments are familiar with my views" and "It is, of course, for the Member States to decide, but I feel sure that—" point up the Secretary-General's assertion of himself as "the most highly qualified representative of the international spirit." [9] Not only has the "international synthesis" found a voice which, as might be expected, reiterates United Nations ideals and resounds United Nations contributions, but it has found one strong enough to speak out upon controversial issues

(as in praise of the Marshall Plan and in blame of undue emphasis upon regional alliances). The international ideal has found,
moreover, a spokesman thoughtfully courageous enough to come
forth with proposals for the solution of problems which confront
the Organization directly (the Italian colonies, the admission of
new members) and indirectly (development of measures for the
control of bacteriological warfare) — proposals which reflect a
United Nations, rather than a national, bias.

The influence of the annual reports is naturally hard to gauge.
They unquestionably provide a framework for the General
Assembly's deliberations; whether they actually give these deliberations direction is a question of the totality of the Secretary-
General's influence, which is exercised through the reports and
a number of other channels. Of itself, the annual report is a
significant section of that totality and is thoroughly studied and
pondered in the foreign offices of the world.[10]

→ *Agenda*

The Secretary-General's concern with the General Assembly's
agenda is two sided, and more technical than political. The political elements are substantial enough for isolation, however, and
quite important enough for comment.

Of the greatest significance is the right of the Secretary-General
to add to the provisional agenda "all items which [he] deems it
necessary to put before the General Assembly." [11] There is nothing exclusive about the phrase, "all items"; and it is the Secretary-
General's assumption that he is thereby entitled to place political
and security, as well as less dynamic, subjects upon the Assembly's provisional agenda. Mr. Lie acted upon this assumption
at the Fifth Session of the General Assembly, offering for its
agenda his "Memorandum of Points for Consideration in the Development of a Twenty-Year Program for Achieving Peace
through the United Nations" [12] — his highly political "ten-point"
proposals.

Placing items such as these on the Assembly's provisional
agenda puts the Secretary-General in a position vis-à-vis the
Assembly somewhat comparable to that in which Article 99
places him relative to the Security Council. The essential right

of Article 99, it will be recalled, is that of the Secretary-General to place upon the Council's provisional agenda any matter which he sees threatening the maintenance of international peace and security. As Mr. Lie has interpreted his Assembly agenda rights, he could well add to that body's provisional agenda any question which he might draw to the Council's attention under Article 99. Thus the decision of the San Francisco Conference not to extend Article 99 to include the Assembly has been in fact reversed.

This is not to say that the Secretary-General's Assembly agenda rights wholly equate with those he enjoys under Article 99. The Security Council, after all, has "primary responsibility" in security matters.[13] It is, moreover, more likely that the General Assembly might decline to take up a security item submitted by the Secretary-General than that the Security Council would do so; for if the Council refused to consider such a security question, it would be frustrating an express intention of the Charter. Furthermore, a matter raised under Article 99 would tend to draw far more publicity than another political item submitted for the Assembly's crowded schedule.

Agenda priorities are another important sphere of the Secretary-General's influence.[14] His authority in this regard is exerted in two directions: toward the completion of the members' more important business first, and toward the distribution of that business, in terms of its being handled by the Secretariat, so as to employ the resources of the Secretariat with the maximum efficiency. These two ends may often overlap; and the second, of course, is a technical operation with only the most remote political overtones. This work involves first of all extensive activity on the Secretary-General's part in reconciling the differing views of the delegations on agenda items. It involves promoting agreement on what points of the provisional agenda, the supplementary list, and the additional items submitted shall be included upon the working agenda; what priority these shall have; and to what committees they shall be allocated. There is usually a good deal of intercommittee "juggling," of shifting of items among committees, especially toward the latter part of an Assembly session, and in this process also the Secretary-General is helpfully influential.

Action in these matters is generally taken not by Mr. Lie himself but by his Executive Assistant, Andrew W. Cordier. Mr. Cordier, for example, saw all the delegations on all the issues that came before the General Committee of the Fourth Assembly — in itself an accomplishment in liaison. Many of these consultations concerned agenda matters and were in large measure responsible for making the General Committee of that Assembly distinctly more efficient than those of earlier sessions.

It is generally not a question of the Secretary-General's taking a position for or against the inclusion of particular items, though upon occasion he has taken such a stand, notably in his successful opposition, at the Fourth Session, to the inclusion on an overcrowded agenda of the item submitted by Panama for the revision of the calendar. Rather, it is a matter of expediting and inevitably, in some measure, indirectly influencing the nature of the agreement of the delegations upon what the Assembly shall consider, and when.

The Secretary-General, additionally, must concern himself with fitting the agenda, and to an extent the decisions, of the Assembly (and the other organs as well, particularly the Economic and Social Council) to the physical capacity of the Secretariat to be of effective service. This means not simply limiting the work of the organs to the capacity of the Secretariat, but also employing the resources of the Secretariat to the best advantage. These resources have limits, of course, ultimately set by the delegates, who may, if they wish, expand them. All this, however, is more of a technical problem than a political one.

## Interventions in Plenary Session and Committee

In contrast to the very limited oral participation of the Secretaries-General of the League in Assembly proceedings, the verbal activity of the Secretary-General of the United Nations, both in plenary session and committee, is the more notable. The importance which the Secretary-General attaches to his oral interpositions is indicated by the fact that the Secretariat "conducted a campaign," in the words of a senior official of the Organization, to insure Mr. Lie an unrestricted right of intervention. The Assembly's provisional rules accorded the Secretary-General the right to address meetings "upon the invitation of the President." [15] It turned out that invitations were not always forthcoming. The first Assembly President, Paul-Henri Spaak, upon several occasions denied the Secretary-General the opportunity to speak, declining to extend an invitation which the Secretary-General expressly sought; whereupon the "campaign" was launched which a year later successfully culminated in the alteration of the rule to provide that "the Secretary-General, or a member of the Secretariat designated by him as his representative, may at any time make either oral or written statements to the General Assembly concerning any question under consideration by it." [16]

The episode is noteworthy in two respects: that the Secretary-General achieved his unrestricted right; and that that achievement was in large measure the result of pressure applied by him. It is a particularly good example of the Secretary-General's initiative in a matter of distinct political connotation.

Similar energy was displayed with regard to the revision of other rules by the Committee on Procedures and Organization, the Secretary-General's representatives taking an active role in the committee discussions. And the Secretary-General sustained his influence in the determination of the Assembly's procedures in the 1949 meetings of the Special Committee on Methods and Procedures of the Assembly, which was set up to explore means of conserving the Assembly's time. His Executive Office took what an informed official [17] describes as "a major role" in its work, proposing many changes in the rules, opposing others, and the like.

The Secretary-General's addresses to plenary Assembly have not been frequent, averaging but two or three per session. They nonetheless form an important part of his public record of political initiative. To an extent they parallel the introductions to his annual reports: at first these speeches were largely restricted to calling upon the Great Powers to restore the coöperative spirit which animated the Yalta declaration; [18] then, beginning with the Third Session, in 1948, they mounted to bolder assessment and carefully phrased criticism of the Assembly's prospects and decisions.

In his closing address to the Second Part of the Third Session, for example, Mr. Lie, in reviewing the United Nations effort to conciliate the Berlin dispute, noted that the "neutrals" on the Security Council had undertaken a study of the currency question and had, "with the active assistance of the Secretariat, made a good effort and a good report. That report, however, was not accepted when it was submitted to the Big Four last winter." The implied criticism of the country which refused to accept a "good" report (the United States) is clear. Further along in the same speech, the Secretary-General stated that the United Nations would "face tests" in the Balkans and Korea which would "require the full coöperation of all the Member Governments" — a diplomatic plea to the Soviet Union, in effect, to end its boycott and blocking of the work of the United Nations Balkan and Korean Commissions.[19]

Again, in his address to the last meeting of the Fourth Session, the Secretary-General commented upon all of the more important political resolutions which met with his favor. Conspicuous in its absence was any comment upon the resolution for the internationalization of Jerusalem (the passage of which Mr. Lie, in the words of a prominent United Nations delegate close to the Jerusalem issue, "did everything in his power to frustrate"), or upon the "peace essentials" resolution sponsored by the United States. Not a word about the latter; rather, Mr. Lie chose to recall once again the spirit of the Mexican resolution, which was entitled "Appeal to the Great Powers to Renew Their Efforts, to Compose Their Differences, and to Establish a Lasting Peace." [20]

Admittedly, this is guarded criticism, so subtly worded that it appears pale beside the output of the postwar intercourse-by-insult school of diplomatic address. It is nevertheless criticism, important in itself as a token of the Secretary-General's political personality and as a clue to the nature of the substance of his major effort at influencing United Nations policy, an effort which takes not the form of speeches but of behind-the-scenes negotiation and conciliation.

Intervention in committee by the Secretary-General (or, as is generally the case, by his representative, usually the Assistant Secretary-General concerned) is of course more frequent than in plenary session and, more often than not, of a purely informational or procedural character. His participation in the work of the Fifth (Administrative and Budgetary) Committee is considered separately; otherwise, interpositions in the proceedings of the Sixth (Legal) and, to a lesser extent, the Third (Social, Cultural, and Humanitarian), Second (Economic and Financial), and Fourth (Trusteeship) Committees are common. For example, in the twenty-three meetings of the Sixth Committee of the Second Session held between September 16 and November 26, 1947, there were nine interventions by the Assistant Secretary-General for Legal Affairs, Dr. Ivan Kerno, or by the General Counsel, A. H. Feller. These interventions ranged from a defense by Mr. Feller of the right of his department to prepare for the Secretary-General a legal memorandum on the question of succession to membership by India and Pakistan, which Dr. José Arce of Argentina challenged, to a statement by Dr. Kerno voicing the satisfaction of the Secretary-General with the Headquarters Agreement.[21]

Whether or not the Secretary-General has the right to advance proposals, present resolutions, and move amendments before Assembly committees, in much the same manner as a member state, is an issue about which there is still some conflict. But since the Secretary-General places many items on the Assembly's agenda and reports on still others, there would seem to be a natural propensity toward his exercising full rights of proposition in committee.

These rights have been realized in practice. Certain governments have upon occasion challenged their exercise, however, and the Secretary-General, while employing the substance of these rights, has not been provocative in asserting their form. Thus, at the Fifth Session, the Assistant Secretary-General for Legal Affairs suggested a minor administrative amendment to a resolution of the Sixth Committee concerning reservations to multilateral conventions. The delegate of Iran then formally proposed the addition of a paragraph in accordance with Dr. Kerno's suggestion. The proposed amendment was withdrawn because of procedural difficulties, but the delegate of the Soviet Union nevertheless took the floor to reprimand the Assistant Secretary-

General for violating the rules of procedure. Dr. Kerno, he held, was not entitled to introduce a proposal in the name of the Secretary-General. The committee chairman, a Czech, agreed that the Secretary-General could not submit specific proposals to the committee, but recalled that Dr. Kerno's suggestion had been formally advanced by Iran. Yugoslavia and South Africa, while not commenting directly upon the Secretary-General's right to make proposals, put forth the view that Dr. Kerno's administrative suggestion was in order.[22]

Six weeks later, the committee considered draft rules prepared by the Secretary-General for the calling of nongovernmental conferences. An amendment to these rules was proposed, but, when the voting stage was reached, the chairman pointed out that there was no draft resolution to be amended — some delegation first would have to sponsor the Secretary-General's draft. The delegate of Yugoslavia recalled that the committee had "often" voted upon drafts presented by the Secretary-General, but, if needs be, Yugoslavia would serve as sponsor. Dr. Kerno interposed to remark that it was true that the draft rules presented by the Secretary-General required a sponsor before they could be put to a vote. But, he suggested, those delegations which had already indicated support for the draft could be regarded as sponsors. Moreover, the Assistant Secretary-General noted, the chairman of the Fifth Committee had recently put directly to the vote a draft submitted by the Secretary-General.[23] No one disputed Dr. Kerno's inconclusive suggestions.

These proceedings of the Sixth Committee, however, take on the aspects of much ado about nothing when compared with the practice of the other committees of the same session of the Assembly and, indeed, on other occasions, of the Sixth Committee itself. This practice indicates that the Secretary-General's rights of proposition are virtually unfettered.

The Third Committee, for example, centered its discussions on children's aid about two resolutions, one of which was "the draft resolution submitted by the Secretary-General." [24] The Second Committee, in considering technical assistance for Libya, considered no resolution but that submitted by the Secretary-General. The delegates discussed and amended and adopted it just as if it were the proposal of a member state whose interests in and knowledge of the subject at hand were great.[25]

The Secretary-General moved an amendment to a resolution on Korean relief, under consideration by the joint Second and Third Committee, and the delegates, far from challenging his right to do so, seemed unperturbed when the delegate of the United States said he would withdraw his amendment if the committee would accept the Secretary-General's.[26]

Nor has the Secretary-General refrained from criticizing other people's resolutions. The Assistant Secretary-General in charge of Trusteeship suggested that a joint Cuban-Mexican draft resolution was either "unnecessary" or was intended to put the Secretariat in a "very delicate position." [27] Again, he said, according to one interpretation, a certain Egyptian draft resolution "did not contain any new element," and according to the other possible interpretation, "would be a step backward." [28]

Even in the punctilious Legal Committee, Dr. Kerno suggested to the representative of India that she withdraw an amendment.[29] And in the Fifth Committee, which considers the affairs of the Secretariat proper, the right of the Secretary-General to make proposals, present draft resolutions, move amendments, offer his support, or express his criticism has been, in accordance with long-standing custom, repeatedly exercised.[30]

Upon occasion, the Secretary-General's representative has done battle in the supercharged debates of the First (Political and Security) Committee and its counterpart, the *Ad Hoc* Political Committee, usually to defend the Secretariat's good name against imputations of partiality. The debates of the *Ad Hoc* Political Committee of the Third and Fourth Sessions, and of the Assembly's Special Committee on a United Nations Guard, on the Secretary-General's proposals for the creation of a Guard (later pared down to the Field Force), form a whole chapter of high-level Secretariat participation in committee proceedings. And much of this participation was defense against the vigorous attacks of the Soviet bloc upon the Secretary-General's suggestions and authority.[31]

The Guard question also provides further apt illustration of Mr. Lie's political initiative — an initiative here purposefully and justly presented as nonpolitical, but quickly made a political issue by the nature of the opposition it raised. Mr. Lie first let go a "trial balloon" in a speech at the Harvard Commencement in June 1948; placed the item on the Assembly's provisional agenda later in the summer; saw it through the General Committee; proposed to the *Ad Hoc* Political Committee, once significant opposition or doubt about his plan had manifested itself, that a special committee be set up to review the whole question of a Guard and report back to the following Assembly; met many of the objections to his plan by presenting a modified version of it to the special committee, once the latter had been set up as he had suggested; and, throughout, in committee and in plenary session, forcefully maintained his integrity and that of his staff in proposing the plan against sometimes vicious assaults. He won out when the Assembly declared itself of the opinion that "the Secretary-General has authority to establish the United Nations Field Service." [32]

These interventions as a group, though preëminently nonpolitical in character, thus are not altogether without their political aspects, and as such they are part of the Secretary-General's political armory.

## Budgetary Relations: Advisory Committee and Fifth Committee

The relations of the Secretary-General with the Advisory Committee on Administrative and Budgetary Questions and with the Fifth Committee of the Assembly,[33] if not strictly political, must certainly be politic. The power and permeating influence of the party that controls the purse strings need no elucidation. These relations again illustrate the superior stature of the Secretary-General of the United Nations as compared to that of his League forebears. The latter were subjected in budgetary and administrative matters to the severe scrutiny and at times the domination of the Supervisory Commission. Any item of the Secretary-General's draft budget that could not be fully justified "was ruthlessly reduced or suppressed" by the Supervisory Commission prior to the submission of the estimates to the Assembly.[34] But this procedure did assure Commission support in that body.

The Advisory Committee of the United Nations is of another

nature altogether. A nine-member body of experts, appointed by the General Assembly for three-year terms, it is not supervisory but advisory; moreover, it does not advise the Secretary-General (at least formally), but confines itself to making recommendations to the Assembly's Fifth Committee. It is not a governmental body for administrative review; it is an expert commission for budgetary analysis and suggestion.

The budget which the Secretary-General submits to the Assembly is his budget and not the Advisory Committee's. The committee cannot, as could the League Supervisory Commission, compel the Secretary-General to alter his estimates in any degree. The process is rather one far more becoming to the situation of the Secretary-General: as a matter of judicious grace, he submits to the Advisory Committee his budget while it is still in the state of galley proof; the Advisory Committee, after study, writes a report to the Assembly, recommending certain cuts; the Secretary-General then reconsiders, deciding to what extent, if any, he will accept the recommendations. If he takes the cuts, the task of the Fifth Committee is simple; if not, the Fifth Committee must sustain either* the Secretary-General or the Advisory Committee.

Officially, the Secretary-General, represented in these matters by the Assistant Secretary-General for Administrative and Financial Services, Byron Price, and the Advisory Committee pursue their respective tasks in worlds apart. Actually, there is a great deal of luncheon conversation between Mr. Price and Thanassis Aghnides, of Greece, Chairman of the Advisory Committee and a former Deputy Secretary-General of the League — so much that it constitutes running consultations between the Secretary-General and the committee before the latter's opinions crystallize. Additionally, of course, the committee calls in the Assistant Secretaries-General and their principal officers as witnesses when their departmental estimates are being analyzed. The Secretary-General will, prior to the committee's final decisions, inform its members what he can and cannot accept of their recommendations (which may or may not deter the committee). He has even been known upon occasion to suggest *sub rosa* to the committee that it recommend a particular cut, noting that there are times when a reduction will strengthen the Secretary-General's hand in internal administration.

Although the Advisory Committee is formally advisory only to the General Assembly, in practice the Secretary-General often seeks its views on a variety of administrative and financial matters, and these views are always forthcoming. The committee's advice is useful for its own sake; moreover, such consultations are helpful in securing the support of nine United Nations members, for although the committee is composed of experts, it is made up of men of influence with their governments who often serve on their country's delegation to the General Assembly. Consultations between the Secretary-General and the committee sometimes are and other times are not reported to the General Assembly.

Until the Fourth Session, the Secretary-General had had no serious dispute with the Advisory Committee, accepting its suggestions for the most part. In 1949, he found them overly harsh and fought them vigorously. This put the members of the Assembly's Fifth Committee "on the spot." They had come with mechanical instructions to vote for the report of the Advisory Committee, but at the same time they were loath to impair the Secretariat's work; and the Secretary-General and his representatives were firm in asserting that the committee's recommendations, if accepted, would affect their work adversely. The Secretary-General ultimately won on all important points at issue, primarily because he demonstrated to the Fifth Committee's satisfaction that the recommendations of the Advisory Committee were unreasonable. At the Fifth Session, in 1950, the Advisory Committee and the Secretary-General achieved a much wider measure of agreement, the Secretary-General declining to accept the former's recommendations only on the question of staff allowances. This time the committee fared rather better than the Secretary-General.

There has been some dissatisfaction among certain delegations concerning the nature of the Advisory Committee. Two proposals for reconstructing it were discussed at the Assembly's Second Session. The first suggested that the committee be transformed into a governmental, rather than an expert, body; the second proposed that it be made supervisory of the Secretary-General rather than advisory to the Assembly — both clearly measures to cut down the administrative and budgetary independence of the Secretary-General. The first was "headed off in the corridors"; the second was defeated when proposed in the course of revising the Assembly's rules of procedure.

The deliberations of the Assembly's Fifth Committee are the last serious lap in the budgetary-administrative course, and one in which the Secretary-General and his chief adjutants fully participate. Mr. Lie as a rule will give a general justification of the budget at the opening meeting of the committee at each session. He remains on frequent call to bolster up any Assistant Secretary-General who is having a particularly hard time and to reply to the more important of the numerous criticisms of his administrative practices — criticisms which often are heavily dosed with political content and considerations.[35] Mr. Price's replies and interventions are constant; and the relevant Assistant Secretaries-General appear as their phases of budget and administration are reviewed.

In summary, the Secretary-General's relations with governments are to a considerable extent concerned with administrative affairs — affairs which of themselves often are peripherally political, and which are further important to the purposes of this study because of the bearing they have upon the position and prestige of the Secretary-General as a whole. The Secretary-General, of course, is a "whole," and the relations of the same man with the same governments concerning administrative and political matters naturally intermingle and interact.[36]

### Role in Assembly Resolutions

The Secretary-General is concerned with the resolutions of the Assembly in two distinct aspects: he and his senior associates take part in the drafting of a large number of the resolutions; and certain of the Assembly's resolutions endow the Secretary-General with *ad hoc* powers, often of a political nature.[37]

A key United Nations official estimates that the Secretariat, under the Secretary-General's direction, drafted roughly 30 per cent of the resolutions of the Fourth Session. Further, the Secretariat "had a hand in most all of them." That is not to say, of course, that the essential substance of these resolutions originated with the Secretariat. Rather, in the majority of cases, it was a question of delegations drawing upon the skill and experience of the Secretariat in drafting resolutions which aptly gave expression to the policies they favored. This in itself leaves a marginal area of influence to the Secretariat — an area which is greatly widened in the case of those fewer resolutions which do originate in substance with the Secretary-General. The resolution on the Palestine Refugee and Works Agency,[38] for example, initially was drafted by the Secretariat. "The Secretary-General," notes the official cited above, "met with the delegations repeatedly about it. His draft went through a dozen changes, in all of which the Secretary-General had a hand, by the time it finally emerged from committee."

Certain of the Assembly's resolutions (not necessarily those in the drafting of which the Secretary-General played a part) accord the Secretary-General a measure of discretion in the effecting of the duties which the resolutions assign. A few illustrations: The First Special Session authorized the Secretary-General to reimburse the expenses of the representatives on the Special Committee on Palestine "on such basis and in such form as he may determine most appropriate in the circumstances." [39] The Third Session, "desiring to improve the administrative control of expenditures incurred by missions away from headquarters," directed that "decisions relating to the itinerary and duration of journeys of missions meeting away from headquarters shall require the consent of the Secretary-General." In authorizing a technical assistance program, it prescribed that "the amount of services and the financial conditions under which they shall be furnished to the various governments shall be decided by the Secretary-General." The same session requested "the Secretary-General to take all necessary steps to extend aid to Palestine refugees" and "to appoint a Director of United Nations Relief for Palestine Refugees, to whom he may delegate such responsibility as he may consider appropriate." [40]

The Secretary-General's willingness to devote part of his energies to quasi-political and technical activities such as those concerned with the Palestine refugees and the abducted Greek children (or vacationing Greek children, whatever the case may be) provides still another contrast to the approach of the Secretaries-General of the League.[41] There was a reticence at Geneva to take on operational duties — so much so that Secretary-General Joseph Avenol actually resisted the attempt to make the League the world center with respect to intergovernmental action on behalf of the German refugees.[42] The contrast is the more noticeable in view of the resolution adopted by the United Nations General Assembly's Fourth Session requesting "the Secretary-General to prepare detailed draft provisions" for the establishment in January 1951 of a High Commissioner's Office for Refugees and prescribing that "the High Commissioner should be elected by the General Assembly, on the nomination of the Secretary-General." [43]

The political substratum of some resolutions which on the surface appear primarily administrative was revealed by the criticism directed at the Secretary-General's execution of a resolution of the Fifth Session. This resolution empowered him, in conjunction with the President of the General Assembly, to select the city in Europe most suitable for the site of the Assembly's Sixth Session. Mr. Lie journeyed to Europe, surveyed facilities, and negotiated with governments, but found that the governments concerned (France and the United Kingdom) then felt that they were unable to extend an invitation. The Secretary-General accordingly recommended that the Assembly reverse its decision to meet in Europe in 1951 and suggested that it meet instead at Flushing Meadow, New York. The reasons for Mr. Lie's recommendation seemed plain enough to most of the delegates, but Semyon K. Tsarapkin, of the Soviet delegation, could perceive the realities to which the others were blind. Mr. Lie's recommendation was the result of "machinations" and "skulduggery" by the United States Mission, which, Mr. Tsarapkin pointed out, wanted the Assembly to meet in New York because the atmosphere was "more propitious." [44]

Unequivocal political power was entrusted to the Secretary-General by the resolution entitled "United Action for Peace" passed by the Fifth Session — perhaps the most important resolution that the General Assembly has yet adopted. Section C of this so-called "Acheson plan" is devoted to the creation by the member states of elements of their armed forces suitable for service as United Nations units, upon the call of the Security Council or of the General Assembly. After recommending the constitution of such elements, the resolution "requests the Secretary-General to appoint, with the approval of the [Collective Measures] Committee . . . a panel of military experts who could be made available on request to Member States wishing to obtain technical advice regarding the organization, training and equipment for prompt service as United Nations units of the elements referred to."

The next section of the resolution establishes a Collective Measures Committee of fourteen members and directs it, "in consultation with the Secretary-General and with such Member States as the Committee finds appropriate," to study the methods which might be used to maintain and strengthen international peace and security, and to report its conclusions to the Security Council and the General Assembly.

The resolution further requests "the Secretary-General to furnish the staff and facilities necessary for the effective accomplishment" of the purposes set forth in the sections described above.[45]

In presenting the Acheson plan, John Foster Dulles noted that the panel of military experts would be "under the authority of the Secretary-General." [46] This provision provoked criticism not only from the Soviet bloc, which fought the plan's vital provisions, but from a state as friendly both to the plan and the Secretary-General as Israel.[47] But, as usual, Mr. Vishinsky supplied the most colorful assaults.

"This provision," the Soviet Foreign Minister informed the Political and Security Committee, "is basically and fundamentally incompatible with the Charter. It short-circuits the Military Staff Committee and the Security Council. . . It is even more bizarre than that: it speaks of military experts and advisers whom it suggests . . . will be under the orders of the Secretary-General. . .

"Apparently, the military experts will be at the beck and call of the Secretary-General. He is to be the commander-in-chief of the armed forces of the General Assembly. . .

"However, under the Charter the Secretary-General can only command his workers in the Secretariat. . . He does not have military experts with or without special panels. He has mimeograph machines. . . One does not need military experts to run mimeograph machines. . .

"The weakness and illegality of this proposal are patent." [48]

Mr. Vishinsky's description of the Secretary-General as the commander-in-chief of the Assembly's armies is of course exaggerated. But the political influence the Secretary-General might wield through his appointment of military experts is not negligible. It is a power which fits in with his initiative in promoting the formation of the United Nations army in Korea. As to the legality of his exercising that power, Mr. Lie need only look to the clause of Article 98 which provides that the Secretary-General "shall perform such other functions as are entrusted to him" by the General Assembly and the three Councils.

The Secretary-General publicly indicated his support of the Acheson plan while it was being debated by the Assembly, and, once it was adopted, he moved quickly in its implementation. He appointed a special coördinating committee of senior Secretariat members, attached to his Executive Office, to organize the plan's execution. In the effecting of the Assembly's resolution on "United Action for Peace," he noted, "I have taken the responsibility and leadership myself." [49]

### Other Assembly Activities

The Secretary-General's Assembly role is filled out in a number of other respects which do not accommodate themselves to the preceding categories. There is first of all his endless negotiating and conciliating activity among the delegations: this informal, largely "behind-the-scenes" endeavor, however, is a general characteristic of the Secretary-General's work; it cuts across his relationships with all of the organs and for the most part is not peculiar to the Assembly.

There are, however, certain types of his informal activity which spring from the structure of the Assembly and which should be here illustrated. For example, the Secretary-General is most active and influential at the opening of the Assembly, and in the weeks preceding, in the selection of the chairmen of the Assembly's six (sometimes seven) committees and, indeed, of the President of the Assembly himself. The permanent delegations seek out the Secretary-General's views upon the likely candidates; and the Secretary-General, while by no means forwarding a slate, responds, conscious of the importance of securing a vigorous President and competent chairmen.[50]

An innovation of the Executive Office also closely related to the Assembly's capacity for accomplishment are the Tuesday luncheons, initiated at the Third Session's Paris meetings by Mr. Cordier, which bring together the President, the committee chairmen, and the principal secretaries of the committees with Mr. Lie and the top members of his office. The custom has taken hold and has proved an exceedingly valuable coördinating device, "notably expediting" the Assembly's labors.[51]

Altogether, the relations of the Secretary-General with the General Assembly are important, varied, and pervasive. They form a significant segment of the whole of his political activity, and a segment that tends to grow as the role of the General Assembly within the United Nations itself progressively expands.[52]

CHAPTER **4**

## Relations with the Security Council

The Secretary-General has only once expressly invoked his powers under Article 99 — those powers which unquestionably must be the central consideration of any analysis of his relations with the Security Council. His caution, quite justifiable in the light of the surrounding facts of his relations with the Council and the members, would be depressingly anticlimactic to a study of his political authority if it connoted a record of little significant Security Council activity. But this is not the case. If the substance of Article 99 has not often appeared, its shadow has. Moreover, the "capacity" in which Article 98 prescribes the Secretary-General shall act has, through a series of initiatives and precedents, been defined so as to accord the Secretary-General a Security Council role of present importance and pregnant possibilities.

### "Upon the Invitation of the President"

It will be recalled that the provisional rules of procedure prepared for the Security Council by the Preparatory Commission lacked provision for the Secretary-General's addressing written or oral communications to the Council.[1] The Committee of Experts of the Security Council met in May of 1946, in the course of the drafting of the Council's revised rules, to remedy the deficiency. There was no question of the Secretary-General's being given some sort of relevant role. His representative, the Assistant Secretary-General for Security Council Affairs, Arkady A. Sobolev, informed the committee at its first session that the Secretary-General was "considerably embarrassed" at the lack of any provision permitting him to convey his opinion to the Council on matters under discussion.[2] The point at issue was whether his rights of communication would be restricted or unrestricted, a question which resolved itself largely into whether his interventions would be at the pleasure of the President of the Security Council or at the discretion of the Secretary-General.

Mr. Lie was modest in his approach, suggesting the adoption of a rule similar to that of the Economic and Social Council, which did contain the imminently controversial phrase, "upon the invitation of the President." [3] Professor Joseph E. Johnson (United States) proposed a rule along the lines of that of the General Assembly, one which was slightly narrower in the extent of the powers accorded the Secretary-General.[4] Professor Boris Stein (U.S.S.R.) dissented. The rule suggested was "insufficient, since it gave the Secretary-General the right of intervening only upon the invitation of the President." The Chinese delegate was of another mind, all for the inclusion of the phrase at issue, and Mr. Johnson backed him up.

The delegate of Australia then entered the discussion with fresh instructions to support the Soviet position. The Secretary-General's right of intervention was "absolute and not limited." [5] The debate thus joined ran on for five meetings. The Secretary-General, suggested the Soviet representative, "should be allowed to speak upon making a gesture to the President." He possessed, Dr. Rudzinski (Poland) affirmed, general powers to participate in the discussions of the Council. Professor Johnson, however, questioned whether the Charter could be interpreted as giving the Secretary-General an "absolute and unlimited right of intervention" — he was "not at all sure that the Charter can be construed as authorizing the Secretary-General to make comments on political and substantive matters." [6] The British delegate, true to national form, was for deleting nothing and defining nothing, but advocated that the committee "let experience show how the powers of the Secretary-General should be put into practice."

The modesty of the Secretary-General became disproportionate: Mr. Sobolev, apparently with instructions to press for the Economic and Social Council version of the rule, did just that. Australia refused to give way, but, with her allies, was outvoted, and the "invitation" phrase was provisionally adopted.[7] The British delegate arrived just afterward, late, with new instructions to support the Australian-Soviet view. The British shift apparently was sufficient to tip the balance in the direction of deleting the "invitation" phrase. For Brazil, Mexico, and Poland quickly fell in line, and Mr. Sobolev then promptly came forward to suggest the immediate drafting of a new text, which, adopted the same day, reads: "The Secretary-General, or his deputy acting on his behalf, may make either oral or written statements concerning any question under consideration by the Security Council." [8]

The Committee of Experts went on to draft a second rule,[9] which stated: "The Secretary-General may . . . be appointed as rapporteur for a specified question" ("rapporteur" as here employed meaning, as Professor Johnson put it, that the Secretary-General might be "appointed for the political task of reconciling two divergent views"). The committee's report included a provision that the Secretary-General's appointment as rapporteur would require his "approval and consent," so as to avoid imposing upon him duties of political mediation which might in his view impair his "impartial position." [10]

The Security Council has not as yet appointed the Secretary-General rapporteur for a question, although he has informally served in that capacity. The rule is nonetheless notable as a recognition by the Security Council of the Secretary-General's mediatorial and political capabilities.[11]

The committee specified that the Secretary-General's rights of communication should equally apply to subsidiary bodies of the Security Council. In this, however, it exempted from consideration the relations of the Secretary-General with the Military Staff Committee. The exemption was a significant one, the Military Staff Committee going so far as to refuse the Secretary-General the right even to be present at, let alone participate in, its discussions. Mr. Lie, considerably distressed, fought the issue out and won.

The role which the Secretary-General played in acquiring his rights of Security Council intervention appears from the record to have been a passive one. The record in this regard is deceptive. The Secretary-General in fact engaged in a "bitter fight" [12] to win his communication rights in the Councils and the Assembly. It seems that pressure was brought to bear privately by the Secretary-General upon certain of the delegations to which the representatives serving on the Committee of Experts were responsible. The British shift, in particular, seems in response to an unusual pressure from somewhere, for it does not conform to the general pattern of British thought respecting the Secretary-General. The United Kingdom, as will be discussed later, has been antipathetic to the Secretary-General's political activity. On the other hand, the British may possibly have altered their stand simply because free procedural interventions by the Secretary-General could facilitate the Council's work. At the time of the committee's drafting, after all, the Secretary-General had attempted no wholly political interventions (his Iranian intervention was primarily legal and, contrary to general impression, "all right" [13] in the British view). The United Kingdom might have not anticipated political interventions. Whatever the reason for the British shift, in the affair as a whole the Secretary-General played a more active role than appearances indicate.

It was in this way that the Secretary-General won the right to speak freely to the United Nations organ charged with "primary responsibility for the maintenance of international peace and security" [14]

### Implementation of Article 99

To say that the Secretary-General has but once invoked Article 99 is not to say that he has not often employed Article 99. Insofar as it comprises the greater part of the Charter's express affirmation of his political authority, the article may be said to be in fact "self-operating." Its presence of itself, without formal invocation, provides the virtually incontrovertible legal justification for that great part of the Secretary-General's political action which may reasonably be presented, if it must be justified at all, as coming within Article 99's compass.

More than that, however, it may be disclosed that "Mr. Lie has had in his pockets several times speeches which would have taken a strong political line and invoked Article 99." "A number of times the Secretary-General made it known [in restricted circles] that he was planning to employ his powers under Article 99. . . . There is no doubt that this intention, which the Secretary-General discussed with the principal members of the Security Council, was a stimulus to the raising of the issues in question by governments." [15]

Article 99 has thus often received *de facto*, if not *de jure*, recognition. It has come into its own as a new force on the international scene. The manner in which it has arrived, moreover, is, from the point of view of the Secretary-General, the optimum. For, if he often had had to call the article into play formally, he would have, on the one hand, exhausted part of his ammunition: there would seem to be a pragmatic limit to the frequency with which the Secretary-General could effectively employ so intense and dramatic a weapon. So many shots conserved leave so many more to be fired, should the need arise. And, on the other hand, had he publicly drawn the Security Council's attention to a matter threatening the maintenance of international peace and security, and had the Council failed to deal with the matter successfully, the Secretary-General's prestige would, in some degree at least, have sagged with that of the Security Council. As it generally has worked out, Mr. Lie has achieved some of the results of employing Article 99 without sustaining the disabilities its invocation might entail.

It is difficult to judge to what precise extent the governments that raised the questions in point were motivated by their knowledge that the Secretary-General was willing to do so if they did not. On the face of it, however, it seems likely that, once an issue was to be raised anyway, the governments concerned might well be impelled to do so themselves — not because of solicitude for the Secretary-General, but because it might well suit the strategy of a party to a dispute to display sufficient interest in and consciousness of its obligations under the Charter to take the initiative in raising the matter. Further, a state, in exercising its rights under Article 35, is not subject to the disabilities of the Secretary-General in invoking his comparable rights under Article 99. For a state is evidently not in like danger of "wearing out its welcome" by raising a situation or two before the Council; and, should the Council fail to settle a dispute to which the state raising it is a party, the state in question, if it coöperates reasonably with the Security Council's effort, is not as likely to participate in the Council's loss of face. Who can blame a state for drawing to the Security Council's attention a situation or dispute to which it is itself a party? But the Secretary-General is not a party to a dispute and is thus more vulnerable. (This is not to say that only a state party to a dispute may raise an issue before the Security Council — any member state may. But, as a rule, it is a party, or a state sympathetically linked to a party, that will raise an issue. In the latter case, the points made apply, though with less force.)

The Secretary-General explicitly cited, though he did not invoke, Article 99 before the Security Council in the course of its consideration of the chronic Greek question in September 1946. The case in point is of interest in five respects: it was a formal citation of the Article; the substance of the citation asserted the Secretary-General's investigatory powers; this assertion went unchallenged; in fact, it was endorsed by none other than Andrei Gromyko in the strongest possible terms ("in this case, as in all other cases, the Secretary-General must act"); and it was offered in the context of a resolution proposed by the United States which, though failing, foreshadowed what was to become an important function of the Secretary-General: the appointment of United Nations officers to special assignments charged with a high degree of political responsibility. The Secretary-General's affirmation of his investigatory authority, moreover, was the more far-reaching in that it claimed not merely the right to make inquiries or investigations without authorization from United Nations organs but the right to initiate such investigations even in cases where the Security Council has decided not to look into the matter. The importance of this possibility is increased by the fact that a proposal to the Council to investigate a dispute or a situation seems to be subject to the veto.

Ambassador Herschel Johnson (United States) proposed a resolution asking "that the Security Council . . . establish a commission of three individuals to be nominated by the Secretary-General, to represent the Security Council on the basis of their competence and impartiality, and to be confirmed by the Security Council" to investigate the facts of the Greek frontier situation. The discussion, a moment later, proceeded as follows:

THE SECRETARY-GENERAL: Just a few words to make clear my own position as Secretary-General and the rights of this office under the Charter. Should the proposal of the United States not be carried, I hope that the Council will understand that the Secretary-General must reserve his right to make such enquiries or investigations as he may think necessary, in order to determine whether or not he should consider bringing any aspect of this matter to the attention of the Council under the provisions of the Charter.

THE PRESIDENT [Andrei A. Gromyko]: As the representative of the Union of Soviet Socialist Republics, I would like to say the following in connexion with the statement made by the Secretary-General. I think that Mr. Lie was right in raising the question of his rights. It seems to me that in this case, as in all other cases, the Secretary-General must act. I have no doubt that he will do so in accordance with the rights and powers of the Secretary-General as defined in the Charter of the United Nations.[16]

There was no immediate further comment upon the Secretary-General's words, and no hint of a challenge of them from any quarter.[17]

Surpassing this formal citation of Article 99 was the Secretary-General's statement to the Security Council of June 25, 1950, on the Korean question. Then, "for the first time," Mr. Lie later affirmed, "I invoked Article 99 of the Charter." [18]

The Secretary-General apparently considers his Korean intervention an invocation of the article despite the fact that the emergency session of the Security Council was called at American initiative.[19] Clearly the United States, by requesting the meeting of the Council expressly to consider the Korean breach of the peace, first drew the Korean crisis to the Council's attention. The United Nations Commission in Korea, to be sure, in its initial report to the Secretary-General after the outbreak of the fighting, suggested that he consider employing his powers under the Charter to bring the Korean question to the Security Council's attention.[20] But the American call for an emergency Council session was made before the Secretary-General had received, let alone acted upon, the commission's report.

When the Council met, however, the President recognized the

Secretary-General first of all, for the purpose of his delivering any "interim reports on the present situation" which he might have received from the United Nations Commission in Korea.[21] Mr. Lie took this opportunity to define the "present situation" as "serious" and "a threat to the international peace" — a declaration clearly in the spirit of Article 99.[22]

The Secretary-General seems to regard his statement as also having fulfilled the letter of Article 99, apparently in the view that his drawing the Council's attention to a matter may constitute invocation of the article, even if his action supplements the earlier raising of the same issue by a member state. In describing his declaration of June 25 as an invocation of Article 99, the Secretary-General thus seems to define the article as admitting joint, as well as exclusive, action. While this interpretation is not unreasonable, it does not appear to be the one anticipated by the Preparatory Commission.[23]

The distinction is not of great importance, however, for Mr. Lie's Korean intervention unquestionably finds its fundamental authorization in Article 99. And since the Secretary-General must be allowed a certain authority which merits deference in the interpretation of "his" article, Mr. Lie's statement of June 25 is throughout this study referred to as the Secretary-General's first formal invocation of Article 99.

Mr. Lie previously had spoken of invoking Article 99 at the press conference at which he announced that he was placing his "ten points" on the General Assembly's provisional agenda. It could not be assumed, he cautioned, that he would not also draw the ten-point program to the attention of the Security Council. "I reserve my right to take such action if circumstances change." In this regard, the Secretary-General expressly noted his powers under Article 99.[24]

Again, in the spring of 1951, at a Belgrade press conference, the Secretary-General reaffirmed his readiness to invoke the article. In response to a question regarding the action the United Nations would take if Yugoslavia were attacked, Mr. Lie declared that, in exercise of Article 99, "I would warn the world that peace is threatened and then it would be for the Security Council and the United Nations to make their decisions. But I am not the master to make decisions. Each organ of the United Nations is its own master." [25]

## Legal Opinions

Some of the most significant interventions of the Secretary-General in the proceedings of the Security Council have taken the form of legal memoranda. The occasions have presented themselves, and the Secretary-General has been quick to take them up. Furthermore, a consideration favoring the submission of legal views may have been not only the desirability of and potentialities for legal exposition in the particular situations upon which the Secretary-General has seized, but additionally the superior defensibility of a position presented in legal terms, as contrasted with one presented in a fashion unabashedly political. Legal exploration does not tend to draw the Secretary-General quite so far out on a limb as may political commitment.

There have been five major legal interventions as of March 10, 1951, excluding advisory opinions on primarily procedural matters: the Iranian agenda question (1946); the powers of the Security Council and the Trieste Statute (1947); the enforcement of the Palestine partition (1948); representation in the United Nations with special reference to China (1950); and the competence of the Security Council to deal with the Korean invasion (1950). The last will be considered in the context of the Secretary-General's Korean activity. All are exceedingly important.

The Secretary-General's Iranian opinion, delivered in April 1946 when Mr. Lie had been in office only two and a half months, marks his first substantive intervention in the Security Council's proceedings. It is noteworthy in this and several other respects.

It will be recalled that in the course of the Council's consideration of Iran's complaint that the Soviet Union was keeping troops upon her territory in violation of treaty obligations, Iran suddenly withdrew her charges, announcing that amicable negotiations with the U.S.S.R. were in progress. The Soviet Union, supported by Poland and France, thereupon took the position that the withdrawal of the complaint by the party which had requested its consideration by the Council removed the complaint from the

Council's agenda, the more so in that the accused party also requested that the item be dropped. An eight-member majority disagreed.

At this point, the Secretary-General offered an unsolicited memorandum setting forth his views on the question. In substance, if not in precise logic, it agreed with the position of the minority.[26] The President of the Council, Quo Tai-chi of China, noting that he had just got the memorandum as he came into the room, proposed referring it to the Council's Committee of Experts. It was agreed that the committee would report back in two days.

After some discussion of Mr. Lie's position, mainly critical, the President, "irritated . . . [at not having] been consulted or advised of the Secretary General's unprecedented decision to intervene on controversial issue" and "ready to ignore"[27] Mr. Lie's communication, asked the Security Council to vote on the Soviet resolution, which proposed the deletion of the Iranian item from the agenda. M. Henri Bonnet (France) and Dr. Oscar Lange (Poland) then took the floor on points of order, the former requesting that the report of the Committee of Experts be had before the taking of a vote, the latter expressing his "astonishment at today's procedure."

DR. LANGE: The Secretary-General has submitted to us a legal opinion . . . and then we went on discussing as if the Secretary-General's opinion did not exist. I submit . . . that the Secretary-General is an important official of the United Nations, invested with special and important powers by the Charter, and that we cannot vote now as if his opinion did not count or exist. . .

THE PRESIDENT: I am quite agreeable to the suggestion that we cannot vote upon the Soviet representative's motion until we have heard from the Committee of Experts. . . In regard to the observation by my Polish colleague that the Secretary-General is a very important official of the Secretariat, in that there is no disagreement, no difference on my part. But I would like to point out to him that in Chapter XV, Article 97, it is expressly stated that, "He shall be the chief administrative officer of the Organization." So whatever observations we may receive from him, and I am sure the Council will wish to give due weight and due consideration to his observations, the decision remains with the Council.

MR. GROMYKO: . . . Since we have decided that the Secretary-

General's memorandum must be referred to the Committee of Experts, how can we immediately vote or take a decision?

As regards the functions of the Secretary-General, the question which arose here was incidental. Of course, these functions are more serious and more responsible than has been suggested just now. It is sufficient to refer to one Article of the Charter in order to come precisely to this conclusion regarding the very great responsibility incumbent upon the Secretary-General. Article 99 [etc., etc.].

The Secretary-General has all the more the right, and moveover the duty, to submit reports on the various aspects of questions that are being considered by the Security Council.[28]

The Council failed to agree upon Mr. Lie's view, but the Secretary-General won something of a victory nevertheless. There was some criticism that he intervened "at a time when the Council had divided so sharply in public debate." [29] There are rumors that hot words passed between Mr. Stettinius and Mr. Lie in the Delegates' Lounge. Be that as it may, Mr. Lie, "certainly not deterred in this case by the fact that he was likely to find the Soviet Union on his side," [30] succeeded in establishing the precedent, which went unchallenged and indeed was subscribed to warmly by the U.S.S.R., of addressing the Council on substantive matters.

It may well be that Mr. Lie thought that an issue upon which he happened to find himself in agreement with the Soviet Union, such as this, would provide a particularly strategic opportunity to set the precedent of substantive intervention. For Mr. Lie could have had reason to doubt the Soviet willingness to admit his right to intervene in the Council's deliberations. That willingness might perhaps be promoted by his choosing for his initial intervention an issue in which his views were consonant with Moscow's.

The results of his Iranian intervention, at any rate, are accepted, in informed circles, as having influenced the Soviet Union in his favor. One key member of Mr. Lie's entourage notes that the Iranian affair antedated the discussions of the Committee of Experts on the Secretary-General's rights of communication with the Security Council. He suggests that Mr. Lie's stand had something to do with the positive attitude displayed by the Soviet Union toward the Secretary-General's powers. At the very least,

Mr. Lie's Iranian intervention was helpful in conditioning the committee as a whole to the idea of the Secretary-General's intervening. At most, it may well have had the crucial effect upon the development of the Soviet attitude toward Mr. Lie which Dr. Rudzinski, former acting chief of the Polish delegation to the United Nations, suggested when he stated: "The Soviet Union, misled by Mr. Lie's intervention in the Iranian affair, favored granting him broad political powers and regrets now her mistake." [31]

But if the Secretary-General's Iranian opinion may be judged to have had such repercussions in the Soviet camp, it is the more likely that it had the effect in Washington which some observers ascribe to it: that of contributing to the impression of Mr. Lie's being tilted toward Moscow — an impression which lingered, particularly in certain Congressional circles, until his Korean initiative. In this light, it may be that the Secretary-General would have done better to have chosen a less controversial issue for the occasion of his first intervention in the proceedings of the Security Council.

Dr. Herbert V. Evatt indicates, indeed, that the Iranian interposition has had a deterrent influence upon the Secretary-General's political activity, because of the adverse reaction to it in certain Western quarters.

The Secretary-General and his staff have not as yet fully availed themselves of this valuable opportunity [their rights of communication assured in the rules of procedure] of guiding the work of the United Nations. This may be due to some extent to the particular circumstances of an intervention in the Security Council which the Secretary-General made in the Iranian case, when the view he expressed did not coincide with the opinion of the majority of the members of the Council. I think, however, it would be unfortunate if this particular experience discouraged the Secretary-General from taking a bold part in the work of the organization on appropriate occasions. I think all members of the Organization should encourage him to take more initiative, and even when they disagree with any particular views he expresses or action he takes, they should make it clear that judicious intervention by him or his deputies is both proper and welcome.[32]

But that the Iranian affair has in fact had such a deterrent influence is denied by sources close to Mr. Lie.

The Secretary-General's intervention nine months later in the discussions on the competence of the Security Council to accept the Trieste Statute was perhaps a more important one in its substance, but a good deal less noticeable in its political reverberations.

Australia maintained with characteristic originality against a Council majority of ten (in itself something unique) that the Security Council's jurisdiction did not admit of the responsibilities which would devolve upon it with the acceptance of the Trieste instruments.[33] "In view of the importance of the issue raised [by the Australian stand]," stated Assistant Secretary-General Sobolev, "the Secretary-General has felt bound to make a statement which may throw light on the constitutional questions presented." He then proceeded to set forth the view that "the Members of the United Nations have conferred upon the Security Council powers commensurate with its responsibility for the maintenance of peace and security. The only limitations are the fundamental principles and purposes found in Chapter I of the Charter." And the Secretary-General saw the obligation of all members to carry out the decisions of the Security Council to be "clear." [34]

The view to which the Secretary-General so cogently subscribed was adopted by the Council by a vote of 10–0–1 (Australia abstaining). Nothing was said of the propriety or the impropriety of the Secretary-General's submitting a statement — it seemed to be taken for granted. His intervention cannot be so taken for our purposes, for in addition to its further demonstrating that "the Secretary-General . . . felt bound to make a statement," it illustrates Mr. Lie's consistent endeavor to do what is within his power to see that the United Nations plays its maximum role on the world stage.

The Palestine case involved not so much an intervention by the Secretary-General as a response to a challenge; it was more a denial of his having given a legal opinion than an exposition of one.

The General Legal Division of the Legal Department prepared, at the request of the Palestine Commission — the commission of "five lonely pilgrims" created by the General Assembly's partition resolution of November 29, 1947 — a paper on the rights of the Security Council relative to the Palestine dispute. The opinion acknowledged that there were no precise provisions of the Charter which would authorize the Council to accept responsibilities such as those involved in the implementation of the partition plan. But it recalled the Secretary-General's Trieste opinion and suggested that by its decision in that case the Council "recognized the principle that it has sufficient power, under the terms of Article 24 of the Charter, to assume new responsibilities, on condition that they relate directly or even indirectly to the maintenance of international peace and security, and that in discharging these duties, the Security Council acts in accordance with the purposes and principles of the United Nations." [35] The paper further observed that if the Security Council considered that it was within its competence to accept responsibilities for the carrying out of provisions of a treaty negotiated outside of the United Nations (as in the Trieste case) it would be the more appropriate for it to accept responsibilities for the implementation of a plan adopted by the General Assembly.[36] The legal content of the paper, in short, was virtually identical with that of the Secretary-General's Trieste opinion — an affirmation of the residuary powers of the Security Council.

The paper was drawn up more or less routinely (the General Legal Division prepares a large number of legal papers in the normal course of its work, at the request of the legislative organs and the Secretary-General) and attracted no particular notice until a delegate who had read it referred to it in a speech. It was thereupon circulated to the members of the Security Council, more than a month after its preparation.

Dr. José Arce, then Permanent Representative of Argentina, argued, before a closed meeting of the Council, that the Secretariat had exceeded its powers in preparing such a memorandum. (Dr. Arce, it will be recalled, had earlier challenged the Secretariat's giving an opinion in the India-Pakistan succession case. It may also be pertinent to note that he was unfriendly to the political implications of the Palestine opinion.) Mr. Lie responded that he was giving no opinion on the substance of the case, but reserved his right to do so. The Secretariat, however, as long as he was its chief, would have the right to express opinions if asked for them by a United Nations organ.[37] The Secretary-General's stand was supported by several delegations.

The next day at his press conference, Mr. Lie publicly disassociated himself from the legal memorandum in question, noting that the Legal Department handed down an average of seven opinions a day, and inferring that he could hardly be held responsible for all of these. The Secretary-General added that, should he give his opinion on the subject, he would do so in a statement to the Security Council.[38]

Such was the curious nature of Mr. Lie's Palestinian "intervention." His disclaimer cuts short the political implications of the position taken in the paper. Apparently, Mr. Lie dissociated himself in the belief that it was strategically unsound to commit himself publicly to a view which he unquestionably shared and, in fact, was engaged in promoting to the best of his ability in private negotiations with the governments concerned. The Secretary-General's action may have been politically expedient, but it seems to have been administratively irregular. For it is difficult to reconcile Mr. Lie's disclaimer with his position as "the chief administrative officer of the Organization" (Article 97) and the provision of the staff regulations that "all members of the staff are subject to the authority of the Secretary-General, and are responsible to him in the exercise of their functions." [39]

The Chinese representation case is the star example of the Secretary-General's bringing to bear on one issue his three instruments of political leverage: the opportunities inherent in his relationships with organs; the power of his appeal to public opinion; and, most important, the pressure he may exert in his private negotiations with governments. The latter aspects of his Chinese effort will be dealt with in their place. A word or two now about them, however, to put the "organic" phase of his endeavor — the memorandum entitled "Legal Aspects of Problems of Representation in the United Nations" [40] — in perspective.

The Soviet Union began its six-month boycott of United Nations organs in mid-January 1950. Mr. Lie, declaring a week later that "the shares of the United Nations company are lower than they have ever been before," [41] launched a series of private conversations with the delegations of the members of the Security Council in an effort to break the deadlock over which of the rival Chinese regimes was to represent that permanent member of the Security Council in the Council and other United Nations organs. His belief that the solution lay in according China's seat to the new Peiping regime was indicated publicly as early as January 20, when he stated at a press conference that the 450,000,000 people of China "should not be deprived of representation." [42]

One facet of Mr. Lie's effort was that of distinguishing between the question of representation in the United Nations and the question of recognition of a government by member states. It is this distinction that he set forth with great force and suggestiveness in his memorandum on the legal aspects of representation. The linkage of representation with recognition, the memorandum held, "is unfortunate from the practical standpoint, and wrong from the standpoint of legal theory." Practically, it involves the risk of the majority of members in one organ recognizing one government and that of another organ recognizing the rival government, and, in organs of limited membership such as the Security Council, the additional deficiency of determining representation by the "purely arbitrary fact of the particular governments which have been elected to serve at a given time." Legally, it runs counter to the fact that recognition is an individual act of a state and acceptance of representation a collective act of the members of the organ, it being "inadmissible" to condition the latter by a requirement that it be preceded by individual recognition. The memorandum went on to cite a substantial store of League and United Nations precedent for divorce between representation and recognition, and pointed out that the International Court of Justice had ruled that the lack of diplomatic relations with an applicant state does not constitute juridical justification for a member's voting against the admission of the applicant. "Unbroken practice" demonstrates the cleavage between recognition and representation — a practice which "conforms to the basic character of the Organization [since] the United Nations is not an association limited to . . . governments of similar ideological persuasion" (recognition, it having been shown, being widely regarded as a political act). So the principle of numerical preponderance of recognition cannot correctly decide between rival governments purporting to represent the same nation. "Is any other principle possible?" asks the memorandum in conclusion.

It is submitted that the proper principle can be derived by analogy from Article 4 of the Charter. This Article requires that an applicant for membership must be able and willing to carry out the obligations of membership. . . [These] obligations . . . can be carried out only by governments which in fact possess the power to do so . . . the question at issue should be which of these two [rival] governments in fact is in a position to employ the resources and direct the people of the State in fulfilment of the obligations of membership. In essence, this means inquiry as to whether the new government exercises effective authority within the territory of the State and is habitually obeyed by the bulk of the population.

If so, it would seem appropriate for the United Nations organs, through their collective action, to accord it the right to represent the State in the Organization, even though individual Members of the Organization refuse, and may continue to refuse, to accord it recognition as the lawful government for reasons which are valid under their national policies.[43]

It is difficult to assess conclusively the effects of the foregoing upon the policies of the members. There is no reaction of the Security Council, as such, to survey, nor any report of its Committee of Experts, since the Council was not formally presented with the memorandum. But, to all appearances, the impact of the memorandum, of itself, was limited. It may well have made more of a dent than the words of Ernest A. Gross, deputy United States representative to the Security Council, would indicate. "I don't see how anybody could possibly quarrel with that [Mr. Lie's representation thesis]," asserted Mr. Gross, who then blandly continued: "Because of the fact that we do not recognize the Chinese Communist Government, we therefore will vote against . . . seating the Communist representative." [44] Yet, generally, as a legal approach to a dominantly political issue, the memorandum does not seem to have much influenced the members.

Mr. Lie, of course, has not confined his attempts to resolve the

China deadlock to a legal exposition. And in the context of his broader approach to the China question, the political implications of the memorandum are clear. There is little doubt about which of the two rival Chinese regimes would sit in United Nations organs if the criteria of representation put forth by the Secretary-General were to be accepted by the members. The memorandum's importance, then, lies in its furnishing a sound legal rationale for the Secretary-General's intensive political effort to overcome the China impasse by promoting the admission of the Peiping government. While of itself too "detached" to be of decisive importance in affecting the policies of members relatively unconcerned about the legal strength of their position, the memorandum fits in with and facilitates Mr. Lie's political assault upon a highly political issue.

The representation memorandum brings the Secretary-General's activity in expressing legal opinions to a peak of vitality that will not easily be surpassed. Not only is a controversial position on a crucial question set forth with extreme vigor, but a course of action — inquiry by the Security Council "as a means of reaching a considered decision based on the facts as to which of the two governments 'is in a position to employ the resources and direct the people of the state in fulfillment of the obligations of membership' " [45] — is suggested. The representation memorandum emphasizes what an integral part of the Secretary-General's political armory is the weapon of legal opinion.

The cases cited by no means exhaust the Secretary-General's deliverance of legal opinions. There are, in connection with the Security Council, several dealing with procedure of little political interest; and Council members also frequently consult informally the legal section of the Secretariat which is attached to the Council on a semi-permanent basis and which devotes its energies largely to the Council's legal problems.

The Secretary-General's legal opinions, moreover, are not confined to the Security Council's work. Legal advisers are attached to the committees of the General Assembly and are often asked for impromptu opinions by the delegates, both in the course of the proceedings and, more informally still, outside of them. The

Assembly also requests more considered opinions of the Secretary-General. For example, in 1949 it asked him to present an analysis of the question of the majority required for the Assembly's adoption of amendments to and parts of proposals relating to important questions.[46] At the Fifth Session, the Secretary-General submitted a report, the excellence of which was acknowledged on all sides,[47] advancing the view that a two-thirds majority is properly required.[48] The Assembly adopted a new rule of procedure reflecting the Secretary-General's conclusions.[49]

The Secretary-General similarly advises the Economic and Social Council. Two illustrations, prominent because of their political implications, are his opinion relating to the disposition of the Yugoslav gold assets — an opinion which the minority attacked as being solicitous of American interests [50] — and that concerning the effects of the United States Internal Security Act and its implementation upon the admission to headquarters of the representatives of nongovernmental organizations which enjoy consultative status with the Council.[51] The Secretary-General's endeavor to assure legitimate consultants, regardless of their political persuasion, access to United Nations headquarters, in accordance with the Headquarters Agreement,[52] has not been popular with alarmist elements in the United States.

Not all of the Secretary-General's legal opinions are advisory in nature. Rather, those relating to his administrative functions may have decisive force. Yet at the same time these administrative opinions may be of important political consequence. An outstanding example is the opinion which was drawn up in response to the situation posed by the partition of India in 1947. India was a member state when its territory was divided and two dominions created. Normal duties confronted the Secretary-General with a decision of evident political connotation. Should the Secretary-General — to take the least of the resultant problems — fly the flag of just India, or of India and of Pakistan, or of neither? The Secretary-General decided that the new Dominion of India continued as an original member — that partition did not constitute dismemberment of India, but merely secession of part of its territory. The seceding area, Pakistan, the Secretary-General adjudged to be a nonmember state.[53] This view, while decisive for the purposes of the Secretariat, was advisory as far as the other organs of the United Nations were concerned.

Notwithstanding the subsequent agreement of India and Pakistan upon the Secretary-General's view,[54] Argentina maintained that both dominions should be treated equally and challenged the Secretary-General's right to deliver an opinion on the issue.[55] But the action of the Security Council and of the General Assembly in admitting Pakistan, while regarding India as a member not requiring such admission, ratified the Secretary-General's conclusions.[56] And the Assembly thus tacitly upheld the Secretary-General's right to take a stand on the question.[57]

A less unusual variation of the Secretary-General's being confronted with legal decisions of political implication as the result of routine duties arises from certain resolutions of United Nations organs which direct the Secretary-General to transmit the text of the resolution in point to all nonmember states. The question of what is a nonmember state then appears. Is, for example, the Vatican a state? The Secretary-General has chosen to regard it as one. But the decision with regard to Outer Mongolia, among others, is more difficult.[58]

The legal activity of the Secretary-General of the League of Nations — to conclude this digression from the Secretary-General's relations with the Security Council — was modest, in contrast with that of his United Nations successor. The League Secretary-General would take the initiative in presenting to the rapporteur of the League Council a legal opinion on the question with which the rapporteur was charged. But he did not present formal legal opinions to the Council as a whole.

### Korea

The initiative of the Secretary-General in the Korean question would be in a class by itself even if the Secretary-General did not regard it as his first invocation of Article 99. When viewed in the context of the Korean crisis, it appears as a highly significant factor in the development of the remarkably vigorous United Nations reaction to the North Korean aggression. When viewed in the context of the expanse of the political authority of the Secretaryship General, it bears an importance quite transcendent.

Mr. Lie learned of the invasion of South Korea at about midnight, June 24, 1950. He at once cabled the United Nations Commission in Korea requesting a report — a report which was to comprise the main body of facts upon which the Security Council was to base its finding of an act of aggression. A few hours later, Ambassador Ernest Gross telephoned Mr. Lie at his Forest Hills home to request him to arrange an emergency meeting of the Security Council to deal with the Korean hostilities. The session was promptly called for two o'clock that afternoon.

In the eleven hours between the 3:00 A.M. telephone call of Mr. Gross and the 2:00 P.M. calling to order of the Security Council by its President, Sir Benegal Rau of India, Mr. Lie came to a decision crucial to his career, his office, and to the United Nations. The Secretary-General could have contented himself with formally presenting to the Security Council the report which he had received from the United Nations Commission in Korea. Together with providing the secretarial assistance which the emergency session of the Security Council required, this would have fulfilled all a conservative interpretation of his powers would demand. But Mr. Lie chose a bolder role, highly charged with political connotations. He addressed the Council, at the very beginning of its meeting, before the members had stated the policies of their governments, and he declared, with considerable force:

It [is] plain that military actions have been undertaken by North Korean forces. These actions are a direct violation of the Resolution of the General Assembly [reaffirming the South Korean Government as the country's lawful regime and extending the life of the Korean Commission] . . . as well as a violation of the principles of the Charter.

The present situation is a serious one and is a threat to the international peace. The Security Council is, in my opinion, the competent organ to deal with it.

I consider it the clear duty of the Security Council to take steps necessary to reëstablish peace in that area.[59]

Thus, the Secretary-General labeled the North Koreans as the aggressors, anticipating similar action by the Council; he noted the dangerous international ramifications of an outbreak which the Soviet world would attempt to portray as civil war; he delivered the unsolicited and immeasurably important legal opinion that the Security Council was "the competent organ" to deal with the Korean crisis, a thesis offered in spite of and in opposition to the Soviet view that the Security Council was not competent to act because of the presence of the "Kuomintang clique" and the absence of representatives of the U.S.S.R. and the Chinese Communist government; and he called upon the Security Council to fulfill its "clear duty" to meet the aggressor's challenge. With his Security Council statement, Mr. Lie anticipated and associated himself and his office with the most determined effort the world has yet seen to give reality to the principles of collective security.[60]

The development of the Secretary-General's Korean role has been as dynamic as its debut. The evening of June 26, the day after the Security Council called upon the North Koreans to withdraw to the Thirty-eighth Parallel and the day before it authorized members to render armed assistance to the Republic of Korea to compel the northerners to withdraw, Mr. Lie, in a radio interview, foreshadowed the Council's employment of military coercion by expressing the view that an international police force, if it existed, could be "properly used" in Korea. "If the Security Council had at its disposal military forces as mentioned in Article 43 of the Charter, I believe it could use those military forces in this situation if the order to cease-fire was not obeyed by the North Korean forces." [61]

And in the fabrication of the "ad hoc" United Nations army for Korea, which was formed in the absence of such an international police force, the Secretary-General took a preëminent part. When the Security Council adopted its resolution calling upon the member states to give armed aid to the South Koreans, Mr. Lie followed up circulation of the resolution with a cable of his own, asking every member state to inform him of what type of assistance it might be able to render. Two weeks later, as the troops under General MacArthur's command grew increasingly hard pressed, the Secretary-General, noting that he had been advised that the Unified Command was in urgent need of additional "effective assistance," cabled the fifty member states that had approved the Security Council's call for armed support of South Korea: "I should be grateful . . . if your Government would consider the possibility of such assistance, including combat forces, particularly ground forces." [62] The cables were drafted by the Secretary-General's staff after conferences held at Mr. Lie's initiative with representatives of the United States, of South Korea, and of the Security Council. They proved to be of considerable importance in assuring that the forces implementing the Security Council's decisions would be United Nations forces in some substance as well as spirit.

In the two weeks that intervened between the dispatching of these crucial cables, the Secretary-General's effort to effect and assist United Nations policy in Korea continued unabated. Mr. Lie's aides, in reply to notes from the U.S.S.R. and Czechoslovakia alleging the illegality of the Security Council's Korean resolutions, reiterated the Secretary-General's view that the Security Council's actions were wholly legal. The Secretary-General underlined his support of the Council's stand by appointing a personal representative to the United Nations Commission on Korea, Colonel Alfred Katzin of South Africa, whom he charged with liaison with the Unified Command. At headquarters, Korean coördination was vested in an informal committee of top Secretariat members, which, significantly, the Soviet Assistant Secretary-General in charge of Security Council Affairs, Constantin Zinchenko, was not invited to join. And, in response to reports of atrocities in Korea, Mr. Lie cabled both sides appealing for adherence to the Geneva Convention on the treatment of prisoners — an appeal to which both sides promptly gave favorable response.

The Secretary-General has since sustained the vigor of his Korean policy in the face of some of the strongest attacks which the Soviet Union has made upon him. "The abettor of American aggression . . . humbly aiding Truman and Acheson to wreck the United Nations" [63] (a description to be more fully examined later) took the lead in preparing United Nations relief activity in Korea, a role allotted to him by the Security Council. [64] He participated in the Council's private sessions, designed to persuade the Soviet representative, Jacob Malik, to end his obstruction of the August meetings of the Council, which were held under the Soviet delegate's presidency.

The Economic and Social Council and the General Assembly, in putting Korean relief on a firmer basis, authorized the Secretary-General to appoint the United Nations Agent General for Korean Reconstruction.[65] The Assembly directed the Agent General to "maintain close contact with the Secretary-General," [66] and requested the Secretary-General to make available to the maximum extent "such facilities, advice and services as the Agent General may request." [67] Mr. Lie appointed J. Donald Kingsley, the Director General of the International Refugee Organization, as Agent General.

When, after the Chinese intervention, Peiping sent a delegation to Lake Success under the chairmanship of General Wu Hsiu-chuan, the Secretary-General lost no time in establishing a negotiatory relationship with the Chinese Communist representatives. Mr. Lie gave a dinner at his home for the Peiping delegation. The guest list suggests that the Secretary-General had more in mind than a gesture of proper hospitality. In addition to the four members of the Chinese delegation, the highest ranking United Nations representatives of the United Kingdom, India, Israel, Sweden, and Pakistan — all states which had recognized the Peiping regime — were invited. Assistant Secretary-General Zinchenko was conspicuous by his presence. The conversation reportedly covered the entire field of Communist China's relations with the United Nations. It was at this dinner that the Foreign Minister of Israel, Moshe Sharett, first broached the principles of the cease-fire resolution adopted a month later by the General Assembly.

When the cease-fire committee created by that resolution initiated its attempts to negotiate with the Peiping delegation, Mr. Lie was useful in serving as intermediary between the committee and General Wu. The Secretary-General also carried on a number of private conversations with the Chinese representatives. That the visit from Peiping was not more productive was not the fault of the Secretary-General. Mr. Lie similarly took a constructive part in promoting the initiation of the cease-fire negotiations which began in the field in the summer of 1951.

Before the Chinese intervention and after, Mr. Lie seized every opportunity to rally the United Nations Korean effort and to place that effort in the perspective of United Nations peace aims. The following quotations are typical of his many public statements in this vein:

"There is no road back from Korea, except a victory for the principle of justice over the principle of power politics." [68] "I do not believe that the U.N. contingent will be forced off its bridgehead in Korea . . . [but] even if developments should force the U.N. forces to give up their bridgehead in Korea, our course is clear. . . United Nations action must continue until the North Koreans have withdrawn beyond the 38th parallel, be it by their own free will, by force or through negotiations." [69]

And, "It will not be enough to win from the North Koreans obedience to the Security Council's cease-fire order of June 25 and their withdrawal. . . The aim of the United Nations is and must be a united and independent Korea, in which all the people of Korea are able freely to select a government of their own choosing." [70]

"The job of the United Nations is to do all it can to prevent a third world war, by conciliation wherever possible, by force when necessary. In Korea there has plainly been a well-prepared armed attack by North Korean forces upon the Republic of Korea, which was established under United Nations auspices. That attack is being met, as it should be, by collective United Nations action to repel it and to restore peace in Korea. It is my duty as Secretary-General, as it is the duty of all the Member Governments, to do everything to bring this United Nations action in Korea to a successful conclusion." [71]

"For the first time in the history of the world the enforcement of peace has been undertaken by a world organization. . . The precedent of Korea will not be forgotten. The world will find it more difficult than ever before, if not impossible, to permit any future cases of armed aggression to pass unchallenged. Enforcement action to restore peace should now become a matter of course." [72]

"The attack upon the Republic of Korea by North Korean forces is the latest and worst of a series of dangerous crises . . .

worse even than the deadlock in Berlin. . . [But] if the United Nations is able to emerge intact and successful from the present crisis, its strength and influence will be immeasurably enhanced, and the world will be much closer to lasting peace than at any time since 1945." [73]

When some of these early hopes of constructive by-products flowing from the Korean struggle were dashed by the massive Chinese intervention, the Secretary-General reacted with a mixture of horror, understanding, and determination which did him credit:

"The new events in Korea monopolize all our thoughts.

"For all of us who have shared the labor and the dreams of the past five years, this is a moment when we are sick at heart.

"The peace of the world is in the gravest danger only five years after the end of the second world war and the establishment of the United Nations." [74]

"The collective military defense against aggression and invasion which the United Nations undertook in Korea was the first action of its kind in history. It was not without risk. . .

"Victory for the United Nations' principles . . . was . . . within sight until 4 or 5 weeks ago. It was then that a half million Chinese soldiers were suddenly thrown into the battle. . . The political and military backing which two great powers had previously given to the aggressors now became a direct military intervention as far as one of them was concerned. . .

"The blame . . . could not be placed upon the United Nations. . . The full responsibility would rest with those who have been pulling the strings — who perhaps may hope for selfish advantages through aggression — and who do not seem to hesitate from taking such steps which *might* lead to another world war.

"The United Nations does not wish to get into a state of war with the new China. . . There, a revolution has taken place which, whatever one's own opinion may be, is now proceeding to transform the conditions under which almost half a billion people are living. China is faced with enormous problems and one can only hope that the new Central Government in Peiping will fully comprehend the importance of peaceful international coöperation when it comes to the future of the Chinese people.

"The world has sympathy for China and wishes the best for the Chinese people. It is not correct that history always repeats itself and that there *has* to be or *must* come revolutionary or interventionist wars [as] we had them after the French and Russian revolutions, as the new rulers in China perhaps believe.

"The world would wish to coöperate with China . . . if there should be an opportunity to do so. . ."[75]

"I still hope that the United Nations will be able to bring about a peaceful settlement. . .

"I can assure you that it will *not* be the fault of the United Nations if this peaceful effort fails.

"We must stand firmly for the Charter, but we must seek every honorable means to prevent the conflict from spreading, to bring an end to the fighting, and to renew negotiation on the wider issues that divide the world."[76]

"[But] the position is that . . . aggression . . . must be repelled, sooner or later. . . This basic position . . . the United Nations cannot go back on. . . If the United Nations should lose in Korea we would have reason to ask ourselves: which country may become the next victim?"[77]

It is clear that the strength and influence of the Secretary-General were immeasurably enhanced by the Korean initiative Mr. Lie took. It was an initiative of such thrust and vitality as to itself establish the Secretary-General's political potency; as is, it multiplied that potency many times. With Korea, the Secretary-General emerged as a coördinate arm of the Security Council's attempt to enforce collective security, as earlier he had emerged, in his efforts to overcome the East-West deadlock concerning Chinese representation and other issues, as the catalyst of United Nations conciliation.

The Secretary-General's Korean stand, moreover, exceeds all others in the unmistakability of its political character, not only because it revealed the Secretary-General in the remarkable role of organizer of an international army, but because it showed him as a foremost advocate of employing that army against the declared interests of the Soviet world. This highly political phenomenon raises considerations fundamental to the evolution of the

Secretaryship General. It compels one to qualify the foregoing assessment of the Secretary-General's Korean policy as having expanded the influence of his office. For it is commonly assumed — and we have joined in the assumption — that a prime element of the Secretary-General's influence is his relatively detached position, his opportunity and obligation, as spokesman for the interests of the United Nations as a whole, to avoid partisan identification with any particular Power or group of Powers.

This is not to say that the Secretary-General is to be "neutral," above all else. For neutrality implies political abstinence, not political action, and, in certain circumstances, might well keep the Secretary-General from conscientious fulfillment of his Charter obligations. There is, for example, an "unneutral" predisposition about the Secretary-General's calling the Security Council's attention, under Article 99, to a matter threatening the peace, since it is unlikely that it can ever be in the equal interests of the parties to a dispute, in an exact, precisely neutral degree, that a situation in which they are involved be brought before the Council. Indeed, Mr. Lie himself has indicated that it is not his job to be neutral, but rather to give loyal effect to the decisions of the other United Nations organs.[78] The difficulty is to square this precept of giving loyal effect to United Nations decisions with the nonpartisan role obviously desirable for the Secretary-General. In certain situations, this is as difficult as squaring the circle.

The Korean crisis was such a situation. A deterioration of the Secretary-General's detached position seems to have been unavoidable in this instance of an armed attack upon the United Nations by one of the extremes among which the Secretary-General would normally and commendably attempt to balance himself. Mr. Lie unquestionably compromised his usefulness by his Korean policy, insofar as it depends upon his successfully avoiding a major commitment to one side or the other. This is an unfortunate but, it would seem, inevitable outcome of a situation in which nonpartisanship and political action in the interests of the United Nations as a whole were incompatible. A certain loss of "availability" seems to have been the price Mr. Lie paid for his honest political potency.

To acknowledge that Mr. Lie sustained a certain loss of availability is not to suggest, however, that he is a total loss to the United Nations potential for conciliating between East and West. For the Power he offended by his Korean stand seems to react in a singular way toward its "enemies." There is considerable evidence indicating that the Kremlin feels more at home in negotiating with its sternest opponents than with its wavering friends. It is, in fact, conceivable that Trygve Lie will be more useful as an intermediary between East and West — understood by one side and trusted by the other — than he was in the days preceding his Korean intervention. It would be presumptuous to submit that this is likely. But the fact that Mr. Lie had nine confidential conversations with the ambassador of Communist China, General Wu, in the course of the ambassador's brief stay, perhaps indicates that it is not impossible.

## Other Interventions

The Secretary-General's participation in the Organization's Korean effort outshines his previous Security Council interventions but does not take away from their importance. Many, such as his legal opinions, are significant in themselves. Others, such as those to be considered now, are noteworthy as precedent for present or potential activity of the Secretary-General. These interventions of the Secretary-General in less dramatic spheres undoubtedly paved the way for his Korean initiative, even if the scope and vigor of his Korean activity is without direct precedent. Those interventions relating to Article 99, and those in the form of legal opinions, have already been noted. Prior to his Korean activity, Mr. Lie had further extended his participation in the Security Council's proceedings to the expression, before the Council, of his support of a point of view on a controversial issue which has been with the United Nations from the beginning; to the suggestion, if not the proposition, of resolutions; and to the formal proposal of quasi-political amendments to a resolution. He had, in other words, won tacit recognition by the Council of precedent indicating that the Secretary-General's "capacity" embraces the right to endorse policies, suggest courses of action, and propose resolutions and amendments.

This precedent is cautious and of course not binding. But, when combined with the other elements of the Secretary-General's power and prestige, it provides a base upon which can be constructed with care a structure of organic activity by the Secretary-General of great significance — a structure monumentally proportioned, along Korean lines.

The Organization's continuing preoccupation with the question of the admission of new members began in the summer of 1946. The situation in the Security Council was then the converse of what it has been since. The United States supported the admission of all current applicants; the Soviet Union maintained that each application must be separately considered on its merits. The view which the Secretary-General asserted at that time has been the stable element in the morass of the Organization's consideration of the problem. It was a call for the admission of all the applicants on the grounds that the Organization's interests are the better served the more universal is the membership.[79]

A year later, the Secretary-General moved from support of the principle of universality to specific proposition of a means of implementing the principle. Dr. Kerno, after quoting Mr. Lie's 1946 statement, suggested on the Secretary-General's behalf that the Security Council recommend the admission at once of seven of the twelve applicants, the other five to be admitted without further question "as soon as the peace treaties with these countries have come into force" — a proposal of a political nature, with a good legal rationale. Just before the Secretary-General's statement, the President of the Council, Faris el-Khouri of Syria, had put forth a similar plan. When China declared herself "opposed to the adoption of this [Syria's] resolution or the acceptance of the recommendation made by the Secretary-General," the President, noting the resolution to be unacceptable to one of the permanent members, terminated discussion of it and moved the Council on to consideration of the individual applications.[80]

The amendments earlier mentioned were offered in the course of the Security Council's handling of the Palestine question. The Secretary-General, in the person of Dr. Victor Hoo, Assistant Secretary-General for Trusteeship Affairs, moved the addition of two paragraphs to a United States resolution, the first requesting "the Secretary-General to provide the Mediator with the necessary staff and facilities to assist in carrying out the functions assigned to him," and the second requesting him to "make appropriate arrangements to provide necessary funds to meet the obligations" arising from the resolution.[81]

The amendments followed by a week the Soviet criticism of Mr. Lie's dispatch of observers and fifty United Nations Guards to assist the Mediator; it was, the U.S.S.R. held, "incorrect and without legal basis." [82] The Soviet delegate this time asked the Assistant Secretary-General to clarify the word "staff," in the first paragraph cited, to which Dr. Hoo replied, "guards, automobile drivers, pilots and all people necessary to help the Mediator perform his functions," and added, in reply to a question of Dimitri Z. Manuilsky (Ukrainian S.S.R.) regarding the nationality of such staff, that there were no restrictions but that most members would probably be American owing to their economy of recruitment. To this Mr. Malik (U.S.S.R.) responded that the intentions of the Secretary-General's amendments "not merely fail to conform to the Charter, but would in fact directly contravene it." [83] Mr. Lie's proposals were adopted, 8–0–3, the U.S.S.R., Uk.S.S.R., and Syria abstaining.

Thus the Secretary-General offered and saw through amendments to a Security Council resolution which he no doubt deemed technically and administratively desirable, but which he well knew gave political offense to certain Council members. It is quite likely that the amendments, in fact, were offered so as to meet the earlier Soviet criticism that such assistance to the Mediator had no basis in "any Security Council document." [84]

The amendments are clearly related to the Secretary-General's narrow executive duties and are not the same thing as proposing amendment of the substance of a political resolution. They are, however, amendments, and they constitute a precedent for other amendments, perhaps of a wholly political character. And of course the difference between an amendment to a resolution and a resolution itself can, if the amendment is broad, be so whittled down as to make the power to amend a resolution equate with the right to move one.

## Relations with Security Field Commissions

The relations of the Secretary-General with the United Nations field commissions and the Secretariat missions which service the governmental commissions are a vital chapter of his political activity. The extended and intimate contact between governmental representatives serving on a commission and the expert Secretariat mission staff upon which they rely affords the Secretary-General a particularly good opportunity to exert his influence. And, in the case of one of the most notable United Nations field actions — that in Palestine — personalities and circumstances combined to endow the Secretary-General with the maximum interest and effectiveness.

The character and degree of the Secretary-General's influence upon United Nations field work depends upon the case in point. In all, there is the minimum, largely apolitical, task of providing the commission (or the Mediator) with the physical services indispensable to the performance of its duties.[85] (That such functions are not entirely without their political elements, however, is demonstrated by the already cited Soviet criticism of the Secretary-General's assistance to Count Bernadotte.) In some instances, depending upon the needs of the situation, the attitude of the governmental representatives composing the commission, the wishes of the parties to the dispute, and, in no small measure, the caliber of the Principal Secretary who is the chief of the mission, the impact of the Secretary-General far transcends the modicum inherent in the process of simple servicing.[86]

For example, a glance at the interim report of the United Nations Commission for India and Pakistan (Kashmir Commission) gives the impression that the Secretary-General's representative and the governmental representatives of the commission itself worked closely together in a collaborative, non-hierarchical fashion in which the Secretary-General's influence, as exerted through the former, and the commission's policies, as presented by the latter, had a coördinate effect.[87]

The Secretary-General's role in the United Nations mediation effort in Palestine is an outstanding example of the vigor of his relations with field missions. In mere servicing alone, the Palestine experience is impressive: in its scale (more than seven hundred persons were in the field at one time), in its extraordinary efficiency (fifty Guards arrived in Palestine within three days of their request by the Mediator), and in its political ramifications. Far more than that, however, Mr. Lie took a political initiative in the Palestine affair which upon crucial occasions overshadowed that of the Mediator. It is in fact not too much to say that the United Nations' effort in Palestine was a joint field–headquarters endeavor in which the Mediator and the Secretary-General collaborated in an indispensably interdependent fashion, its successful results belonging as much to one as to the other.

The Mediator, by the terms of the resolution which established his post, was to conform in his activities with the resolution and "such instructions as the General Assembly and Security Council may issue"; and he was to render progress reports to the Council and to the Secretary-General "for transmission to the Members." There was no indication that the Secretary-General and the Mediator were to be partners, much less that the latter would be in any way subject to the Secretary-General's instructions.

But Mr. Lie himself says, "With Bernadotte it was a special situation. I had known him for years. He was my suggestion as Mediator. There was close personal collaboration. And I had a close personal relationship with Bunche. There was a constant exchange of cables and telephoning." [88] "In a particular crisis," adds a principal figure of the Palestine field mission, "if we felt it would be helpful if Lie would call in certain delegates and apply certain pressures, we would ask him and he would do so. . . Lie was constantly carrying on conferences here, breaking up logjams."

The extent and intensity of the Secretary-General's field activity in Palestine surpasses that of his work in relation to other field problems, with the possible exception of Korea. Colonel Katzin, as the Secretary-General's personal representative in Korea and a man of wide experience in international organization, was charged with important field work, notably the handling of complex liaison and refugee problems. He took a particularly large measure of initiative, at the instructions of the Executive Office of the Secretary-General, in initially organizing United Nations relief for Korean refugees.

The Secretary-General's field activity in Palestine and Korea are the outstanding examples of a significant phase of his political authority. Altogether, his role in United Nations field work presents, in the words of a high-ranking Secretariat officer intimately concerned with it, "a considerable record of leadership."

If our stress of the Secretary-General's participation in the proceedings of the Security Council perhaps has given the impression of constant and permeating activity greatly influencing all of the Council's work, it has given an unbalanced impression. Before 1950, at any rate, the Secretary-General did not seek to turn the scales in the majority of issues with which the Council was confronted. His interventions, both on and off the record, while important, were, in proportion to the number of items considered, few and selective. Perhaps it was a matter of not crying wolf so often as to wear out the effects of his voice, even if the wolves frequently were actually there. In all events, Mr. Lie's pre-1950 Security Council activity tends to fit in with the relatively cautious approach of the earlier years of his administration.

As the chronic United Nations crisis deepened in 1950, however, Mr. Lie came forward to assume a leading role in grappling with the problems which, above all others, beset the Council: Chinese representation and the related question of the Soviet boycott, and the Korean invasion. His ability to move to the forefront in 1950 was of course helpfully conditioned by the important, if relatively restricted and little publicized, initiative of his first four years of office.

# Political Aspects of the Secretary-General's Relations with Nonpolitical Organs

It is not surprising that there are political aspects to the Secretary-General's relations with the "nonpolitical" organs and affiliated bodies of the United Nations: the Economic and Social Council, the Trusteeship Council, the International Court of Justice, and the specialized agencies. The infusion of political considerations into bodies predominantly technical has been a characteristic of the development of the United Nations. This phenomenon naturally has affected the range and quality of the Secretary-General's activity.

## Economic and Social Council

Much of the Secretary-General's participation in the work of the Economic and Social Council and the Trusteeship Council, and their subsidiaries, is essentially similar to his Assembly and Security Council activity: influencing of agenda priorities; interventions, for the most part procedural; some legal advice; and the like. To speak of the "Secretary-General's participation" in economic, social, and trusteeship matters, by the way, is to speak more often of the Assistant Secretaries-General for Economic, Social, and Trusteeship Affairs than of the Secretary-General himself. The Secretary-General concentrates, though not exclusively, on security matters, and because of the very ramifications of the work of the nonpolitical councils, especially of the Economic and Social Council, he finds it impossible to take a part in their proceedings comparable to that which he takes in the Security Council.

The Economic and Social Council and the Trusteeship Council have, in their rules of procedure, accorded the Secretary-General rights of intervention slightly less extensive than those which he enjoys in the Security Council and General Assembly.[1] But this has not conspicuously impeded his participation in their work. In fact, the influence of the Secretary-General upon the operations of these Councils in some ways surpasses that which he exerts upon the activities of the General Assembly and the Security Council. The political elements of that influence are naturally not so prominent in a nonpolitical sphere. But its total extent is perhaps greater.

The breadth of the Secretary-General's influence may be traced to two factors. In the first place, the Secretariat's normal function of preparing the informational framework of documentation, draft reports, and so forth, within which the delegates take decisions, assumes greater significance in the highly technical and specialized economic, social, and dependent-peoples fields than it tends to in political areas, where delegations incline to be more self-reliant and where the Secretary-General's views may, to some, be politically suspect. Thus, much of the debate of the Economic and Social Council revolves around the conclusions of the World Economic Report. And the draft report which the Secretary-General prepares on technical assistance plays a key role in the Organization's determination of the United Nations "Point Four." (That is not to say that Mr. Lie, or even A. D. K. Owen, Assistant Secretary-General for Economic Affairs, drafted the technical assistance report. Technical Secretariat work of this level of importance most certainly is directed by the top tier of United Nations officialdom, however, and is flavored with their outlook.)

Secondly, because of the "nonpartisan" nature of technical work, the resolutions of the Councils and the Assembly in these matters often endow the Secretary-General with a measure of authority not so often granted in the political sphere. The Secretary-General appointed the Director of the International Children's Emergency Fund and nominated the High Commissioner for Refugees; he was requested to take "all necessary steps to extend aid to Palestine refugees";[2] and he was empowered to determine the amount of the technical assistance to be granted to the member states requesting it, and the financial conditions under which it should be furnished. These are illustrations of a type of authority not uncommonly accorded the Secretary-General.

Moreover, these two factors are cumulative in effect. The Councils have habitually come to rely upon the Secretary-General's staff to provide the data out of which their decisions are hammered; and the propensity to entrust the Secretary-General with broad powers for the execution of certain of these decisions is one that feeds on precedent. Taken together with the elements of the Secretary-General's political practice earlier discussed, many of which here apply, these factors spell a significantly influential role for the Secretary-General in the wide area of United Nations technical activity.

With regard to the first factor, there is no implication, of course, that the process is one of the Secretariat's presenting a certain set of facts from which necessarily follows a set of governmental decisions. The facts as the Secretariat so ably documents them are the larger part of the "environmental" element in the decisions which emerge; but a factor of often greater dynamism is the element, so to speak, of "free will" — that is, of the instructions and biases of the delegates which may or may not be amenable to the Secretariat's documentation.

A notable example both of the extreme initiative the Secretary-General may at times assume in the areas under discussion and of the "free will" of the delegates is provided by the criticism offered by Henri Laugier, then Assistant Secretary-General for Social Affairs, of the work of the Human Rights Commission, and the governmental reaction to that criticism. M. Laugier, in a speech to representatives of nongovernmental organizations, sharply attacked the commission's drafting of the Covenant on Human Rights as a "disaster." Describing the draft Covenant as "narrow and feeble," he took issue with the commission's restricting to governments alone the right of petition, in case of the violation of human rights, and further criticized the commission's limiting the Covenant to civil and political rights.[3] The Assistant Secretary-General's speech, in short, did not lack vigor, but the commission, apparently unmoved, proceeded to produce a document unresponsive to M. Laugier's (and, it must be assumed, the Secretary-General's) views.

M. Laugier's speech, as a daring frontal attack upon the policies of the majority of the members of a United Nations Commission, is of course not typical of the usual character of the Secretary-General's initiative, an initiative which as a rule is more subtle. Nor is it representative of the degree of the Secretary-General's influence in these areas of United Nations activity, an influence which is very broad indeed. In fact, even in this case, the rebuff to the Secretary-General may have been more apparent than real, in the light of the General Assembly's subsequent instructions to the Human Rights Commission. The Fifth Session of the Assembly took a position on the content of the Covenant markedly similar to that expounded by M. Laugier the previous spring.

Finally, the Secretary-General's influence has been enhanced in certain technical fields by an unusual competence of local Secretariat leadership combined with a pressing governmental need for the Secretariat services in question. The work of the Secretariat of the United Nations Economic Commission for Europe, under the direction of Gunnar Myrdal, is the outstanding illustration.

### Specialized Agencies

The Charter assigns to the Economic and Social Council the coördination of the activities of the specialized agencies.[4] The Council, in turn, has in practice delegated a measure of this coördinating power to the Secretary-General. This he exercises in his capacity as chairman of the Administrative Committee on Coördination, a committee established by the Secretary-General at the request of the Economic and Social Council and composed of the Directors General of the specialized agencies and the Secretary-General, with the purpose of "taking all appropriate steps, under the leadership of the Secretary-General, to ensure the fullest and most effective implementation of the agreements [5] entered into by the United Nations and the specialized agencies."[6]

The Administrative Committee considers a wide range of procedural, administrative, and programmatic coördination. In all this, the voice of the Secretary-General is dominant. Decisions must be unanimous, and in the reaching of these decisions the Secretary-General is preëminent. The committee itself meets but two or three times a year, but in the interim periods the Executive Office of the Secretary-General assumes a leadership among the deputies of the administrative heads of the specialized agencies akin to that which the Secretary-General assumes in the committee itself.

The Secretary-General's executive powers of coördination are limited to his chairmanship of the committee, and the chairman is endowed with no particular prerogatives. It is his committee — it was for a time called "The Secretary-General's Committee on Coördination" [7] — and in it he looms large, but this is a matter of practice rather than a question of investment with substantial coördinating authority. The Secretary-General "never dreams of interfering with the agencies' internal matters"; and, for their part, the Directors General "look to the Secretary-General as the focal point of international, interagency action." [8]

The extent of the support which the administrative heads of the specialized agencies accord the Secretary-General — and more, the influence upon the agencies of Mr. Lie's politically slanted conception of the functions of the international secretariat — was most dramatically illustrated by the statement which the committee unanimously adopted in May 1950, in the midst of the Secretary-General's famous Washington–London–Paris–Moscow tour. At a time when the Secretary-General's "peace mission" was being widely criticized, particularly in the United States, the agency chiefs threw their weight behind Mr. Lie's favorite theses of the need for universal United Nations membership and the necessity of negotiation among the Great Powers. By implication, they backed his efforts to facilitate the admission of Communist China and the return of the Soviet world to the United Nations. The committee declared:

> We believe it would be a disaster if efforts to realize the principle of universality in practice were to be abandoned now. . . We also believe that it is necessary for all the Governments to renew their efforts to conciliate and negotiate the political differences that divide

them and obstruct economic and social advancement. Specifically, we believe that it is essential to the future of both the United Nations and the specialized agencies that the present political deadlock in the United Nations be resolved at the earliest possible moment. The peace and well-being of all peoples demand from their Governments a great and sustained new effort by the nations of the world to achieve constructive and durable peace.[9]

The influence of the Secretary-General in the more normal range of the committee's operations is generally as conclusive. A typical example is his consultation with the agency chiefs on the appointment of the executive secretary for the Technical Assistance Board. The Secretary-General's candidate was accepted almost automatically. But it is an influence invoked discreetly, a matter not of directives but of suggestion issuing from the Secretary-General. "The Secretary-General is a coördinator, not a dictator. Mr. Lie has a great flair for intuitively finding the common factor upon which all the agencies may agree." [10]

Agreement has not been invariably forthcoming. Notably, there was a difference of view between the Secretary-General and the Directors General on coördinating the technical assistance program, a difference which was resolved by the Economic and Social Council in Mr. Lie's favor. Still, agreement is very much the rule — as has not always been the case in United Nations bodies. All in all, the position, prestige, and effectiveness of the Secretary-General have been enhanced by the start which has been made under his direction toward coördinating the "proliferation" of United Nations work.

### International Court of Justice

The relations of the Secretary-General with the Court — the other principal organ of the United Nations not composed of representatives of governments — are a case *sui generis*. His substantive activity springs from requests by United Nations organs for advisory opinions by the Court.[11] When the Court is asked to give an advisory opinion, the Secretary-General transmits "an exact statement of the question upon which an opinion is required"; supplies, in accordance with Article 65 of the Statute of the International Court, "all documents likely to throw light upon the question"; and, in certain cases, submits to the Court a written and perhaps, additionally, an oral statement relating to the question. The second and third of these functions leave room for exercise of a degree of influence by the Secretary-General. As regards the provision of documentary material, the contents of the dossier, here as elsewhere, may prove influential. The Secretary-General's statements to the Court may serve as a more direct path of his influence.

Six opinions have been delivered at United Nations request. The first concerned the criteria for the admission of new members to the United Nations. The second dealt with reparations for injuries incurred in the service of the United Nations. The third took up the Argentine contention that the General Assembly is not bound by the Security Council's membership recommendations. The fourth concerned the question of the obligations under the peace treaties arising from the alleged violation of human rights in Hungary, Bulgaria, and Rumania. The fifth advisory opinion considered the legal status of South-West Africa, and the last the question of reservations to the Genocide Convention.

When the case of admission criteria came up, Dr. Kerno, the Assistant Secretary-General for Legal Affairs, delivered on the Secretary-General's behalf a factual explanation of the documentation supplied. He made no oral statement in connection with the Argentine case, but, at the beginning of the Court's consideration of the legal status of South-West Africa, he gave a two-day speech, surveying the background and posing the knotty juridical questions of the problem.

The Secretary-General was particularly concerned with the three remaining opinions, those regarding reparations, human rights, and reservations to the Genocide Convention. The last relates to the Secretary-General's functions as the depositary of treaties and will be discussed in that connection. It suffices to note that the Secretary-General took the initiative in bringing the question to the General Assembly's attention, and that both written and oral statements were submitted on his behalf to the Court — statements which were an important element in the Court's consideration of the problem.

Under the peace treaties with Hungary, Rumania, Bulgaria, and Italy, the Secretary-General was charged with appointing the third member of the arbitral tribunal which was to be set up in case of dispute between the United Nations government and the former enemy state, if and when the disputants failed to agree upon a third member. Such tribunals were to be established in response to a dispute concerning the interpretation of most clauses of the treaties with the Balkan states, including those relating to human rights, and, in the case of Italy, with regard to certain economic clauses. This empowering of the Secretary-General to appoint the third member is evidently another feather in his cap — one placed there, it is interesting to note, by the United States with the support of France. Britain had proposed that the function in question be assigned to the President of the Court, while the U.S.S.R. would have delegated it to the Ambassadors of the United Kingdom, France, the United States, and the Soviet Union in the capital of the former enemy state.[12]

As a result of the Mindszenty trial and related affairs, the General Assembly asked the Court for an advisory opinion concerning whether a dispute existed within the meaning of the treaties among the parties thereto, and whether, if so, the parties were obliged to appoint the members of the arbitral tribunals. The Court ruled in March 1950 that a dispute in fact existed and that it would oblige the constitution of the tribunals.

Hungary, Rumania, and Bulgaria refused to appoint their representatives within the required thirty days of the Court's decision, however, thus bringing on "phase two" of the human rights opinion. For the Court then had to decide whether, despite the failure of one party to appoint its representative to the arbitral commission, the Secretary-General was authorized to appoint the third member upon the request of the other party. If it answered this question affirmatively, the Court would then be called upon to decide whether this two-member arbitral commission would be competent to make a definitive and binding decision in settlement of the dispute.

The Court answered the question negatively. It found that the Secretary-General's power to appoint a third member derived solely from the agreement of the parties.[13]

In all this, Dr. Kerno took a conservative role. He presented to the Court written and oral statements of fact, taking care to point out that the Secretary-General assumed no position on any of the questions of the case. Thus, the Secretary-General was not re-buffed by the Court's decision, though, clearly, his powers under the treaties were interpreted so as to make them at least theoretically less important than they might be.

In the Court's consideration of the question of reparations for injuries incurred in the service of the United Nations, the Secretary-General was able to play a more influential role. His representatives, Dr. Kerno and A. H. Feller, General Counsel of the United Nations, regarded the United Nations as a party and pleaded the case on its behalf.[14] The United Nations "won," the Court declaring, in a decision of the most fundamental importance, that the Organization is an "international person," possessing international rights and duties and the capacity to protect its rights by bringing international claims.[15]

The Secretary-General's contribution toward the verdict was considerable. To begin with, the reparations question was placed on the agenda of the Third Session of the General Assembly at his request. He presented to the Sixth (Legal) Committee of the Assembly a memorandum which held that the United Nations possesses the legal capacity to present a claim under international law against a state. When the stage of court proceedings was reached, the Secretary-General's representatives submitted a strong and positive argument affirming the international juridical personality of the United Nations. The Secretary-General was afforded some guidance, but no instructions, in the discussions of the question by the Sixth Committee. The United Nations' presentation was in fact the Secretary-General's.

The Secretary-General's initiative in the reparations case sets a precedent of active participation in the Court's proceedings that parallels his activity in other organs. The presenting of written and oral statements here and in other instances further parallels the general contrast of the initiative of the Secretary-General of the United Nations with that of the Secretary-General of the League. The latter confined his relations with the Permanent Court to mere transmission and documentation and submitted neither written nor oral statements.

The Secretary-General has other legal functions which, while not directly connected with the Court, may be conveniently mentioned here. Under Article 102 of the Charter,[16] every treaty and every international agreement entered into by the members after the coming into force of the Charter must be registered promptly with the Secretariat and published by it. Two discretionary functions of possible political implication flow from the duties imposed upon the Secretary-General by this article. He must, on occasion, decide what is a treaty and what is an international agreement within the meaning of the article. And he must cope with the difficulties which arise when a signatory to a multipartite instrument wishes, at the time of signature or of the deposit of its ratification, to make a reservation to the treaty in point.

With regard to the scope of the obligation to register treaties, the Secretary-General has acted upon the principle that the broad wording of Article 102 does not admit of exceptions and qualifications.[17] But the question of reservations to multilateral agreements has proved more intricate. The prominent example of the importance of the Secretary-General's discretion in this latter regard arose from the United States ratification of the Constitution of the World Health Organization, with a reservation providing that Washington retained its right to withdraw from W.H.O. on a one-year notice. According to the traditional law of treaties, the Secretary-General, before accepting the deposit of the American ratification, should have secured the consent to the reservation of all other signatories of the W.H.O. Constitution (including, perhaps, those that had not yet ratified). But this would have been a time-consuming process, involving the risk of canceling the United States ratification merely through the objection of any one signatory. And, as it happened, the United States instrument was deposited with the Secretary-General just three days before the opening of the first World Health Assembly. So to have followed normal procedures would have meant excluding the United States from W.H.O.'s constitutive session — a loss which would have been of the greatest seriousness to the organization.

In these circumstances, the Secretary-General contrived the ingenious procedure of in effect asking the W.H.O. Assembly, as the body competent to interpret the W.H.O. Constitution, if it agreed that the apparent reservation of the United States need not be considered inconsistent with the Constitution. The Assembly was only too happy to agree that there was no inconsistency; whereupon the Secretary-General advised all of the states that were parties to the Constitution that the United States became a party from the date of the deposit of its instrument of acceptance.[18]

The Secretary-General found this discretion regarding reservations to multilateral conventions so uncongenial, however, that in 1950, when difficulties loomed in connection with ratifications to the Genocide Convention, he placed the whole matter on the Assembly's agenda. The Sixth Committee, after considering the relevant reports of the Secretary-General [19] and the International Law Commission,[20] decided to request, for the Secretary-General's future guidance, an advisory opinion of the International Court of Justice. That opinion, delivered the following spring, saw "a new need for flexibility in the operation of multilateral conventions." It took the controversial view, by a vote of 7 to 5, that a state which has made and maintained a reservation which has been objected to by one or more of the parties to the Genocide Convention, but not by others, can be regarded as being a party to the Convention "if the reservation is compatible with the object and purpose of the Convention." The majority specified that its view related to the Genocide Convention and not necessarily to other multilateral treaties. For this reason, and because of the variables which inhere in the majority criterion for judging the effect of reservations, the Court's opinion would not seem to resolve the Secretary-General's difficulties.[21]

### → Secretariat

The Secretary-General, as the chief administrative officer of the Organization, is in a position to exercise considerable authority over the Secretariat. This power is modified, to be sure, by his responsibility to the General Assembly and its Advisory Committee on Administrative and Budgetary Questions, and by the provisional staff regulations which the Assembly has adopted for his guidance.[22] It is modified in a sense, too, by pressure member states may exert in an extra-Assembly, sometimes un-official, manner with regard to staff appointments and related matters. The Secretariat, moreover, elects a Staff Committee to represent its interests, and has been accorded an Administrative Tribunal, a Joint Appeals Board, and a Joint Disciplinary Com-mittee, which may hand down "advisory opinions" to the Secre-tary-General concerning differences which may arise with respect to the fulfillment of contracts and the like. But these reservations to the totality of his administrative power are, in any sense of tying the Secretary-General down juridically, not too significant; they leave to him an area of option which is liberal.[23] The most important limit to his discretion is his discretion itself.

This limit is a very real one; there is no purpose to the Secre-tary-General's employing his wide administrative powers out-rageously. In practice, his administration tries to strike a balance between the imperatives of efficiency and an economy-minded Assembly, and the natural desires of the staff for maximum salary, privileges, promotional opportunity, independence, and author-ity. It is a sensitive operation in which the Secretary-General's ultimate administrative power is neither wholly muted nor daily shaken in the faces of the staff.

To speak of the Secretary-General administratively is actually to speak not of Mr. Lie but of Mr. Price. The Secretary-General has formally delegated to the Assistant Secretary-General in charge of Administrative and Financial Services virtually all of the administrative job.[24] This is all to the good, both in theory and practice. For such delegation frees the Secretary-General to concern himself with the external, political phase of his respon-sibilities. He is not burdened with the administrative load which the League Secretaries-General carried. The League Secretaries-General devoted a considerable portion of their time and energies to internal affairs and concurrently managed to carry on substan-tial political activity of an informal nature, but the latter suffered from preoccupation with the former. For the Secretary-General of the United Nations to lead such a dual existence is probably an impossibility, not only because of his expanded political functions, but because the administrative demands of running the United Nations, an organization far larger than the League, are much heavier than were those of the Geneva Secretariat. The Secretary-General, moreover, has added to the good judgment shown in delegating his administrative responsibility by placing his internal authority in the competent hands of Mr. Price.

The arrangement has but two reservations, again one of administrative theory and another of actual application. Mr. Price is but one Assistant Secretary-General among eight and ranks no higher than any one of them. At the same time, he is charged with handling certain aspects of general administration for all departments. The difficulties which tend to crop up in such a situation are evident.

Mr. Price, further, is a citizen of the United States, and, in his position, that is a handicap. For, owing to the predominance of Americans in the Secretariat — a predominance which is numerical and which, furthermore, is noticeable in vital policymaking positions close to the Secretary-General — there is a widespread sensitivity toward American domination. This sensitivity is perhaps heightened by the prominent role which the United States plays in the United Nations as a whole and international affairs in general. Other elements of the feeling may be the not uniformly commendable reception of the United Nations and its Secretariat by American citizenry, and, of course, the usual nationalistic biases of which even the Secretariat is not absolutely free. In addition, there is some discontent with what appears to many as an overdose of American administrative procedure. In these circumstances, the Assistant Secretary-General must move with especial circumspection.

The delegation by the Secretary-General of his internal authority seems to be working out well. Its success may be traced in part to the fact that Mr. Lie, who is of course the final arbiter, has consistently supported the Assistant Secretary-General when his support has been needed. By way of example: It is reported that Mr. Price was told by a certain United Nations body to "mind his own business," in response to his directive concerning the elimination of a certain Secretariat post. Mr. Price replied that if the body wished to keep the man, they might pay his salary — the Assistant Secretary-General in charge of Administrative and Financial Services would not. The body appealed to the Secretary-General, and Mr. Lie, "as always," upheld Mr. Price.

There are seven other Assistant Secretaries-General, and together with Mr. Lie and Mr. Price, they compose the cabinet. It is not, of course, a cabinet of the British type, in which the Secretary-General corresponds to the Prime Minister. Rather, it is one similar to the American — there is policy discussion, but no voting, and the Secretary-General, like the President, takes sole responsibility for all decisions.

Its sessions are frequent; usually there are two a week. They cover both external and internal affairs, both general and departmental problems. They provide an opportunity for broad review and the advising of the Secretary-General by his assistants. The cabinet's emphasis, however, is distinctly specialized: it is more a question of reporting the work of the departments than of evolving general policy. This is perhaps unfortunate, but entirely understandable; the Assistant Secretaries-General are by occupational conditioning narrowly inclined, attached as they are to the three Councils or to specialized functions; of the present Assistant Secretaries-General, "not all happen to be broadly developed individuals"; [25] and they are not, in all instances, wholly the personal choice of the Secretary-General.

It is difficult to assess the relationship between the weakness of the cabinet in general policy formation and this last factor — that the Assistant Secretaries-General are essentially political appointees — but that there is some relationship of consequence is likely. One extremely well-informed observer declares that "Lie takes it for granted that what he tells the Assistant Secretaries-General will get back to their governments sooner or later." Another wholly reliable source confirms this judgment as having been valid at one time, but adds that the Secretary-General now feels able to rely upon his cabinet. Even so, this source notes, "they don't know everything"; but he points to the apparent fact that there was no leakage of intelligence concerning Mr. Lie's conversations with Stalin as evidence of the increased reliability of the Assistant Secretaries-General. (Of course, the main suspect, the Soviet Assistant Secretary-General, could in this case have been "let in" from Moscow's end.) Any distrust by the Secretary-General of the loyalty of any of the Assistant Secretaries-General obviously would tend to restrict the importance of the subject matter put before the cabinet and to vitiate its impact in general policy formation.

It might be thought, on the other hand, that this very element of political appointment in the composition of the cabinet would be a source of its strength. For if the Great Powers and prime regions of the world have a hand in the choice of the Assistant Secretaries-General, these officers in turn should have a particular influence with their respective sponsors. This theoretical presumption holds good up to a point. Mr. Lie has found it useful to employ the United States Assistant Secretary-General in the most crucial negotiations with Washington and the Soviet Assistant Secretary-General in like negotiations with Moscow — if not for their influence with these capitals, at least for their understanding of them. But, as the unfortunate League experience with certain Under Secretaries-General demonstrates, advantages of this kind are more than canceled if there is any doubt about whose "man" a particular Assistant Secretary-General is. If there is any equivocation in the direction of the primary loyalties of the Secretary-General's highest associates, the fundamental principles of the international secretariat are undermined at the very center.

In sum, it is hard to evaluate the influence of the three factors suggested as promoting the specialized character of the cabinet: occupational conditioning, personality, and the political aspects of the appointment of the Assistant Secretaries-General. Certain of these factors, at any rate, combine to make the cabinet less an integrated organ of policy formation than a useful mechanism through which the Assistant Secretaries-General may advise their chief on matters within their departmental jurisdiction.[26]

General staff functions are performed by the ranking members of the Executive Office of the Secretary-General, with Andrew W. Cordier, Executive Assistant, acting as "chief of staff." The office advises the Secretary-General on matters of his concern and assists him in the performance of his duties, both external and internal. Externally, it handles liaison with governments (especially that arising from General Assembly affairs). It further manages the coördination of the specialized agencies and economic and social matters, and it serves as the hospitable resting place of high-ranking officers with special external assignments whose functions or prestige makes their lodging in less exclusive quarters inappropriate. Internally, the office performs the job of general coördination. All Secretariat letters and cables which "involve questions of policy or engage the responsibility of the Secretary-General" must obtain clearance from the Executive Office before dispatch, while copies of all important official communications are scrutinized by the office after dispatch.[27]

There are, moreover, what an associate of the Secretary-General describes as the "four wheels of the coördinating effort of the Office": the regular meetings of the top-ranking directors of all departments under the chairmanship of the Executive Assistant, following upon previous intradepartmental gatherings of senior personnel; the activity of the Missions Coördination Board; [28] the functions of the indefatigable Mr. Cordier, as chairman of the United Nations Publishing Board, in reviewing the publishing schedule and "keeping tabs on the research work of the U.N."; [29] and the services of the Director of Coördination for Specialized Agencies and Economic and Social Matters in coördinating affairs in these areas.[30]

There was for a time a "fifth wheel" in this coördinating effort: the experimental Assistant Secretaryship General for General Coördination, created in January 1948. Attached to the Executive Office, the position was particularly designed to coördinate work with overseas missions and specialized agencies and to eliminate any deadwood which might have accumulated in the Secretariat. Commander R.G.A. Jackson of Australia was appointed to the post.

The experiment did not work out happily, owing to organizational and emotional difficulties. Commander Jackson, though on the same official level as the other Assistant Secretaries-General, had at times to wield the Secretary-General's power — an equivocal situation. It seems to be less difficult for Mr. Cordier, who is outranked by the Assistant Secretaries-General, to speak for the Secretary-General — he is received on easier terms. Moreover,

Commander Jackson, apparently a man of great energy and ability, seems not to have been as tactful in his approach to an admittedly difficult job as he might have been. The well-known example of his exuberance of initiative was his impromptu telephoning to Pope Pius XII to settle a little matter, without clearance or ado of any sort. The Commander's relations with Mr. Lie, Count Bernadotte, Mr. Price, and Mr. Sobolev, among others, seem to have been troubled. His position was abolished nine months after its creation. Much appeared in print attributing political motives to the dissolution of the post, but there seems to be no basis whatever in fact for these allegations.

The Executive Office acts both as shield and right arm of the Secretary-General. It distills the problems with which he must deal, resolves the secondary issues, and presents to him for decision matters of substantial policy; and it executes those decisions. Its relationship to the effective authority of the Secretary-General is central and crucial.[31]

Internal administration bears directly upon external relations in matters of personnel appointment. Patronage is not only a national phenomenon. Pressure upon the Secretary-General by member states for the employment of their nationals, though common and not totally without effect, is a much less important factor in United Nations personnel policy than was comparable pressure in the League — perhaps because the legal basis of the Secretary-General's independence in recruiting matters is more solid than was that of the Secretaries-General of the League.[32] Pressure is "present," though "diminishing," and, all in all, "less than in Washington"; [33] moreover, its effects are modest. It may facilitate the securing of a position if a proper one happens to be open and if the candidate otherwise meets the qualifications; but patronage pressure of itself is by no means sufficient to impel the hiring of any particular national.

Such pressure is mainly exerted by the smaller states, whose citizens are attracted by the prestige and salary of Secretariat position. Some of its seeming success stems from the fact that it is brought to bear by small states which often are underrepresented in the number of their citizens employed by the United

Nations, and whose nationals are entitled to first call. The Great Powers do not indulge in the practice. Large numbers of Americans, Frenchmen, Englishmen, and Chinese are members of the Secretariat. The Soviet Union, far from concerning itself with patronage, is notably underrepresented — so much so that the Secretary-General has been said to have attempted to induce the U.S.S.R. to nominate candidates. There was widespread support among the lesser powers for a Colombian resolution, introduced at the Third Session of the General Assembly, which would have forced the Secretary-General to recruit along strict geographic lines.[34] If the resolution had been adopted, the leverage which the Small Powers might exert on behalf of their nationals would have been notably increased. The combined resistance of the Secretary-General and of the more responsible states managed to defeat it by one vote.

Governments have been known to turn their attention to firing as well as hiring. The events in Czechoslovakia in 1948, in particular, are reported to have given rise to pressure emanating from Prague for the dismissal of certain Czech members of the Secretariat.[35] If governmental pressure has had little success in recruitment, it has had none in removal.

An interesting sidelight to demands for dismissal of Secretariat members has been the criticism expressed in certain public and journalistic quarters in the United States about the United Nations harboring American citizens allegedly communistic. There has also been talk to the effect that the United Nations serves as a convenient entree for foreign spies, this theme having been given a boost by the Gubitchev case. Both views, spiced with attacks upon Mr. Lie as a communist tool, were sensationally expounded by "Witness Number 8" before a Senate judiciary subcommittee in July 1949. Among the charges were allegations that Commander Jackson had been discharged because he had stood up to Mr. Lie's so-called pro-communist doings. Mr. Price, then Acting Secretary-General, addressed a strong protest to the Secretary of State, noting that if the Secretary-General were to "be answerable . . . to committees of national legislatures, all possibility of the successful existence of the United Nations as an international organization would be destroyed." He protested the "unfounded and irresponsible attacks" upon the Secretary-General and reminded the United States of its obligations under Article 100 of the Charter. His protest elicited an affirmation by the United States government of complete confidence in Mr. Lie.[36]

To say that the Secretary-General is not responsive to governmental, and still less to private, pressure with respect to dismissals is not of course to say that he takes pleasure in appointing members of the Secretariat who are *personae non gratae* to their governments. On the contrary, much recruiting is not "direct" but upon the basis of governmental nomination. It is reliably reported, in a related vein, that Chinese of Nationalist persuasion have had a peculiarly difficult time in gaining admission to the Secretariat ever since their government was driven from the mainland. Firing is one thing; but another thing is the loading up of the quota of a country with persons who do not enjoy the confidence of the regime which controls their homeland.[37]

The appointive power of the Secretary-General is not confined to the Secretariat. It extends to the influencing of the choice of special United Nations officers who are entrusted with *ad hoc* missions, often political, by the legislative organs of the Organization. In some cases, the Secretary-General is empowered by resolution to appoint the official outright (the Plebiscite Administrator for Jammu and Kashmir,[38] the Executive Director of the International Children's Emergency Fund,[39] the Director of the United Nations Relief and Works Agency for Palestine Refugees,[40] the Agent General for Korean Reconstruction[41]). He has even been authorized to appoint a whole commission — the *Ad Hoc* Commission on the repatriation of war prisoners.[42] In other cases, he is charged with naming the officer, subject to the confirmation of the competent organ (the Acting Mediator for Palestine,[43] the High Commissioner for Refugees [44]). With regard to the appointment of still other officers, he plays a consultative role which is often close to decisive (the Mediator for Palestine [45] and the United Nations Commissioner for Libya).

The Secretary-General's appointive rights usually have been widely supported by the member states. A notable exception has been Nationalist China, which, before Mr. Lie's efforts to facilitate the accrediting of the Peiping regime, was unfriendly to the Secretary-General's initiative, and since, not surprisingly, has gone out of its way to criticize the Secretary-General. When the resolution of the General Assembly concerning the establishment of the office of the High Commissioner for Refugees percolated down to the Social Committee of the Economic and Social Council for detailed exposition, the Nationalist delegate, Mr. Yu Tsune-chi, took the floor to condemn as "dangerous" the provision for the Commissioner's nomination by the Secretary-General. Mr. Yu stated that, in the interests of the dignity of the office, the person or organ nominating the High Commissioner should have "appropriate standing"; and to confer this power upon the Secretary-General, "an administrative officer," the delegate added, would be "dangerous . . . and not sufficiently democratic." Mr. Yu indicated that his government had doubts about the soundness of Mr. Lie's judgment and "regretted to have to point out that past experience had left it with the impression that the Secretary-General had not always been completely impartial and had allowed himself to be influenced by political considerations." Mr. Yu won scant support, the Social Committee proceeding to endorse unanimously the Secretary-General's appointing the High Commissioner (China abstaining), amid expressions of confidence in the Secretary-General's integrity and of the necessity of the Commissioner's being able to work closely with the United Nations Secretariat. The British representative, in the course of his diplomatic remarks in this vein, noted, interestingly enough, that his government had been opposed to the arrangement when it had been worked out at the Assembly, but would not now challenge an Assembly decision.[46]

The power of appointment to office is so traditional an implement of political influence as to need no elaboration. That the member states will invest the Secretary-General with this power in many instances, and defer to his views even when they retain the final power, is another, and a striking, demonstration of the reality and reach of the political authority of the Secretary-General.

CHAPTER **6**

## The Secretary-General's
## Relations with Governments

*If what I do is published, I lose my influence. . .
It isn't the Secretary-General's job to make head-
lines.*                                    TRYGVE LIE

*The real power of the Secretary-General is exer-
cised outside the public debate.*   MARTIN HILL

*Mr. Lie's lobbying is a curious combination of
high politics and pedestrian mechanics.*
                               THOMAS J. HAMILTON

*There is steady pressure, my steady pressure,
behind the scenes.*                 TRYGVE LIE

The record of the Secretary-General's relations with the organs
of the United Nations is but the outer manifestation of the inner
substance of his political activity. His most significant work is
direct and usually private negotiation with the member states
themselves. The experience of the Secretaries-General of the
League supplies substantial precedent in this regard. The Report
of the Preparatory Commission further provides official basis for
the building of the Secretary-General's structure of "governmental" relations,[1] for it notes that "the Secretary-General may
have an important role to play as a mediator and as an informal
adviser of many governments." [2]

How important this role is, and something of its extent and
character, is indicated by Mr. Lie's response to inquiry regarding
the nature of his behind-the-scenes political activity: [3]

Hundreds of such cases have been brought to my attention. . . I see the parties at lunch, or give a small dinner party. I can bring them together, or sometimes I mediate without bringing them together. Then I ask one something with the knowledge of the other and back again. It is my daily work — the most important part of the daily work of the Secretary-General. . .
It is very much like the processes of settling labor disputes. Investigation, mediation, arbitration. It's very much the same kind of work. You know that was my life before I entered the Government. I was legal adviser to the Norwegian trade unions. I gained great experience with the trade unions. . . That was my life, my experience — mediating, negotiating, settling labor disputes. It's about the same sort of thing.

A close associate of Mr. Lie adds that "delegations use the Executive Office when direct contact with another delegation is not expedient. The Office of the Secretary-General serves as a means of uncovering what's possible in the way of agreement among differing delegations." And he sums up the extent of these consultations as "endless": "They go on every day. The delegations consult the Secretary-General on almost everything. It's a state of continuous consultation." [4] "Almost everything" embraces matters administrative as well as political. In fact, the greater part of this activity is probably concerned with administrative questions. The area remaining to the political is nevertheless wide and is kept so by the initiative of both the Secretary-General and the delegations.

An aspect of these consultations which may be comfortably categorized as neither political nor administrative is the Secretary-General's attempt to promote intragovernmental coördination. On occasion, a delegate of a state will vote for a project in the Economic and Social Council the funds for which his compatriot will vote against in the Assembly's Fifth Committee. This laxity of intragovernmental coördination is by no means uncommon and has a seriously pernicious effect upon the United Nations capacity for accomplishment. The Secretary-General does what he can through conversations to rationalize a government's policies when the need arises, and he takes every opportunity to stress the necessity of consistency in intragovernmental policy in his reports to United Nations organs.[5]

It is of course impossible to analyze the "hundreds of cases" of behind-the-scenes political activity of which Mr. Lie speaks. We shall therefore examine in detail five of the cases in which this activity has been most important: Palestine; Berlin; and the interlocking questions of Chinese representation, the Washington–London–Paris–Moscow "peace tour," and the ten-point peace program. We shall then touch upon a few of the more notable illustrations of his activity.

### The Palestine Effort

The Secretary-General's Palestine effort marks his first sustained, large-scale attempt to influence the determination of a political problem with the resolution of which the United Nations has been charged. In it, he took as his guiding directive the Assembly's partition recommendation of November 29, 1947. His adherence to that directive was reinforced by his conviction that the well-being of the United Nations would be fundamentally affected by its response to the Holy Land challenge and to the Arab attempt to frustrate the Organization's will by the employment of armed force. He threw his weight behind that recommendation with such vigor and consistency, however — even when support of it by the member states had considerably weakened — that sources both objective and partisan agree that his Palestine activity was further enlivened by a bias in the Israeli favor.

In January 1948, as the Palestine disorders mounted in intensity, the Secretary-General sounded out a number of the smaller Powers (Belgium, Sweden, the Netherlands, Norway, Brazil, and Mexico) about the possibility of their sending troops to the Holy Land, under United Nations auspices, should more serious fighting develop. A few days later, in opening the first meeting of the Palestine Commission, he gave public demonstration of his support for the partition plan. "You are entitled," he said, "to be confident that in the event it should prove necessary, the Security Council will assume its full measure of responsibility in implementation of the Assembly's resolution. You have a right to assume, as I assume, that in such a situation the Security Council will not fail to exercise to the fullest, and without exception, every necessary power entrusted to it by the Charter in order to assist you in fulfilling your mission." [6]

Mr. Lie's open prodding of the Security Council did not stop there. As it became clear that the Council had no intention of exercising "every necessary power" to implement partition, on the plea that the United Nations lacked legal authority to do so, the Secretary-General responded in a press conference that Britain had in effect bestowed upon the Organization full responsibility and temporary sovereignty over Palestine. Concurrently, he informed the nations most concerned that he intended to do all within his power to carry out the Assembly's resolution.

The Security Council took no effective action prior to the expiration of the Mandate on May 14. The morning after the Arab states launched their invasion, the Secretary-General sent a personal appeal to the five permanent Council members for determined action to meet this first actual challenge of United Nations authority by armed force. He followed up his appeal with the dispatch of a special emissary to London (Assistant Secretary-General R. G. A. Jackson) to point out forcefully to Mr. Bevin that British policy could well destroy the United Nations, or, if altered, do much to resolve successfully the Palestine conflict. A personal representative was likewise sent to Washington, preliminary to conversations which the Secretary-General himself undertook ten days later with Secretary of State George C. Marshall in New York.

Mr. Lie was influential in the selection of Count Bernadotte as United Nations Mediator, and throughout the Count's service and that of Dr. Ralph Bunche, he took the fullest measure of initiative in providing the Mediator with all support, material and political. His part in the Rhodes conversations was particularly prominent. Several times, when the negotiations threatened to collapse, he stepped in at Lake Success to enjoin the Israeli and Egyptian governments not to leave Rhodes.[7] And when the shooting down of Royal Air Force planes by Israeli fighters threatened to set back the Rhodes conversations, Mr. Lie interceded directly with the British, the Israelis, and the Americans to keep a new and emotion-fraught issue from hobbling the mediation effort.[8] Indicative of the acclaim accorded the Palestinian endeavor was the awarding to Dr. Bunche of the Nobel Peace Prize in 1950.

The Secretary-General's Palestine activity has been capped, to date, by his attempt, at the Fourth Session of the General Assembly in the fall of 1949, to prevent the taking of an evidently unenforceable and unrealistic decision on the future government of Jerusalem. The significance of Mr. Lie's not listing the Jerusalem resolution among the achievements of the Assembly, in his closing address, has earlier been mentioned. A delegate close to the Palestine question more directly describes the Secretary-General's intervention as follows: "Lie took a very active role in opposing the Jerusalem resolution. . . It was a personal defeat for him. He did everything in his power to frustrate it." That a resolution voted by a majority of more than two-thirds of the member states of the United Nations can be characterized as "a personal defeat" for the Secretary-General is a demonstration of the breadth and force of his informal political initiative.

## The Berlin Negotiations

The most important and most underrated of the Secretary-General's efforts in private negotiation, prior to his intense and crucial activity of 1950, was his careful, resourceful attempt, in Paris in the autumn of 1948, to overcome the impasse over the Berlin blockade. The precise nature of that attempt is still very much in the realm of top secret. Some partial idea, more or less accurate, of Mr. Lie's Berlin effort was leaked to the press, however (not through the Secretary-General's doing), and the following account is based upon these press reports.

Two weeks after Mr. Vishinsky's veto of the Security Council resolution for the settlement of the Berlin crisis, it was revealed that Mr. Lie was engaged in the preparation of a new compromise proposal.[9] Essentially, it concerned a revision of the Moscow directive of August 30. That directive had sought to exchange the lifting of the blockade for the simultaneous introduction of Soviet-zone currency in Berlin. At the same time, Dr. Juan Atilio Bramuglia, President of the Security Council for September and spokesman for the Council's six "neutrals," was also preparing a plan. His effort and that of Mr. Lie were not connected. There was some consultation between Dr. Atilio Bramuglia and Mr. Lie once their separate approaches were advanced, but no attempt at a "merger."

The day the first reports of Mr. Lie's effort appeared in the press, the Secretary-General acknowledged that "as part of his duty to keep himself informed of all matters before the United Nations, he was making a study of the currency problem in Berlin." [10] His study, it was reported, foresaw advance agreement upon the introduction of Soviet marks and the end of the blockade, to be followed by negotiations among the Big Four themselves on the detailed and relatively secondary issues of Berlin administration. It was further reported that Mr. Lie's representatives had been in contact with experts of certain of the Powers concerned with the dispute. Chances of his effort's succeeding were then described by informed sources as "fifty-fifty."

Neither Mr. Lie's activity nor that of Dr. Atilio Bramuglia did bear tangible fruit — why, press reports do not indicate. Upon the suggestion of Dr. Evatt, then President of the General Assembly, the Secretary-General took an additional tack in joining with him in an open letter of appeal to the Big Four to compose their differences in the spirit of the Mexican conciliation resolution for which they had voted [11] and to begin by resuming negotiations on Berlin. Dr. Evatt had had nothing whatever to do with the Secretary-General's earlier private negotiations, the open letter coming as a fresh contribution of the former Australian Minister of External Affairs. Mr. Lie also joined forces, upon the invitation of Dr. Atilio Bramuglia, with the currency committee of the Council's six neutrals, appointing a seventh representative — Gunnar Myrdal — who played a key role in the committee's work. The report, which Washington ultimately rejected on the grounds that the situation had changed from the time when it and the other parties had agreed to the study, was nonetheless praised by the Secretary-General as a "constructive and solid approach" to settlement of the Berlin currency problem. [12]

Mr. Lie's role in the Jessup-Malik conversations a few months afterward was modest; it is widely assumed to have been nothing more than the bringing of the two together at his home to facilitate their conversations. His contribution was in fact something more substantial than that, although he did not directly participate in the negotiations which finally led to the lifting of the blockade. The sum of the Secretary-General's effort, all in all, together with that of the Security Council and the Assembly President, while it did not resolve the Berlin crisis, is generally conceded to have eased it.

### Chinese Representation

The efforts put forth by Mr. Lie in the six months between the initial Soviet boycott of the Security Council, in January 1950, and the Korean invasion, in June of the same year, were of such intensity and importance, and were so widely publicized, that it seemed as if the Secretary-General had entered upon an entirely new order of endeavor. The little-known and little-cared-about behind-the-scenes initiative of the Secretary-General suddenly catapulted into the public eye. The deep-rooted appeal of any promise of peace and the unsurpassed glamour of a midnight meeting with Stalin combined to focus popular attention upon the Secretary-General in a way that it never had been focused before.

Actually, there was nothing very new in the form, in the procedure, of Mr. Lie's activity from January to June. The Secretary-General had had private talks with Stalin before (in 1946) — and with the President and the Prime Ministers of France and Britain as well. This was not the first time that the Secretary-General had attempted to break an impasse between East and West or to facilitate the resumption of negotiations between them (witness his Berlin efforts). Mr. Lie's initiative in the first half of 1950 was distinguished rather because of the vigor with which it was sustained, the advanced stage to which it was brought, and the more serious character of the international context in which it was offered. In those six months, the Secretary-General met almost daily with the representatives of the states most directly concerned. He gathered information, exchanged views, and suggested possible courses of action on an unprecedented scale. And he did this in a period of virtual diplomatic rupture between East and West, a period in which, with the U.S.S.R. boycotting United Nations meetings and with productive diplomatic intercourse among the protagonists in the cold war at an apparent standstill, the Secretary-General of the United Nations alone seemed to offer hope of renewal of negotiations between East and West.

The supreme object of Mr. Lie's effort was to bring about this renewal of negotiations. But no action could be taken to break the deadlock, the Secretary-General felt, "until the Chinese question is settled, so that we may have present again all nations who have been elected as members of the different organs." [13] Thus, he devoted his initial activity to overcoming the impasse concerning Chinese representation. Not that the Secretary-General treated the Chinese question as a mere auxiliary to the central problem of East-West relations. He recognized throughout the importance of the question in itself, though he later came to lay somewhat greater stress on East-West relations as a whole than the following explanation of his China activity, given in the course of a speech delivered in March in Washington, would indicate:

I have been trying to help the Member Governments settle the question of who is to represent China in the United Nations. I am not doing this because the Soviet Union and its neighbors have refused to attend meetings at which China is represented by Nationalist delegates. I have never thought walking out of meetings and staying away from meetings was a good way to settle differences of opinion.

It is a serious matter to have the Soviet Union staying away from United Nations meetings, but that is not the first consideration. The first consideration is the people of China. There are 450,000,000 people in that country — the greatest in the world and in the United Nations in terms of population alone.

The 450,000,000 people of China are collectively original members of the United Nations by the terms of the Charter itself. They have a right to be represented by whatever government has the power "to employ the resources and direct the people of the State in fulfillment of the obligations of Membership" in the United Nations. I repeat, whatever government is thus qualified, regardless of its ideology.[14]

Aside from the light it sheds on the Secretary-General's activity on the Chinese problem the foregoing is of interest in its direct criticism of the Soviet policies of walk-out and boycott. It parallels Mr. Lie's earlier statement that "all Members of the United

Nations have an obligation to participate fully in its work. This is especially true of the Security Council, which under Article 28 must be so organized as to function continuously. Refusal to participate in United Nations meetings is not the way to help solve such problems as the question of China." [15] And it anticipates his later declaration: "The Soviet refusal to attend meetings at which China is represented by the Nationalists is resented strongly by many governments and is also a practice with which I certainly do not agree. I have made this plain on several occasions here, and I made it plain during my visit to Moscow." [16] This last forthright expression came just nine days before Senators Knowland and Bridges, in acknowledgment of Mr. Lie's China efforts, called upon Washington to instruct its representatives at United Nations headquarters to seek to replace Mr. Lie as Secretary-General unless he "at once" revised his attitude on China. Their statement referred to Mr. Lie as "the Soviet partisan incumbent." [17]

If sentiment in favor of accrediting the Chinese Communist regime were enough to justify this description, the Senators' designation would have been apt. For Mr. Lie has clearly favored the admission of the Peiping government. His legal memorandum, it will be recalled, distinguished between the question of recognition of a government by states and representation in the United Nations, and suggested that an inquiry be undertaken by the Security Council to determine which of the two rival governments was actually in a position to direct the population and resources of China in fulfillment of the obligations of membership. Obviously, no inquiry could possibly judge the Formosa government to be in such a position. And if there were any doubt about what the Secretary-General believed the outcome of his proposed inquiry would be, it was resolved by his rather casual admission, offered in the course of his explanation of the memorandum to a Paris press conference, that "we hoped to see the new Republic of China in the United Nations." [18]

The Secretary-General made every effort to realize this hope. He held round after round of private conversations with the members of the Security Council (Nationalist China excluded). He concentrated particularly on the "pivotal four" — France,

Egypt, Ecuador, and Cuba — the votes of any two of which would have swung the Security Council balance in favor of Peiping's accreditation. In these conversations, the Secretary-General did not directly attempt to induce these states to switch from support of the Nationalists to support of the Communists. Rather, in the words of a top member of Mr. Lie's entourage, "the Secretary-General tried to persuade them to take into account certain considerations, among them those set forth in his legal memorandum — considerations which would have led them to reconsider their positions." [19]

Though "China was not the main issue on the agenda for my trip," Mr. Lie later noted — ("the main issue for me was how to get peace, once the China situation is settled" [20]) — the Secretary-General carried his efforts on behalf of the Peiping government to Washington, London, Paris, and Moscow. Again, it was a matter of suggesting certain considerations, not a process of frank lobbying. "I do not think it would be fair or just for the United Nations Secretary-General to go to countries and ask them to vote in a certain way. That would be more or less pressure. I am not quite sure that Member nations would accept my travelling around to get votes." [21] Shielded with this gentle distinction, Mr. Lie continued his talks, apparently bringing them, by the eve of the Korean invasion, to the verge of success. Before Mr. Lie's visit to London, Britain's policy had been to vote for the admission of Peiping when it appeared there would be available the necessary six other affirmative Security Council votes, but until that day to abstain. After the Secretary-General's departure, British policy seemed to shift to active support of the candidacy of the Communist government.[22] This shift, and Mr. Lie's Paris efforts, evidently were among the factors inducing the French government to reverse its opposition to accrediting Peiping — a reversal of policy which, it seems, did not see the light of day in the summer of 1950 largely because of the Korean crisis. It was widely agreed in informed circles that if France publicly revised her stand to favor Mao Tse-tung's government, Ecuador or Egypt would follow along, providing the seventh vote which would have assured the admission of the Peiping regime to the Security Council. The Chinese question would thus have been "settled"; the U.S.S.R. presumably would have returned to United Nations organs; and the way would have been cleared for Mr. Lie to propose formally to the Security Council his ideas for the resumption of East-West negotiations.

While in Moscow, it is interesting to note, Mr. Lie took the initiative in arranging a meeting with the Chinese Communist Ambassador, the representative of a regime not recognized by the United Nations. According to press reports, Mr. Lie requested him, among other things, to raise with his government the question of its discharging the international obligations contracted by the Nationalist government.

With the Korean invasion, the Secretary-General turned his energies toward the enforcement of collective security. But his position concerning the representation of China, he noted, remained without change. "The question should be decided on constitutional grounds and not in connection with other considerations, such as events in Korea, or boycotts, or ideologies, or questions of recognition or non-recognition. The people of China have a constitutional right, under the Charter, to be represented at all times in the United Nations by the Government that has the power to represent them." [23] Mr. Lie's refusal to link the Chinese question with "events in Korea" took on particular point as the contrary Soviet strategy of attempting to tie a Korean settlement to Peiping's accreditation unfolded.

### The Ten-Point Memorandum and the "Peace Mission"

The deterioration of relations between leading Members of the United Nations has created a situation of most serious concern for the United Nations and the future peace of the world. In my capacity as Secretary-General, I have felt it my duty to suggest means by which the principles of the Charter and the resources of the United Nations could be employed to moderate the present conflict and to enable a fresh start to be made towards eventual peaceful solutions of outstanding problems.[24]

This introductory paragraph to the letter accompanying his ten-point memorandum, which Mr. Lie sent to each of the member states in June 1950, indicates the rationale behind the bulk of the Secretary-General's epochal activity of the first half of that year. Mr. Lie's effort was directed toward exploring the possible areas of fruitful negotiation between East and West. It was not an attempt at mediation. It was a step prior to mediation. "I wanted to find out," Mr. Lie explained, "if the cold war was just going to go on month after month with no end but ultimate disaster in sight, or whether there was a basis for the renewal of general negotiations between the two sides on at least some of the outstanding issues of the so-called cold war." [25] It was, in his words, "an exploring mission" — and one in which the Secretary-General took the lead in suggesting what promising areas might be discovered.

The first public sign of Mr. Lie's conciliation effort came in March in his Washington speech. The Secretary-General then put forth what was to become the first of the ten points of his "Twenty-Year Program for Achieving Peace through the United Nations": his suggestion of special periodic meetings of the Security Council, to be attended by foreign ministers or heads of governments. These sessions would be designed to provide a high-level review of outstanding issues before the Organization, accompanied by private consultations on these issues among the foreign ministers. "Great results" could not be expected from any one of these meetings, the Secretary-General cautioned, but they could supply the occasion "for the restoration of an atmosphere of mutual confidence more favorable to . . . peaceful settlement." "I do not believe in political miracles," said Mr. Lie. "It will take a long series of steps to reduce the tensions of conflict. . . What we need, what the world needs, is a twenty-year program to win peace through the United Nations." [26]

The Secretary-General followed up his suggestion by conversations with high-ranking officers of the State Department. A few days later, he circulated among the six nonpermanent members of the Security Council a draft of a six-point agenda for a possible special session. It anticipated many of the items he was shortly to take up in Washington, London, Paris, and Moscow: Chinese representation, atomic energy and the problem of the hydrogen bomb, the creation of an international police force, the admission of new members, the reduction of conventional armaments, and the holding of future periodic high-level Security Council meetings.

In mid-April, it was announced that the Secretary-General would shortly visit the capitals of Western Europe and would perhaps extend his tour to Moscow. If Premier Stalin was in Moscow at the time, Mr. Lie remarked with customary simplicity, "I think I shall see him." [27]

The Secretary-General and his Department of Public Information made every effort not to overplay the tour. Mr. Lie's parting words, as he sailed from New York, are of interest both as an illustration of this attempt to avoid exciting false hopes among the public and as a guide to the nature of the trip's objectives:

I do not expect any immediate results from my journey. It is more along the lines of groundwork which has to be done, and which I have to do. I am going to various countries convinced that I am doing my duty, and I hope something may result from it later. I believe that all decent people desire in their hearts that the cold war be ended. But it will take time. I do not expect too much. I shall see the leaders of various countries and obtain information from them, and I should know more about where we all stand when I return. [28]

The precise nature of what the Secretary-General said to Harry S. Truman, Dean Acheson, Clement Attlee, Ernest Bevin, Kenneth Younger, Sir Gladwyn Jebb, Sir Hartley Shawcross, Anthony Eden, Vincent Auriol, Georges Bidault, Robert Schuman, Joseph Stalin, Viacheslav Molotov, Andrei Vishinsky, Andrei Gromyko, Arkady Sobolev, Wang Chia-hsiang, Dirk Stikker, Max Petitpierre, and Gunnar Myrdal, and what they said to him, is known only to these gentlemen and the relatively small circles of their intimate associates.

From the parts of the story which have been made public, however, and from deductions from certain speculations, the validity of which have been confirmed by wholly reliable sources close to Mr. Lie's tour, some incomplete reconstruction of the essentials of these talks may be offered, concerning their subject matter, accent, and results.

As for subject matter, Mr. Lie himself reported: "Our conversations covered a great many subjects. They ranged over the whole field of United Nations problems and activities. For example, the cold war, China, periodic meetings of the Security

Council, control of atomic energy, disarmament, and many, many others. Some matters were brought up by the statesmen to whom I talked and some by me. In this connection, I had several memoranda in my briefcase." [29]

One of these memoranda was the Secretary-General's legal opinion on the question of representation in the United Nations; another was his "Memorandum of Points for Consideration in the Development of a Twenty-Year Program for Achieving Peace through the United Nations." The ten points of the latter comprise a good number of the total of those taken up by the Secretary-General. They are as follows:

1. Inauguration of periodic, top-level meetings of the Security Council, together with further development of other United Nations machinery for negotiation, mediation, and conciliation. Among such other machinery, Mr. Lie suggested the reëstablishment of the regular practice of consultations by the representatives of the Big Five, and a renewed effort to secure agreement on the limitation of the use of the veto power in the pacific settlement procedures of the Security Council.

2. A new attempt to establish international control of atomic energy. The Secretary-General particularly noted two possibilities of a "fresh approach": his calling a conference of scientists whose discussions might provide a reservoir of new ideas on the control of weapons of mass destruction and the promotion of peaceful uses of atomic energy; and an interim control agreement that "would at least be some improvement on the present situation of an unlimited arms race, even though it did not afford full security."

3. A new approach to control of other weapons of mass destruction and conventional armaments in general, which should "go hand in hand with any effort to reach political settlements."

4. A renewal of serious efforts to reach agreement on the armed forces to be made available to the Security Council. An interim accord for a small force sufficient to prevent or stop localized outbreaks should be negotiated pending a final solution.

5. Acceptance and application of the principle of universality of membership. "Application" would include the admission of the fourteen nations then applicants and the promise of the ad-

mission of Germany and Japan once the peace treaties are concluded.

6. A sound and active program of technical assistance and encouragement of capital investment in underdeveloped countries.

7. More vigorous use of the specialized agencies. Here, Mr. Lie suggested the membership of the Soviet Union in these agencies, and the ratification of the Charter of the International Trade Organization.

8. Continued development of United Nations work on human rights.

9. Use of the United Nations to promote, by peaceful means instead of by force, the advancement of dependent and colonial peoples toward independence.

10. Active and systematic use of all the powers of the Charter and all the machinery of the Organization to speed up the development of international law toward an eventual enforceable world law for a universal society.

Points one and seven of this program were particularly accented by Mr. Lie in his conversations, the former in all four capitals and the latter in Moscow. The Secretary-General tried to persuade the Soviet Union to take an active part in the technical assistance program (for which it had voted at the Fourth Session of the General Assembly but had not backed since) and to join the specialized agencies (in spite of its having given notice of withdrawal from the World Health Organization, one of the few in which it held membership). Apparently, the Secretary-General had no success in either regard.

As for his proposal for periodic meetings of the Security Council, all four capitals seem to have reacted favorably but with various degrees of warmth, Washington being the coolest. But at the time, it seemed that no such meetings would be possible until the Chinese question had been settled; and when the U.S.S.R. returned to the Security Council, in spite of the presence of the Nationalist representative, the Korean situation then made pressing for periodic sessions inopportune.

With regard to the more general results of the tour, it was Mr. Lie's view that, "if anyone won the first round, it was the United

Nations and its Secretary-General." [30] "I have drawn from my conversations," he noted, "a firm conviction that the United Nations remains a primary factor in the foreign policy of each of these Governments and that the reopening of genuine negotiations on certain of the outstanding issues may be possible." [31]

The Secretary-General did not reveal the basis of his "firm conviction" concerning the chances of the renewal of East-West negotiations. It may be disclosed, however, that the Secretary-General received certain assurances from Premier Stalin which in Mr. Lie's view, if not in Washington's, constituted concessions sufficiently significant to promote the "reopening of genuine negotiations."

Mr. Lie's reception in Moscow, interestingly enough, was extremely cordial. "I have been received in a most friendly way," he reported, "and the exchange of views and ideas has been of a positive kind." [32] He was shown a variety of unusual courtesies, among them a remarkably full coverage in the Soviet press of his visit and his ten-point memorandum. The text of the latter was printed in full in Russian newspapers, despite the limited space they generally devote to international affairs.

The Secretary-General was full of amiable impressions of the Soviet Union and, upon his return, shared them with his press conference. He noted the physical progress made in the U.S.S.R. the last few years and spoke, with unconscious paternalism, of the rising Soviet living standards. "They wore shoes," he remarked, in referring to a crowd of Muscovites he had seen at a soccer match, "and they had ties now, and they had suits like anyone else. Looking around, I said to myself: That crowd could be transferred . . . to Ebbets Field on a Sunday afternoon." [33]

The Secretary-General's reception in Western Europe was likewise warm. President Auriol, Prime Minister Bidault, and Foreign Minister Schuman were "most cordial." [34] Expressions of public support were strong. In London, Mr. Lie was received in a "friendly spirit," [35] 144 members of the House of Commons signing a motion praising his efforts.

In Washington, it was another story. No one thought of circulating a laudatory resolution among the members of Congress on either the occasion of Mr. Lie's pre-European or post-European visit. Indeed, the chill was so penetrating that it traversed the Atlantic, where Kenneth Younger, British Minister of State, acknowledged to Commons that there was "a certain suspicion" of Mr. Lie's mission in the United States. "I can assure the House that there is no suspicion here," he added. "We realize Mr. Lie's position — that of a very important international figure who has the duty as well as the opportunity to resolve the difficulties which have been frustrating the United Nations." [36]

To be sure, Mr. Acheson, in commenting upon the Secretary-General's tour and ten-point memorandum, began by saying, "I think it is proper for Mr. Lie in his capacity as Secretary General of the United Nations to take whatever steps he thinks desirable in his effort to reduce the existing tensions in the world. The Secretary General of the United Nations occupies a unique position and deserves our encouragement and support." [37] But the cool tone of most of the remainder of his statement seems to have been a more accurate indicator of the true temper of the feeling of official Washington concerning Mr. Lie's efforts. While declaring that the United States was willing to consider any "practical" possibilities for negotiation put forth by Mr. Lie, the Secretary of State emphasized not the immediate renewal of negotiations but the creation of situations of strength in the free world.

Mr. Lie, refusing to be discouraged, insisted that he was "really satisfied" [38] with Mr. Acheson's words. He had earlier described his initial talk with President Truman as a "good one" [39] and his Moscow exchanges as "positive." On leaving Paris, he said he was "satisfied," and in London, that "no door is closed." [40] He was preparing to depart for Europe again to press his efforts further when the Korean invasion came.

In response to the Korean crisis, the Secretary-General suspended these plans. "But," he affirmed, "that does not mean that I have abandoned, or have any intention of abandoning, my efforts for peace by negotiation, mediation and conciliation. On the contrary, when the peace enforcement action of the United Nations has succeeded in Korea, the need for the United Nations in its conciliating and mediating role will be greater than ever." [41]

Mr. Lie's activity of the first half of 1950 has been the subject of so much criticism, commendation, and confusion that it merits a summation of its nature and an examination of the commentary directed toward it.

The Secretary-General's efforts concerning the question of the representation of China in the United Nations were clearly aimed at facilitating the admission of the Central Peoples' Republic. Sufficient reason for Mr. Lie's Chinese stand is the evident fact that the Peiping regime controls China and is thus in a position to fill effectively the seat which China is assured by the terms of the Charter. It is further safe to assume that the Secretary-General was additionally motivated by his anxiety over the Soviet boycott, which took as its excuse the presence of the "Kuomintang clique."

Mr. Lie's four-capital tour, and the ten-point memorandum which he circulated in the course of it, seems to have had the following objectives: (a) resolution of the Chinese impasse, primarily through shifts in Anglo-French policy and preferably acquiesced in by the United States; (b) dramatization of the dangers of the continued duration of the "cold war," and illustration of the potentiality of the United Nations for lessening those dangers; (c) persuasion of the Soviet Union to participate in the technical assistance program and specialized agencies of the United Nations, both because of the intrinsic value of its participation and because of the contribution the gesture of its joining would make toward improving the atmosphere for political negotiation; and (d) exploration of the areas of possible constructive negotiation between East and West, and, if possible, the securing of indications from both sides of what concessions they might be prepared to consider on certain of the issues outstanding between them, in order to clear the way, once the Chinese question was settled, for the reopening of "genuine negotiations."

The results of Mr. Lie's efforts are less clear. As stated, he seemed very close to success on the Chinese issue when the Korean invasion so radically altered the picture. And not until the Chinese question had been settled could the outcome of his attempts to lay the groundwork for a renewal of East-West negotiations have been judged. As for his aim of dramatizing the dangers of the cold war and drawing attention to the potentiality of the United Nations for meeting them, in this the Secretary-General seemed successful and, in view of the Korean outbreak, clairvoyant.

There was little responsible criticism of the right of the Secretary-General to take the initiative during the first half of 1950 — a significant demonstration of how far Mr. Lie had advanced the status of his office through skillful use and broad construction of his constitutional powers. His efforts attracted wide support, both from most of the permanent representatives at Lake Success and from the world public. But some criticism of the Secretary-General's activity was offered — not as concerned his right to carry it forward, but regarding the objectives of that activity and the means which Mr. Lie chose in attempting to reach those objectives.

Certain United Nations delegates deplored Mr. Lie's emphasis on settling the problem of China before achieving East-West negotiations. Negotiations, they felt, were the important thing. Mr. Lie would have done the cause of peace a greater service if he had worked for the resumption of negotiations outside the framework of the United Nations, pending settlement of the Chinese question.

Aside from the incongruity of suggesting that Mr. Lie labor for the initiation of negotiations by-passing the Organization of which he is Secretary-General, there seems to be some validity to this criticism. The Chinese issue did have certain "fake" characteristics which were thrown into clear relief when Mr. Malik returned to the Security Council on August 1 — characteristics of a procedural knot which any substantial desire on Moscow's part could untie. Sources close to the Secretary-General report, however, that he decided against trying to bring about negotiations outside the United Nations because of several statements of President Truman — and one of Mr. Attlee, in rebuttal to Mr. Churchill's campaign proposal of a Big Four meeting — to the effect that the United Nations was the proper forum in which to negotiate. For the West to have agreed to talks outside the United Nations would have seemed an admission of the validity of the Soviet boycott.

There was, of course, criticism of the substance of Mr. Lie's China activity, mainly from extreme supporters of the Nationalists and certain United States Senators. But more detached sources also took issue with his espousal of Peiping's accreditation. They did not dispute the rectitude of his supporting the admission of the Communists *per se*, but they did criticize what seemed to be his willingness to "appease" the U.S.S.R. on the question.

It is perhaps enough that certain elements in Washington too often seem to content themselves with a policy simply because it is the opposite of that of the Soviet Union; but to ask the Secretary-General of the United Nations to adopt the same approach is asking a great deal. Mr. Lie, of course, was influenced not only by the merits of Peiping's case but by the desirability of active Soviet membership in the Organization. Such a consideration, from the point of view of the Secretary-General, is entirely normal and legitimate, even if the U.S.S.R. makes adherence to it as difficult as possible.

Certain observers criticized the ten-point program as "anemic." They asserted that most of the points were merely restatements of obvious desirables. To call for "vigorous and continued development of the work of the United Nations for wider observance and respect for human rights" (point 8), for example, was not to voice a provocative thought contributing much to overcoming the East-West deadlock.

It is true that there was not a great deal in the "Twenty-Year Program for Achieving Peace" that was fresh or ingenious. But Mr. Lie was aware of that when he wrote, "What is suggested here is only an outline of preliminary proposals for a program; much more development will be needed." [42] And as for the one point which the Secretary-General publicly carried beyond the outline stage — his plan for periodic, top-level meetings of the Security Council — this suggestion was fresh and it is ingenious. For it did away with two of the prime objections to an East-West conference on the highest level: it envisaged not one grand attempt, to be followed by a more awful depression in the distinct possibility of failure, but a series of meetings, in which the lack of progress at one session might be made good at another; and at the same time, private Great Power negotiations were to be engineered, not outside the United Nations, but under its auspices.

Mr. Lie offered in the course of one of his press conferences a further explanation of his plan for periodic meetings, and of the purposes of the memorandum as a whole, that is well worth quoting. If the Chinese question is settled, he said,

> as I hope, then the time will come for me to send to the President of the Security Council . . . my memorandum together with a letter, and to ask him to place it on the Security Council's agenda. . . I would recommend not to call a periodic session at once. I think the basis for work would be for them [the members of the Council] to establish themselves a sub-committee . . . to try to find in private consultations, in informal closed meetings, whether there is a chance to get agreement about some of the points in my memorandum. . .
>
> My memorandum will therefore, as far as I can see, be just a working document, a basis for friendly, genuine talks and negotiations among the members of the Security Council, in the hope that they will be able to find some issues which they think can be settled at the first periodic session.[43]

There has been some objection to the secrecy surrounding the tour, particularly as concerns Mr. Lie's conversations with Stalin. Many observers, delegates among them, have questioned the right of the Secretary-General to refuse to divulge the substance of his conversations and have deplored his tendency "to act importantly in the worst traditions of secret diplomacy." Mr. Lie has refused to bow to these criticisms:

> No Member Nation has the right to know the contents of my conversations. . . For example, if I spoke to the officials of the Government of Pakistan, the Government of India has no right to receive information from me about that conversation. I have the right to tell them or not to tell them. . . It is for the governments to decide when and in what manner they will express their opinions about the present situation and my memorandum. . . We cannot have everything discussed in the press.[44]

It is difficult to see how the Secretary-General could be an effective political force if he had to make public his diplomatic negotiations. To require him to do so — at times convenient to the night editor — would be in effect to deprive him of all right

of political initiative. It would contradict the clear intention of
the founders of the Organization when they wrote, in the Report
of the Preparatory Commission in a tone of unchallenged assumption, that since the "Secretary-General is a confidant of
many governments . . . no Member should offer him, at any
rate immediately upon retirement, any governmental position in
which his confidential information might be a source of embarrassment to other Members." [45]

Less thoroughgoing criticism relates to the timing of Mr. Lie's
tour. There was considerable annoyance in Washington at the
Secretary-General's going to Moscow on a "peace mission" while
Mr. Acheson was in London trying to persuade his French and
British colleagues to agree on a rearmament program. The contrast which could be invidiously made, and the distraction of
public attention from "the real thing" to Mr. Lie's dramatic
doings, was understandably distressing to American strategists.
Unquestionably, Mr. Lie's timing, ideally speaking, could have
been better. Sources close to the Secretary-General explain that
the coincidence was inadvertent — that while Mr. Lie, and not
Moscow, chose the period of his visit, the Secretary-General's
duties permitted him to select no other time.

A further criticism as to timing is of the hindsight school.
"Here Lie was in Moscow and everywhere else talking about
peace," runs this commentary, "while the Russians were preparing Korea." Mr. Lie, in short, was the unconscious tool of the
Soviet peace campaign, designed, among other things, to create
a peaceful atmosphere well suited to the surprise attack in Korea.
Such criticism might be more impressive if American intelligence,
with channels of information in this case incomparably superior
to those of the Secretary-General, had been any less surprised than
was Mr. Lie by the Korean invasion. But it appears that Washington could not have been more surprised.

The most that can be said for this brand of criticism, in fact, is
that it was "bipartisan." "Only recently," wrote Lev Oshanin, in
the Moscow *Literary Gazette*, "after he donned the mask of
objective arbitrator, Trygve Lie traveled about European capitals on a 'peace mission.' Newspapers wrote much about his
'valuable initiative.' What is such a 'mission of peace' worth after

Trygve Lie's openly coming forth against peace and in defense of an aggressive war?

"Evidently, this 'valuable initiative' was no more than a maneuver designed to detract attention from the war venture being prepared by the Americans in the Far East." [46]

This criticism, as voiced in the West, does verge, however, upon a questioning of Mr. Lie's activity of a more intelligent and fundamental character — a questioning which concerns not Mr. Lie's means but his immediate end: the resumption of negotiations between the Soviet Union and the Western world. Exponents of this latter view challenge Mr. Lie's assumption of the inherent desirability of negotiations. Negotiations are of value, they hold, when the parties agree on fundamentals. As long as Mr. Malik insists on calling black white, negotiating with Mr. Malik cannot be productive. Unless, of course, negotiations are not so much a matter of genuine give-and-take within a framework of understood principles, as — in the words of Mr. Acheson — a recording of "situations of strength." The Soviet Union will only compromise in response to the strength of the other party and not in any degree in response to the merits of the issue or the arguments put forth. Thus negotiations will be inopportune and even deleterious, insofar as they confuse the issue, until the point is reached where they may record the facts of Western strength. "A prior condition [of] . . . successful and meaningful negotiations with the Soviet Union," Mr. Acheson put it, ". . . is for the Soviet leaders to be convinced that they cannot profit from a policy of expansionism — that their own self-interest as well as that of the rest of the world would be advanced by a settlement of some, at least, of our outstanding differences." [47] As for the role of the Secretary-General in this world where negotiations are worse than useless, these critics suggest that rather than attempting to mediate between East and West, Mr. Lie should bring his weight down on the side which has demonstrated its respect for the Charter's principles.

Mr. Lie has not hesitated "to bring his weight down" in instances of the most flagrant challenge of the Organization's authority — in Palestine, for example, and, more pertinently, in Korea. But his adherence to the negotiatory process is firm. Two days after Mr. Acheson's initial declaration that negotiation with the U.S.S.R. would be useful only after the United States had created "strength instead of the weakness which exists in many quarters," the Secretary-General asserted: "The United Nations was founded on the belief that peaceful negotiation of differences is not only possible, but necessary, no matter how difficult the circumstances, or how great the differences, or how deep the misunderstanding or distrust on both sides." [48] "I do not know how you can ever resolve differences or reduce distrust except by negotiation honestly entered into by each side." [49] "The United Nations has no alternative except to try all measures of pacific settlement," one of the Secretary-General's most influential advisers further explained, "even if failure is probable. That is an obligation of the Secretariat, and the United Nations as a whole." [50]

That is the Secretary-General's view. Whether his concept of his responsibilities is in the best interests of the Organization is a question which cannot be answered, except over a period of years.[51]

### The General Assembly and the Ten Points

The anticlimax to Mr. Lie's activities of the spring of 1950 came the following fall, when the General Assembly took up the Secretary-General's ten-point program. The Assembly decided to debate it in plenary session, without prior discussion in committee. It concluded its debate by adopting, by a vote of 51 to 5, a mild resolution commending the Secretary-General for his initiative in preparing and submitting the memorandum and referring the points to the various organs for further study, requesting them to inform the Assembly at its Sixth Session of the results of their consideration.[52]

The debate was of interest in four respects. It was opened with an excellent introductory speech by the Secretary-General, which adjusted the memorandum to the subsequent events in Korea and suggested, among other things, that the periodic meetings proposed be rotated primarily among the capitals of the permanent members of the Security Council (excepting Washington).[53] Secondly, the debate produced considerable governmental comment upon the Secretary-General's proper role. Thirdly, it loosed a fresh torrent of Soviet criticism of Mr. Lie. And, lastly, it witnessed the unusual occurrence of the Secretary-General's rebutting such criticism in a blunt and telling fashion.

The comments of the delegates upon the political powers of the Secretary-General were uniformly friendly. General Carlos P. Romulo suggested that "our Secretary-General, by the terms of the Charter, is one of the principal guardians of the peace of the world . . . in moments of grave emergency and crisis he must be regarded as having also the implied authority and, indeed, the duty to bring to the attention of the Organization any suggestions which, in his considered judgment, would help to ensure the maintenance of international peace and security." [54]

Yugoslavia was "of the opinion that the Secretary-General, by the very function he exercises in accordance with the United Nations Charter, was not only authorized but bound to take a certain initiative." [55]

The United States, Senator John Sparkman proclaimed, did "not believe that any voice should be raised in criticism of the Secretary-General for the action he has taken in preparing and publishing his Memorandum. True, it was an unprecedented action. It is, however, fully within the scope of the powers of the Secretary-General, as we construe them. . . In our view he should always feel free to bring to the attention of governments and of peoples everywhere any proposals he may have which are calculated to bring about a more peaceful world." [56]

The memorandum, the delegate of Chile affirmed, "clearly shows that the Secretary-General knows how to carry his duty and how to fulfill the provisions of the Charter." [57] "It seems to my Government," added the British Minister of State, Mr. Younger, "that the Secretary-General was fully entitled to take the initiative which he did, and that he ought to receive the thanks of all Members for having done so." [58]

Even the delegate of Poland, who maintained that the memorandum reflected "an American point of view far removed from the principles of the Charter," agreed that "it is no less unquestionable that it is the duty of the Secretary-General to take the initiative and to use all the means at his disposal under the

Charter to lessen present conflicts and to open up a new era to the peaceful solution of disputes." [59]

But Mr. Vishinsky could bring himself to say no more than that the Secretary-General "is supposed to be . . . the custodian" of the Charter.[60] His criticism of the ten points was thorough-going: "It has been said here that Trygve Lie came back from Moscow with his Memorandum. No; he came to Moscow with his Memorandum, which had been already sanctioned by the State Department . . . , subsequently visaed by the Foreign Office in London, and, later, countersigned by Schuman in Paris. In other words, it was approved by that whole company of plot-ters against peace, and finally it appeared before our eyes in Moscow.[61] . . . The program of United States monopolies is set forth in the Secretary-General's Memorandum." [62]

The Soviet Foreign Minister's adjutant, Mr. Malik, later em-broidered upon his chief's theme. "The fact that the contents of the Memorandum had been agreed upon in advance with the State Department in Washington is not disputed or denied by anybody. I shall not name the persons who actually wrote the Memorandum and I shall not state who participated in Washing-ton in the work; those facts are well known to representatives here and there is no need to speak about that. The fact that the Memorandum was agreed upon in advance with Washington arouses no doubt on anybody's part. The authors of the Memo-randum will not deny it." [63]

But the author did deny it. When the Soviet Deputy Foreign Minister sat down, Mr. Lie got up to respond:

"Mr. Malik's statement from this rostrum imposes upon me the necessity of pointing out that something which has been said here is not true and will not be made true by repetition.

"It has been said that my Memorandum was sanctioned, or even drafted by, the Governments of the United States, France and the United Kingdom. This is not true, and those who say it must know that it is not true. I must make it absolutely clear that the Memorandum was my own conception and that I myself drafted it in consultation only with my eight — I repeat: eight — Assistant Secretaries-General, and other principal assistants. The text which I discussed in Moscow was precisely the same text which I brought to Washington, London and Paris, and it appears in my communication to the Member Governments without the alteration of a single word or a single comma." [64]

In sum, the Assembly's action on the ten-point program, while not spectacular, tended to confirm the essential political character of the Secretaryship General.

### Other Diplomatic Endeavors

As indicated at the beginning of this chapter, the foregoing summation of Mr. Lie's behind-the-scenes activity is illustrative and not exhaustive. Other examples of particular interest which may at least be mentioned are his efforts directed against the Bevin-Sforza plan for the division of Libya and the allocation of the other former Italian colonies, and those exerted against the rescinding of the Assembly's resolution requesting the withdrawal of ambassadors from Franco Spain and affirming the ineligibility of Fascist Spain for membership. Mr. Lie was also active, at the Fourth Session of the General Assembly, in supporting the candidacy of Czechoslovakia against that of Yugoslavia in the fight for Eastern Europe's Security Council seat.

One last example: The Secretary-General took part in the private negotiations of the conciliation commissions which the Third and Fourth Assemblies set up to deal with the Greek imbroglio. Dr. Evatt was the moving spirit of the Greek mediation attempt at the Third Assembly, and Mr. Lie's experience there no doubt made him of particular value at the meetings of the commission established by the Fourth, from which Assembly Dr. Evatt was absent. This serves to drive home the generalization that while other United Nations officers and delegates come and go, the Secretary-General is quasi-permanent. This permanency is an important element of the Secretary-General's strength.

### Governmental Attitudes

THE UNITED STATES

What of the attitude of the member governments toward the political practice of the Secretary-General? There has been, with the exception of the Soviet bloc, extremely little formal, direct criticism by governments of the Secretary-General's political activity. There has been a good deal of criticism in the press at the indirect instance of United Nations members, and, upon occasion, certain delegates have informally spoken to the Secretary-General in a chastening manner.

Altogether, the attitudes which these criticisms express fall into two broad categories and a number of lesser ones. Generally, the Great Powers are inclined to look with disfavor upon the political activity of the Secretary-General as the introduction of a new force upon the international scene they dominate, and a force which may not necessarily sustain their particular interests; the Middle and Small Powers, on the other hand, tend to applaud such activity as further strengthening a United Nations which has given them a world forum for expression of their views in international affairs.

The Great Powers are not identical in their outlook on this question, however, and some of the smaller Powers — particularly the Netherlands and Belgium — are partial to the strictly administrative interpretation of the Secretary-General's role. Moreover, all of the member governments seem subject, in varying degrees, to the pragmatic outlook which Mr. Lie frankly describes: "Everything is in order as long as I agree with a particular Government, but as soon as I don't — 'Aren't we paying you? Aren't you a servant of the Governments? You are an administrator, why do you talk!' " [65]

A source close to the Department of State verifies the conformity of the United States with the Secretary-General's view: "Our attitude is too much like that of the others . . . the all too prevalent, unconscious attitude assumed by the regular Department personnel concerned with shaping our policies that anything that helps is good, anything that stands in the way bad. . . it takes for granted that when the Secretary-General is moving our way, he is doing well; but when he's against us, he's clearly beyond his powers." By way of illustration, this informant points out "the contrast of Trieste and Palestine. Mr. Lie's support was taken for granted on Trieste. But when we took a different position on Palestine — a narrow interpretation of the Security Council's powers, hard to reconcile with Trieste — there was little attention to and some annoyance at Mr. Lie's expression of a broad view of the Council's powers."

In the same conversation the author mentioned, in passing, the criticism made by another well-informed person that the Secretary-General had employed Mr. Price, Mr. Feller, and Mr. Cordier in negotiations with Washington. "The United States government hasn't shown great interest in Lie," was the reply. "Mr. Lie hasn't often been invited to the White House or to state dinners by the Secretary of State. So he feels constrained in his Washington relations and chooses an American, who knows his way around and won't be slighted too easily, to do his negotiating in Washington." It should be added that Mr. Lie's relations with the United States Mission to the United Nations have been warmer, particularly with Ambassador Warren Austin.

Officials of the United States government have not been above stimulating press criticism of activity of the Secretary-General which has displeased them. It can be stated upon absolutely reliable authority, for example, that a high-ranking official of the State Department inspired the article which appeared on the front page of the *New York Herald Tribune* of November 14, 1948, attacking Mr. Lie and Dr. Evatt for their Berlin letter and invidiously implying that the Secretary-General and the President of the Assembly had fallen victim "to the corridor efforts of Mr. Vishinsky." [66]

In its few pertinent official statements, however, the United States has displayed a more congenial attitude. "I would not want to leave the impression," said Ambassador Ernest A. Gross — after having announced that the United States would continue to vote against unseating the Nationalists, Mr. Lie's memorandum on Chinese representation notwithstanding — "that I have doubts that it [the Secretary-General's Chinese intervention] is within his responsibilities.

"I think the Secretary-General, in a matter which is obviously of so much concern to him, would feel that it is part of his responsibilities to make whatever suggestions he considered were constructive." [67]

Mr. Gross' declaration is paralleled by the later statements of Mr. Acheson and of Senator Sparkman, in relation to the Secretary-General's tour, which have been quoted earlier. More important than such statements, however, is the great upsurge in genuine coöperation between the Department of State and the Secretary-General which has been noticeable ever since Washington "discovered" the United Nations in connection with the Korean crisis. Washington's new-found warmth and attachment to the Secretary-General were emphasized — perhaps even with unwarranted ardor — in the struggle over continuing Mr. Lie in office at the expiration of his initial term.

THE SOVIET UNION

The assumption is widespread in informed circles that the Soviet Union, of all the Powers, would naturally tend more than any other to oppose a politically potent Secretary-General. For the totalitarian state has an ingrained difficulty in comprehending, let alone promoting, the institution of the objective international secretariat. The attitude of Germany and Italy in the League, and of Spain nowadays, demonstrates the near inability of the totalitarian mind to admit the validity of the concept of a secretariat impartially dedicated to supranational interests. An interesting illustration of the trouble the totalitarian mentality has in distinguishing the supranational responsibilities of the member of the secretariat from his national obligations was supplied by Spain in 1947. In response to an anti-Franco declaration of Trygve Lie, Spanish spokesmen threatened to bar Norwegian shipping from Spanish ports.

Indeed, one extremely competent observer declares that the attitude of virtually all of the members is responsive to the particular stand of the Secretary-General which may be in question, and that only the Soviet Union and its associates have a set policy which is steadily antipathetic to the Secretary-General's political initiative. "The last thing the Russians want," still another source puts it, "is a Secretary-General who will forcefully assert United Nations ideals and recommend courses of action. What they want is a silent guy who at least gives them 50 per cent of the breaks." Certainly the record of Soviet participation in the United Nations as a whole lends support to this thesis. It has been the Soviet Union, above all others, that has reiterated the theme of national sovereignty and protested against the expansion of the area of international jurisdiction.

But the record of Soviet statements concerning the Secretary-General does not indicate such negative consistency. Rather, early in the Organization's life, the Soviet Union and its Polish associate went out of their way at the closed meetings of the Security Council's Committee of Experts in which were drafted the rules of procedure, and during the Council's public meetings on the Iranian and Greek questions, to assert vigorously the Secretary-General's broad rights of political intervention. Later, this pattern changes. Officially, we find Jacob Malik asking a plenary meeting of the General Assembly, at which the Secretary-General's proposals for a United Nations Guard were under discussion, "Who has thus found it necessary to impose this patent violation of the Charter? We cannot fail to observe that this proposal, regardless of the actual intentions of the Secretary-General, is merely one of the links in a general system of measures which have been carried out lately by the leading circles of the United States of America and which are designed to violate the United Nations Charter overtly and to transform the United Nations into the obedient tool of that country." [68]

And *Pravda* wrote, in a critique of the third annual report of the Secretary-General:

Trygve Lie twice refers to bacteriological warfare. Is not the definite purpose of this to distract the attention of the General Assembly and of world public opinion from the existing unresolved question of atomic energy? . . . Under cover of a study of questions connected with bacteriological warfare, the question of the use of atomic energy for war purposes will be shelved.

This attitude of Trygve Lie is in accord with the interests of the Anglo-American bloc, but in no way conforms with the interests of peace and security of the peoples of the world. Thus Trygve Lie is not only unobjective. In actual fact, he sides with the Anglo-American bloc, supporting those of its actions which are directed towards the circumvention and violation of the United Nations Charter and those which are contrary to the aims of the Organization. [69]

That the preceding represents the more restrained in Soviet taste in polemics is indicated by the following, written by Professor Taris, a member of the Soviet Academy, again in *Pravda*:

Having visited the capitals of Europe, Mr. Trygve Lie has returned from far afield, and having awarded a group of members of the Security Council, who are the lackeys of American imperialism, the name and functions of the Security Council,[70] he is now sending appeals to all nations in the name of the United Nations to help the American aggressors in their scandalous undertakings.

Mr. Trygve Lie, having discarded his mask, has given up all pretense at abiding by the United Nations Charter, which he, as U.N. Secretary-General, should strictly respect. He has joined the ranks of the direct and active associates in the armed intervention in Korea. . .

Whence comes this sudden burst of energy, full of slavish obedience and denial of all principles of international law? . . . The Secretary-General of the United Nations has now freed himself of all the ties which but so recently constrained him somewhat to political and moral responsibility.[71]

Thus the Soviet Union's attitude, far from being consistent, is radically inconsistent, at first upholding the right of the Secretary-General to speak out and praising the substance of what he says; later, attacking that substance and impugning the Secretary-General's integrity in an unrestrained fashion. Whether the U.S.S.R. initially had hopes of finding an ally in Mr. Lie, and reacted so hotly upon its hopes being dashed, is impossible to say. The estimate of Dr. Rudzinski,[72] who, as legal adviser to the Polish delegation, was in an unusual position to assess the motives of the Soviet bloc, would lead one to assume as much. On the face of it, however, the Soviet Union would seem to have been guided by the general standard: Support the Secretary-General's political initiative when it's in our favor, fight it when it is not.

THE UNITED KINGDOM

It is difficult to find documentary confirmation of what one hears on all sides: that the United Kingdom is the chief exponent of the primarily purely administrative interpretation of the Secretary-General's role. Sources of unquestionable authority assert this as an unqualified fact; and it is generally accepted in United Nations circles to be the case.

Possible explanations of the British attitude are not wanting. The United Kingdom, as a Great Power, may be expected to share the Great Power bias against an international factor not necessarily amenable to its will; and the United Kingdom is further reputed to be "sour" on a United Nations which has several times thrown its weight against what Britain judged to be her interests, notably in Palestine and in the British colonies (and this disgruntlement would naturally extend to a Secretary-General who has taken an active part in United Nations dealings with both Palestine and nonself-governing territories); moreover, the British tradition supports a civil servant's impartiality and detachment from political affairs. These may well combine to give rise to a British attitude which at any rate has been distinctly unfriendly to the political initiative of the Secretary-General.

The friendly words, earlier quoted, of Kenneth Younger, British Minister of State, concerning Mr. Lie's tour, perhaps presage a later revision of the British attitude. Another similar sign has been the United Kingdom's more amicable reaction, beginning in 1950, to the remarkable measure of initiative which the secretariat of the United Nations Economic Commission for Europe has consistently taken. Considering the traditional realism of the British response to the *fait accompli*, it would not be surprising if her policy toward the political initiative of the Secretary-General were in process of revision.

### CHINA

The Chinese have, by and large, followed the British lead. From the very beginning (note the Iranian and rules of procedure cases) they have tended to speak of the Secretary-General as all administrator and no politician.

The attack of the Nationalist delegate, Dr. T. F. Tsiang, upon the Secretary-General for the issuance of his China representation memorandum was something else again — more in the line of direct reaction to a view evidently not in the interests of the regime Dr. Tsiang represented than a doctrinaire expression upon the Secretary-General's proper role. Charging that Mr. Lie's memorandum had the "purpose of appeasing the Soviet delegation by sacrificing the National delegation of the Government of China," Dr. Tsiang wrote the Secretary-General: "Today, with such bad politics and bad law, you have intervened against the interests of my country. Tomorrow you can do the same thing against the interests of other countries.

"The organization of international security is vitiated by an element of insecurity at its very center, particularly for the smaller and weaker countries." [73]

Earlier, Dr. Tsiang had characterized the Secretary-General's memorandum as "a deliberate attempt to prejudice China's case before the United Nations. It oversteps the duties of the Secretary General and undermines confidence in his impartiality." [74]

"I have been asked to comment on Dr. Tsiang's attack upon me," Mr. Lie replied. "I do not wish to engage in controversy with Dr. Tsiang. He is doing his duty as he sees it and I am doing mine as I see it. He calls my memorandum 'bad law and bad politics.' As to the law, I am quite willing to leave that to the judgment of any representative group of jurists or the opinion of the International Court of Justice should it be decided to bring the question before the Court. As to the 'politics' of my position, I am quite content to leave that to the considered judgment of the Member nations and to history." [75]

THE ADMINISTRATIVE THEORY

Those states which oppose the political initiative of the Secretary-General put forth reasons more theoretical than the practical ones suggested above. The Secretary-General should not take political positions, their spokesmen privately argue, since there in fact exists no "international synthesis" for which he may speak. "The Secretary-General cannot speak for the whole lot," one of the most distinguished of United Nations figures puts it, "since they disagree. . . The Secretary-General cannot be a spokesman for supranational interests, since there is dispute among the nations as to what those interests are." Political statements, insofar as they reflect supranational interests upon which agreement is lacking, would be mere "utopian pronouncements." Insofar as they do not reflect these interests, they are partisan.

The reply of the advocates of a potent political role to this persuasive line of reasoning is that there are in fact solutions to problems which are genuinely in the supranational interest, though admittedly the member states may not agree as to what these are.

Taking advantage of his quasi-permanent, supremely informed position at the center of world diplomacy, however, the Secretary-General is peculiarly competent to discern these solutions — a proposition that goes back to fundamentals such as the objectivity of the human mind, the decent inclinations of the human character, the tendency of man to identify his ego and loyalties with the interests of the organization of which he is an integral and creative part, and the like. Moreover, the experience of the League in demonstrating the practicality of the concept of the objective international secretariat lends pragmatic support to this proposition. "Righteous men who adhere to the Charter" — the phrase is Gunnar Myrdal's [76] — do exist.

The Secretary-General's proposing solutions to international problems which, by virtue of his fulfillment of the ideal of his position, are "supranational" solutions, would concededly be "utopian" if his proposals were entirely without effect upon the policies of the member states. But this is not the case. The Secretary-General, as has been shown, does exercise a certain influence; from which it follows that the political initiative of the Secretary-General is valid and meaningful.

LESSER POWERS

A detailed discussion of the individual attitudes of the fifty-odd Middle and Smaller Powers who are members of the United Nations is evidently impracticable. In general, they very much favor the Secretary-General's taking substantial political initiative (though occasionally they oppose it in practice). "The smaller the country," Sir Eric Drummond recounts, "the more trust it placed in the Secretary-General." [77] This League phenomenon is reproduced in the United Nations.

In fact, the attitude is not uncommon among the smaller states (it may have become less so in view of the remarkable spurt in the Secretary-General's political activity in 1950) that Mr. Lie could have accomplished more than he has. "He was of course a product of Big Five agreement. When the general framework of that agreement collapsed, so did much of the potentiality for the Secretary-General's activity. Well, perhaps he couldn't have done more under the circumstances, but it was certainly initially assumed that he would be more active." [78] Sources other than the delegate quoted, however, go farther; they take the view that the East-West split is all the more reason and opportunity for the Secretary-General's filling a vigorous political role. [79]

A second, subtler explanation of what some small states regard as the Secretary-General's inadequacy of political initiative is offered by one of the most distinguished of Small Power representatives:

Mr. Lie has his strong points and his weak points. Undoubtedly his weakest point is the fact that he comes from a country not fully acquainted with the world, its people and its politics. A Norwegian is not versed in the affairs of India or South America or the Middle East. . .

Lie has a sense of isolationism, coming from Norway. A Frenchman, an Englishman, has a sense of the world. An Englishman has the Empire, the Frenchman feels himself the heart of the world. But a Norwegian tends to have an abstract sense of the world. This is of real significance. A Scandinavian can only be an umpire. He cannot be a leader. . . Lie, being what he is, couldn't have done more. . . A man coming from Oslo — what leadership can he exert? He knows very little, has had relatively little experience. . . But the post he occupies certainly demands great things. . .

A real world figure could do a great deal — Nehru, or a man like Hoover. . . Or perhaps Eisenhower, or Lord Mountbatten. Men of that stature, in that position, could exert a great deal of influence. . . But Trygve Lie had better stick to administration. He is not a great diplomat who can move things. [80]

How widely this view is held it is impossible to judge. It is at any rate clear that there is a noticeable inclination among the small states to urge the Secretary-General on. It will be recalled that it was a Small Power "revolt" at San Francisco which nullified the intentions of the sponsoring Great Powers to have the Secretary-General and his deputies elected by a vote (subject to veto) for three-year terms, and a Small Power drive which came quite close to achieving a substantial expansion of the Secretary-General's political endowment. This early favor of a politically potent Secretary-General is one that has been sustained.

# CHAPTER 7

## The Secretary-General
## and World Public Opinion

*The office I happen to hold — the office of Secretary-General — stands for the hopes for peace and civilization that are bound up in the United Nations.* TRYGVE LIE

*The Great Powers will never allow the Secretary-General to be more popular than their national leaders. He cannot be like Stalin or Attlee or Truman. The Foreign Offices won't permit it.*
A UNITED NATIONS OFFICIAL

The importance of the Secretary-General's popular role was succinctly and officially set forth by the Preparatory Commission in the following terms: "The United Nations cannot prosper, nor can its aims be realized, without the active and steadfast support of the peoples of the world. . . . the Secretary-General, more than anyone else, will stand for the United Nations as a whole. In the eyes of the world, no less than in the eyes of his own staff, he must embody the principles and ideals of the Charter to which the Organization seeks to give effect." [1]

If the Secretary-General's actions speak louder than his words — and considering the overriding importance of his private diplomatic role, they must — his words nevertheless are of the greatest moment to his political authority. He must be a negotiator before he is a speechmaker, and, as is often the case, he must sacrifice the latter for the progress of the former. But his power of public appeal can be a valuable auxiliary to his governmental and organic influence; and in the last analysis, insofar as international opinion is the ultimate source of international law, his public appeal is a prime source of that influence. For the "principles and ideals" which the Secretary-General shall endeavor to embody unquestionably possess an emotional and intellectual appeal for influential sections of opinion, to which, in some countries, governments are responsive. There is a reservoir of popular feeling in favor of the United Nations, or at least in favor of United Nations ideals — feeling which the Secretary-General, who symbolizes the United Nations as a whole, may draw upon to his advantage.

But the process has its limitations. The facilities for publicity and propaganda which the United Nations controls directly, such as its radio and publications, are relatively meager. And even these may be hobbled by unfriendly governmental action, as the difficulties of shipping United Nations printed material into Peron's Argentina demonstrate.[2] The Secretary-General is dependent largely upon national publicity media, and these are not wholly dependable. He cannot count on being able to rally popular opinion against governmental policy when the access to this opinion can, in many countries, be censored by official indication that publicizing the Secretary-General's views is not in the national interest. More practically, the Secretary-General must buck both the competition of the domestic news, which most media are tailored to present, and that of international events of more dramatic news value. The generalities to which the Secretary-General often is confined are overshadowed by the sensational specifics of the cold war.

The Secretary-General's appeals to public opinion take three main forms: his speeches and statements in press conference, the introductions to the annual reports, and those of his suggestions to the member states which he makes public. The latter two categories have for the most part been dealt with; as for his speeches, they closely parallel the introductions and need be considered but briefly. But first a word about Mr. Lie's weekly press conference.

The press conference, as an institution, has a distinctly democratic flavor. Preëminently and significantly an American phenomenon, it is a natural antidote to the possibility of losing touch with reality or to the development of a sense of hauteur. It is thus symptomatic of Mr. Lie's background, instincts, and his concept of his office that the Secretary-General has entered so fully into the practice of a conference each Friday morning, except when the General Assembly is in session.

Mr. Lie often chooses to channel the most important news through these conferences. But they are sometimes lively for other reasons, as the following exchange, a not unusual example of the give-and-take of these conferences, demonstrates:

QUESTION: Is it in your discretion to approve or disapprove the acceptance of the offer of three divisions from Nationalist China? I ask this question because it has been admitted even in the United States that the use of these forces —

THE SECRETARY-GENERAL: This is not a question for me to decide; it is for the Unified Command.

QUESTION: Nevertheless, I ask you this question.

THE SECRETARY-GENERAL: Nevertheless, I will not answer that question.

QUESTION: Do you want questions or do you not?

THE SECRETARY-GENERAL: I like questions.

QUESTION: . . . My question is whether you would approve such an acceptance of such forces inasmuch as you would like to see the war confined to the Korean area.

THE SECRETARY-GENERAL: No comment, my friend.[3]

Mr. Lie handles himself well at these conferences. The correspondents are anything but shy, and the combination is productive of both news and humor. The Secretary-General's relations with the press, on the whole, have been good, although the feeling is widespread in press circles that they could be better. The "no comments" which Mr. Lie relied upon so frequently in the period after his return from Moscow displeased many members of the United Nations press corps.

Virtually all of Mr. Lie's speeches are made up in whole or in large part of some or all of four elements: defense of the United Nations and exposition of its successes and failures; emphasis upon the necessity of Great Power negotiation and accommodation; criticism of aspects of the Great Power conflict; and the proposal of means to strengthen the United Nations. The last two elements are not as uniformly ubiquitous as the first two, but they are surprisingly common.

The importance of the first element — public defense of the United Nations — should not be underestimated. Edward J. Phelan, former Director-General of the International Labor Organization and an intimate associate of Albert Thomas, twenty years ago analyzed the role of the international secretariat in this regard with great insight:

> What is to be done when a decision . . . of the Council is attacked outside — attacked, that is, in the press or in one of the national parliaments? In the majority of cases, the Council cannot defend itself . . . it may have become divided. The position is a curious one, because while there may be an opposition, there is no government. Is the minority alone to put its case before public opinion? Is there to be no one to defend the decision adopted by the majority, the solution which the civil servant has to apply? . . . If the valid decisions taken by a majority in an international body are to be attacked and if there is no defense of them, the cumulative moral effect might be such as to destroy all public confidence in the international institution concerned.
>
> The answer is, of course, that the defense must be made by the civil servant, and that is what actually happens. But when the civil servant is thus called on to explain the real significance of a decision which he is responsible for executing, he runs the risk of being accused of a lack of impartiality. It may be asserted that he is taking sides, entering into controversy, or making that dreadful thing called propaganda. And in a certain sense he is.

Moreover, Mr. Phelan added,

> it is clear that if the civil servant has to envisage the possibility of having to defend such decisions, he will tend to give them not only a technical but a political preparation. He will weigh not only the strictly administrative elements but also the political elements. Thus not only when a decision is challenged or criticized, but throughout the whole function of administration, the political element will enter in, because each decision will in greater or less degree be the subject of political appreciation, and perhaps preparation, by the international civil servant.[4]

Examples may be cited of each of the Secretary-General's four favorite themes, beginning with his defense of the Organization. "What effect is being given to them [the ideals of the Charter] — or can be given to them by the United Nations?

"Some people think that the United Nations has not done much about these goals and will not be able to do much about them. Some fear that the United Nations is impotent because of the veto, that it has been paralyzed by the Great Power conflict, and that it has been consigned to the deep freeze by the cold war. . .

"Nobody should underestimate the dangers and difficulties created for the world and for the United Nations by the cold war. Nevertheless, this impression of the weakness of the United Nations, natural as it is, is very wrong." [5]

"In the past four years almost every major conflict in the world has been brought before the United Nations in one form or another. In every case war has been either stopped or prevented and the forces of peaceful settlement been set to work. This has been true in the cases of the Balkans, Palestine, Indonesia, Iran, Syria, Lebanon, Korea and Kashmir. It has been true in the case of Berlin. Furthermore, the Security Council, veto or no veto, has played a major part in these successes." [6]

An example of the Secretary-General's insistence upon the necessity of East-West negotiation:

"No matter how great the differences may be between the Great Powers, there are only two ways in which these differences can in the long run be dealt with. One way is the way of force. That means a third world war. The other way is by agreement and accommodation. That is the way of peace, and it is the United Nations way." [7]

An illustration of his criticism of certain policies of the members, in this case of the signatories of the North Atlantic Treaty:

"Regional coöperation has to be evalued in the right perspective. If it is conducted in accordance with and not in violation of the regulations and interests of the United Nations it will prove to be advantageous for humanity as a whole. But if it is started in opposition to or in ways which are otherwise against the interests of the U.N., the damage may become irreparable. . .

"I have not wished at this opportunity to touch upon Article 51 of the Charter, which permits collective self-defense in a period until the Security Council has been able to take the necessary measures in the case of an armed attack on a member state. The temporary character of this provision is obvious. I do not believe that it will ever be used, whatever arrangements are being entered into solely in accord with this paragraph. Such arrangements cannot be called regional agreements in the U.N. sense." [8]

The reaction of the world press to a speech of this sort is interesting to note. Since the State Department had declared the Atlantic alliance to find its Charter roots in Article 51, while at the same time speaking of a regional agreement, the point of Mr. Lie's remarks was unmistakable — and was promptly hailed by the press of the Eastern bloc. *Friheten*, Oslo's Communist organ, for example, viewed it as an "attack against the Atlantic Pact" in its issue of August 9, 1949. Mr. Lie, under severe criticism in the West, subsequently issued a "clarifying statement," retracting little but denying criticism of the Atlantic pact. The Communist reaction was typified by the headline in *Svodbodne Slovo* (Prague, August 11), "Trygve Lie Retreats before Reactionaries." The London *Daily Worker* (August 11), in step this time, noted his clarification with the headline, "Trygve Lie Eats His Own Words." Nor did Mr. Lie's clarification satisfy much of the Western press, *Time and Tide* (London, August 13) finding the Secretary-General's "criticism" of the Treaty "quite clear," and the *Economist* (August 13) claiming that Mr. Lie "laid himself open to criticism which will damage not only his own reputation but also the reliability of the Organization."

In this connection, the following statement of the Secretary-General, issued at a press conference in August 1950, would seem to indicate that Mr. Lie is not overly dogmatic and that he is capable of adjusting his views to changing events:

It is understandable and in conformity with their responsibilities that Member Governments, when faced with the failure to make peace and the consequent delay in establishing a United Nations collective security system, should look to their own defenses and form such bilateral and multilateral associations as would, in their opinion, strengthen their security.

At such a time as this I believe there must be strong national defenses and the people must be willing to carry the burden of armaments. Disarmament can come only as part of a collective security system and when an atmosphere of mutual confidence such as prevailed during the war has been re-established. [9]

This apparent reversal brought on the Soviet charge that Mr. Lie is "two-faced and double-dealing." [10]

As indicated earlier, the Secretary-General employs his speeches as direct auxiliaries of his diplomatic endeavors or as "trial balloons" to test public support of action he has under consideration. An example of the latter is his speech at the Harvard Commencement of June 1948, in which he publicly first put forth his ideas for a United Nations Guard; another is his Washington suggestion of top-level Security Council meetings. His private efforts to find a solution to the Chinese representation question have been supplemented by public declarations in favor of China's being represented by the government in fact in the position to do so.

The Secretary-General, furthermore, has used his public addresses as a medium for emphasizing the United Nations as a force against present and potential aggression. His many statements about Korea and his assurance to a Belgrade state banquet in April 1951 — amid reports of the build-up of armies by the Soviet bloc — that "the United Nations will not fail Yugoslavia" [11] are prominent illustrations.

Mr. Lie's Belgrade speech also illustrates the extensive travels which are another element of the Secretary-General's public appeal. Mr. Lie has been energetic in journeying throughout five continents in response to the invitations of member states.

These speeches are "professional jobs," simply and forcefully written. They each generally have a "point," something which the press can latch onto; though because the point is not always a fresh one, press coverage, for this among other reasons, is not consistently front page. This is a deficiency hard to overcome, for the Secretary-General is governed by higher considerations than those of press appeal, and the quantity of new and exposable dramatic material he may employ is limited.

The impact of the Secretary-General's public declarations is of course impossible to assess accurately. On the one hand, his speeches, and even more the introductions to the annual reports and other public statements such as the Berlin letter, have won a fair amount of publicity, particularly in the more literate sections of the world press. On the other, it cannot be said that Mr.

Lie has succeeded in capturing the popular imagination. Important impersonal factors are responsible, as is, to a lesser degree, Mr. Lie's personality. He is naturally at a great oratorical disadvantage, forced to speak as a rule in a language which is not his own and much of which he has had to learn in recent years. More than that, Mr. Lie, though a warm figure and impressive in his sincerity, does not possess the vivid eccentricities and personal magnetism of a Roosevelt or a Churchill; nor does he possess a propaganda machine of a Stalin, capable of impressing a less extrovert personality upon the popular mind. Finally, Mr. Lie does not judge it to be politic, let alone possible, to attempt to build up anything of a "personal myth."

Some of Mr. Lie's critics see further factors in his failure to capture the public mind: a lack of public initiative, a failure of the Secretary-General to assert his position forcefully enough, to come forth with rebukes to the malefactors and commendation for the benefactors of the Organization. This school of thought (to which the Secretary-General refers as the "world leader" school in his remarks, earlier quoted [12]) believes that if Mr. Lie had been bolder in his political activity and public appeal, he would have rallied a popular support about the United Nations and its Secretary-General which would have more than made up for the adverse reaction of the governments to such initiative. It suggests, for example, as one exponent has put it, that "the American people would support Lie against our own Government if he were in the right." [13]

An examination of the record of the Secretary-General's initiative, however, shows that he has been reasonably courageous in criticizing member states, great and small, when they trampled upon United Nations interests; courageous in asserting United Nations ideals; and, to a degree which mounted high in 1950, courageous in suggesting a "United Nations policy" for the consideration of the member states.

And what has been the reaction of the public? Did the American people in fact rally about the Evatt–Lie Berlin letter? Were they swept up by his proposals on Chinese representation (proposals which *Pravda* termed a "timid effort," but which within the bounds of possibility were certainly as bold as could reasonably be expected)? Did they throw their support behind his twenty-year peace program?

Evidently not. Mr. Lie's appeals made some impression, of course — his effort to advance the peace program by his Moscow trip made a deep impression — but they failed to turn the tide of sentiment generated by the cold war; and they failed not because the Secretary-General has not tried. And this is in a country in which pro-United Nations sentiment is substantial and the media for carrying the Secretary-General's words full. In other countries, where the East-West conflict is regarded with more detachment, Mr. Lie's stands sometimes meet with more sympathy, but this often tends to be offset by a greater cynicism and ignorance of the United Nations in general and by the relative difficulty of reaching the public. The frustration of appeals for popular support in totalitarian states, where, as contrasted with the situation in the democracies, public opinion plays so removed a role in the formation of governmental policy, may be taken for granted.

It is primarily the essential nature of his position — and not his personal effort or the lack of it — that constitutes the chief obstacle to Mr. Lie's public appeal. His detachment, his impartiality, the fact that he "more than anyone else . . . stand[s] for the United Nations as a whole" are at once his strength and his weakness. He is the living symbol of that synthesis of international outlook which is surely the force of future progress, and this gives him a unique and potentially vast appeal. But in the context of a bitter cold war, "if you ain't fer us, you're agin' us" — and the premium on impartiality, when it is needed most, is low.

The following quotations, from publications which seldom agree on anything, illustrate what Mr. Lie is up against.

Let us look at the [third annual] Report. Even in the Introduction in the appraisal of the general situation we read the following: "The United Nations has become the chief force that holds the world together against all the conflicting strains and stresses that are pulling it apart."

The Secretary-General of the United Nations does not define these "conflicting strains." He merely equates them, thus creating the false impression that both strains are striving to destroy the unity of the United Nations.

The impersonal form resorted to by Mr. Trygve Lie does not denote objectivity. On the contrary, it is a departure from objectivity. . .

Who can . . . equate the "conflicting strains," who can maintain as does Trygve Lie, that "the conflict between East and West has been the cause, direct and indirect, of many setbacks and disappointments in the work of the United Nations during the past year"? It is quite obvious that the form in which the question is raised and such a presentation of the facts are not in keeping with the truth.[14]

Contrast the preceding with:

Torn from the background of the conflict in the U.N. between the Western nations and [the Soviet], these are fine and constructive phrases [the writer refers to the Secretary-General's "anti-boycott, by-pass, and backdown" speech, made at Hyde Park in April 1948]. "A plague on both your houses," when these houses are being turned into arsenals that command a peaceful street, is a just and humane sentiment. But in the factual circumstances, and in the framework of the office of the U.N. Secretary General at this period, it adjudges the [X] powers . . . guilty of the very practices they charge to [Y] and equally responsible for the threat of war that hangs over the world today.

In one sense this may be called neutrality . . . but it is partisanship. . . The implication in the speech by Mr. Lie is a verdict of equal guilt for all concerned. And that is neither the judgment of many nations served by the Secretary General nor . . . is it for him to pronounce, even were the times less perilous.

At Hyde Park he made no distinction between those powers who have labored for these ends [the Charter's ideals] in the U.N. and those which have subverted them. Yet the postwar facts show a very clear distinction.[15]

Were it not for the lumbering, rhetorical style of the first quotation and the more urbane character of the second, it would be hard to tell which was written by Yakob Victorov, foreign editor of *Pravda*, and which by Arthur Krock, Washington columnist for the *New York Times!*

This is not to say that even-handed criticism of both sides is justified on objective grounds. The Secretary-General, however, runs the risk of losing his value as an intermediary and "third force" if he leans too much to one side or the other. The Korean experience indicates that the Secretary-General may have no choice but to "lean" if he is to play an active part in upholding

the Organization. But Mr. Lie, at any rate, has as a rule attempted
to take an approach which he sums up as follows:

> I think it is a negative and destructive policy to spend one's effort on
> placing the blame for the world's troubles instead of trying to reach a
> constructive solution of them. There is always plenty of blame to be
> shared by everybody. The main question is not whether one nation or
> another should back down or change its position. The first concern of
> all governments should be to uphold and strengthen the Organization
> that is the world's one hope for peace.[16]

In sum, it is clear that the Secretary-General's power of impartial and nonpartisan appeal is severely restricted by the atmosphere of international partisanship which has permeated affairs
since the founding of the Organization. That very atmosphere,
however, makes his appeal the more desirable. It challenges the
Secretary-General to do all possible to make his appeal more
effective.

# PART 3

# The Future of
# the Secretaryship General

# CHAPTER 8

## The Extension
## of Mr. Lie's Term

*Five years ago, we did not object to the candida-
ture of Trygve Lie. Later, however, we realized
that Trygve Lie did not possess the qualifications
required of a Secretary-General of the United
Nations.*                      ANDREI Y. VISHINSKY

*He is unobjective, two-faced, and we will have no
truck with him.*              ANDREI Y. VISHINSKY

*If, as a body, we had lent ourselves to this at-
tempt at the political assassination of a man because he did his duty under the Charter, we
should have assassinated the United Nations
itself.*                       SIR CARL BERENDSEN

The extension of the term of office of the first Secretary-General
was a remarkable event. The Soviet Union, which, five years
before, had proposed the election of Mr. Lie for the Assembly
presidency by acclamation, now promoted the candidacies of
some of its most confirmed opponents, rather than that of Mr. Lie.
The United States, which for five years had been berating employment of the veto, and which, at that very session of the
Assembly, had submitted the Acheson plan for overcoming the
veto, threatened to invoke it against all candidates but Trygve
Lie. Yugoslavia, whose election to the Security Council the Secretary-General had forthrightly opposed, proposed to that body the
reappointment of Mr. Lie. India, which began by advancing a
scheme that would have eliminated Mr. Lie from the race, finished

by cosponsoring the resolution to continue him in office. The Arab wing of the Arab–Latin American voting combination, so often a potent coalition, was cool to the candidacy of the Secretary-General, and the Latin American wing was lukewarm. But the resolution extending Mr. Lie's term was carried by a substantial majority.

Even in its conventional aspects, it was an extraordinary episode. Ambassador Austin, an emotional speaker, made "the most impassioned speech of his long United Nations career" [1] in support of the Secretary-General. Mr. Vishinsky rose to new heights of argumentation, and dropped to new lows of invective, in his assault upon the Secretary-General. The Soviet Union, which so often had cried "illegal" with so little effect, this time found in the enemy camp some who had doubts about the legality of the majority's view. And the office of Secretary-General, admittedly political, was invested by the intensity of the battle fought over it with a heightened political importance few would have acknowledged before October 1950.

Mr. Lie announced in December 1949 that he was not a candidate for reappointment.[2] Six months later, Dr. Ting-fu F. Tsiang, the representative of Nationalist China, declared that, should Mr. Lie become a candidate, he would veto his reappointment. China would, however, consent to the extension of the Secretary-General's term for a year, to avoid complications for the Organization. Dr. Tsiang did not conceal that his government's opposition to the reëlection of Mr. Lie was a result of the Secretary-General's efforts to facilitate the accreditation of the Peiping regime.[3]

At the same time it was revealed that the United States, Britain, and France had reached the conclusion that Mr. Lie was the only available person who would be acceptable — at least for a while — to the permanent members of the Security Council. Although the Secretary-General was an almost sinister figure in more myopic American eyes, the opposition to his reappointment in informed circles was not significant. The United Kingdom and France were agreeable to his reëlection. The Western powers, it seemed, inclined toward Mr. Lie primarily because they felt that the Secretary-General was a competent officer who had managed not to antagonize either East or West. In the days preceding the Korean outbreak, it looked as if Mr. Lie would be continued in office on much the same basis as that of his initial appointment — an East-West compromise.

It was not anticipated that the Soviet Union, then boycotting the Security Council over the Chinese representation issue, necessarily would return to the Council in time to take part in the effecting of this compromise. The West had agreed, however, to select a candidate as if the U.S.S.R. were present — that is, to refrain from exploiting the Soviet boycott by choosing an outright partisan of the anti-Communist forces. It was taken for granted, in view of Moscow's cordial reception of the Secretary-General's "peace mission," that Mr. Lie would be acceptable to the Soviet Union.

With the invasion of Korea, all this changed overnight. The Secretary-General's important support of the Organization's attempt to repel the North Korean aggression provoked unrestrained Communist criticism. His relations with the West, and especially with Washington, rapidly grew far closer than they had been in the past.

By the time of the opening of the Fifth Session of the General Assembly, in the autumn of 1950, there was considerable feeling that the Soviet Union would veto Mr. Lie's reappointment. The Soviet delegation, however, kept its intentions to itself. It sidestepped suggestions for private consultations among the permanent members, made by Sir Gladwyn Jebb, President of the Security Council for September, and twice renewed early in October by the United States delegation. At the first meeting of the Security Council which took up the question of the appointment of the Secretary-General, the Soviet representative confined himself to characterizing as illegal the much-discussed plan of the Assembly's extending the term of office of the incumbent, in the event of the failure of the Council to nominate a candidate. Yugoslavia proposed to this initial meeting the reappointment of Mr. Lie. Its motion did not specify the period of reappointment, the length of the new term being left to the General Assembly, as it had been in 1946. It was assumed, however, that Mr. Lie's renewal in office would be for five years.

The Council met again on October 12. The Soviet Union made

the obviously hollow gesture of nominating Zygmunt Modzelewski, then Foreign Minister of Poland. With the candidacies of Mr. Lie and Mr. Modzelewski before it, the Council voted 9 to 1, with one abstention, in favor of Mr. Lie. The single vote cast against the Secretary-General was that of the U.S.S.R. It was the Soviet Union's forty-sixth veto, and as such precluded the Council's nominating Mr. Lie for a new term. Little justification for his vote was offered by the Soviet delegate. Nationalist China was the abstaining member. Dr. Tsiang was prudent enough to avoid a vengeful veto which would have further weakened the precarious position of the Nationalist regime in the United Nations, offended the Power behind whose fleet his government sheltered, and which, in any case, was unnecessary in view of the probable Soviet attitude. The Council meeting concluded with a majority decision authorizing the President for October, Mr. Austin, to write to the President of the General Assembly that the Security Council was unable to make a recommendation on the appointment of a Secretary-General.

The Western powers at this point accelerated their drafting of a plan for the extension of Mr. Lie's term. The United States was reported to have favored an extension of five years. The United Kingdom, and France still more, preferred· an extension of less than five years, in order to underline the fact that Mr. Lie's term was being extended and not being renewed in the normal fashion. The Secretary-General had previously let it be known that he would accept an extension of no less than two and a half years, a period which, he felt, would be a minimum demonstration of the Organization's confidence in him.

Negotiations seem to have inclined toward the longer extension at first, but when Mr. Lie expressed to the sponsors of the resolution, in response to their inquiry, the wish that he not be asked to serve for more than three additional years, this was the period settled upon. Three years, moreover, was regarded by the sponsors as a span long enough so that the administrative order and stability of the Secretariat would not too soon again be called into question.

The Soviet Union, for its part, at the same time abandoned its reserve. It entered upon an anti-Lie campaign of great vigor and enterprise. The supporters of the Secretary-General had planned that the General Assembly would be called back into plenary session on October 19 to consider — and adopt — their extension resolution. On October 17, however, Jacob Malik, Soviet Deputy Foreign Minister, requested the President of the Security Council to call another meeting. That meeting, and succeeding ones, led to the postponement of the Assembly session until October 31. In the ten days intervening, the Soviet Union electioneered spectacularly. It did its best to inspire numerous candidacies and its worst to discredit the Secretary-General. Because of its efforts, or perhaps in spite of them, Mr. Lie for a time appears to have hovered closer to defeat than is often thought.

When the Security Council met on October 18, Mr. Malik began by declaring there was no need for great haste in this matter of selecting a successor to Mr. Lie. He suggested that the Council might find candidates among a number of foreign ministers, among former presidents of the General Assembly, and among chiefs of delegations to the United Nations. Candidates from Latin America and Asia, he added, should be among those considered.

Sir Gladwyn Jebb countered by pointing out the demoralizing effect of unreasonable delay. At this juncture, Sir Benegal Rau, the representative of India, advanced a scheme which would have effectively reopened the race and closed out Mr. Lie. "In order to convince the General Assembly and the world generally that the Security Council had exhausted all possibilities," Sir Benegal Rau later recounted, "I suggested, on the analogy of the plan by which we elected the judges of the International Court of Justice, that each of the eleven members of the Security Council should put forward two names. These twenty-two names were then to be submitted confidentially to the permanent members, which, after mutual consultation, would submit to the Security Council a revised list comprising only those names that none of the permanent members would veto. From this revised list the Security Council would then proceed to elect a person to be recommended for appointment as Secretary-General." [4]

China, Egypt, and, of course, the U.S.S.R. lent their immediate support to the Indian plan. Cuba, Ecuador, and France were reported to be interested, and even the United Kingdom, it seems, did not at once demur. Ambassador Austin was quick to point out that, if India's suggestion were adopted, the certain result would be the elimination of Mr. Lie, whose name would be promptly scratched out by the Soviet Union. This, he suggested, would be a strange decision for a Council which had cast nine votes in Mr. Lie's favor.

Mr. Austin was, not surprisingly, backed up by Arne Sunde of Norway. But the delegate of France this time did not find himself in agreement with his American colleague. The least that the Council could do, M. Chauvel is understood to have held, was to explore the issue further, to insure that no possibility of finding a candidate who might meet with the approval of the five permanent members was overlooked.

When the Council adjourned in this equivocal situation, the chances of Mr. Lie seemed less bright. Speculation about other possibilities rocketed. Four names came to the fore: General Carlos P. Romulo of the Philippines, Dr. Luis Padilla Nervo of Mexico, Sir Benegal Rau of India, and Dr. Charles Malik of Lebanon. The Soviet Union let it be known that it was prepared to consider favorably any and all of these candidates.

The Council resumed consideration of the Indian plan two days later. The Secretary-General's supporters appeared to have put the intermission to good use. Yugoslavia, the United Kingdom, and Cuba joined the United States and Norway in voicing opposition to the Indian scheme. The necessary Council majority of seven in favor of the plan was thereby precluded, and the Council's attention was directed toward other procedures.

The Council, at its succeeding session, decided to ask the permanent members to meet in private in an effort to reach agreement upon a candidate. The vote in favor of this plan, which was sponsored by the Soviet Union, was significant, particularly in view of the assumption that the U.S.S.R. would not weaken in its opposition to the reappointment of Mr. Lie. Seven states voted affirmatively: France, Ecuador, Cuba, Egypt, India, China, and the U.S.S.R. The United States, Norway, Yugoslavia, and Britain abstained.

This two-way division actually indicated the split of the Security Council into three camps. On one side were the determined supporters of the Secretary-General: the four abstaining states. On the other were the Secretary-General's implacable opponents: the U.S.S.R. and, somewhat less resolutely, Nationalist China. In between were the five states which held the balance of power; states which had voted for Mr. Lie when the vote was first taken, but which were, for a variety of reasons, not so convinced of the desirability of his election that they would be unwilling to consider the designation of another candidate. It was not that they wanted Mr. Lie less, but that they wanted a candidate who could win unanimous Council support more.

There were, perhaps, additional and more earthy considerations which influenced the attitudes of these five pivotal states. It is fair to assume that Egypt would not resist the ousting of the Secretary-General who had opposed its attempts to frustrate the General Assembly's recommendation for the partition of Palestine, especially if he were to be replaced by an able Arab League colleague, Dr. Charles Malik. Ecuador and Cuba, members of the Latin American caucus, might be presumed to have found attractive the possibility of agreement being reached upon their experienced comrade, Dr. Luis Padilla Nervo. Even India, which had risked much to promote East-West agreement, might be thought to have contemplated appreciatively the possibility of an Indian Secretary-General — Sir Benegal Rau, or, perhaps, Sir Ramaswami Mudaliar or Sir Girja Bajpai. In fact, it would seem that the purest of motives could be attributed only to France.

The permanent members met in great privacy on October 23, and it was duly reported in the press the following day that five candidates were then considered. In addition to that of Mr. Lie, the names of General Romulo, Dr. Padilla, Sir Benegal Rau, and Sir Ramaswami were understood to have been put forth. The representatives of the permanent members agreed to consult their governments upon these nominations and to meet in closed session once again two days later.

Mr. Vishinsky, meanwhile, publicly declared that the Soviet Union would be agreeable to the designation of anyone who could win the support of the permanent members. Only Mr. Lie was "impossible" to consider for the post.[5] He spoke favorably of

General Romulo, and of Dr. Padilla, and suggested Dr. Charles Malik as another candidate meriting serious consideration.

The second meeting of the permanent members does not seem to have been a fruitful one. It was brief and was directly followed by a closed plenary meeting of the Council. It was at this meeting that Ambassador Austin dramatically declared that while the Soviet Union had vetoed the reappointment of Mr. Lie, the United States would veto the appointment of any candidate but Mr. Lie. In a statement later repeated publicly, he said:

I feel that the choice of Mr. Lie is a matter that concerns the security of my own country, the security of the Far East, the Middle East, and the Western Hemisphere. . .

Mr. Lie has been the steadfast advocate and executive of the unity of fifty-three nations resisting armed aggression. . . I do not believe that Mr. Lie now must bow down and take the rod on his back from the country that has been arguing the case of the Korean aggressors in the United Nations.

He should have the united support of those members whose cause he has supported.

No other man could take this office knowing that his predecessor had been condemned because he carried out the policies of the United Nations fearlessly and impartially. Anyone holding that office would forever after stand under the shadow of any permanent member that opposed United Nations policies.

I have indicated to the permanent members of the Security Council that I am ready to thwart the Soviet veto of Mr. Lie by every means in my power.

I do not believe a veto will become necessary, but the great moral principle of the unity of the free powers is at stake and I do not fear to use whatever means I can to maintain that unity.[6]

It did not in fact prove necessary for Mr. Austin to resort to the veto. General Romulo, who was nominated by Nationalist China, received but four votes: those of the Soviet Union, Egypt, India, and China. The seven remaining members of the Council abstained, the General thus falling three votes short of the necessary majority. The Soviet representative nominated Dr. Charles Malik, but he too received just four votes. Votes were not taken upon the candidacies of Sir Benegal Rau or of Dr. Padilla, both of whom had indicated they were withdrawing from the race.

The Council meeting was otherwise distinguished by the first full-length exposition of the Soviet justification for vetoing the reappointment of Mr. Lie. The Council, apparently unimpressed, adjourned that evening, after again authorizing its President to inform the President of the General Assembly that it was unable to submit to the Assembly a recommendation regarding the appointment of a Secretary-General. The Soviet Union, however, served notice that it would request still another Council meeting to examine other candidates.

Whether Mr. Austin's threat to invoke the veto was as unnecessary as appearances indicate is a question the answer to which must await the revelation of facts still obscure. While it evidently was not needed to block the election of General Romulo or of Dr. Malik, it might have been needed to forestall the designation by the Council of Dr. Luis Padilla Nervo. For Dr. Padilla could count not only upon the votes of India, China, Egypt, and the U.S.S.R., but upon those of Ecuador and Cuba as well. This would have given him six votes, and, assuming that neither the United States nor Britain would exercise the veto, then just one vote more — that of France — would have given him the winning majority of seven.

Since France had from the beginning made it clear that "the normal functioning of the Organization must take precedence over personal preferences" and that "the normal functioning presupposed a nomination in accordance with the provisions of Article 97 of the Charter," [7] Dr. Padilla had every reason to expect that France would pledge its vote to him. For the unmistakable meaning of declarations such as these was that France, while having nothing against Mr. Lie, would vote for another suitable candidate who gave promise of securing the requisite majority. But M. Chauvel notified Dr. Padilla on October 25 — the day upon which the votes were taken on General Romulo and Dr. Malik, and the day of Mr. Austin's veto statement — that France would abstain in the event of the Council's voting upon his candidacy. Dr. Padilla thereupon withdrew.

Mr. Austin, it should be noted, declared in the course of his public statement that he had indicated to "the permanent members of the Security Council" his readiness to invoke the veto. There is the implication in this that he had made his determination known, not first of all to the Council as a whole, but rather, before the Council meeting, to the representatives of France, Britain, China, and the U.S.S.R. He might of course have communicated the decision to veto, if the veto were to be needed, to his French and British colleagues even earlier; but in any case, there would seem to have been time for M. Chauvel to adjust, in response to Mr. Austin's intentions, the vote his government might otherwise have been expected to cast for Dr. Padilla. For, in the knowledge that his government's vote for Dr. Padilla would not have effectuated Padilla's election, in the face of the United States veto, it is reasonable to assume that M. Chauvel would have altered the probable earlier decision to vote for the Mexican diplomat. There would have been no point, in these circumstances, in casting the seventh vote for Dr. Padilla. It would merely have put France in the embarrassing position of forcing its ally to carry out a threat which could only have results detrimental both to the standing of the United States and the status of Mr. Lie.

One may hazard in turn, however, that had M. Chauvel communicated to Mr. Austin his intention to abstain, the United States delegate would have been freed of the necessity of saying anything at all about his readiness to wield the veto. But this speculation loses much of its point if, as perhaps was the case, the first M. Chauvel heard of Mr. Austin's intentions was the latter's declaration to the session of the permanent members which preceded the Council meeting.

It is difficult to assess the wisdom of Mr. Austin's move without a prior determination of its necessity. But even if one credits the United States with that modicum of diplomatic judgment sufficient to restrain it from making so profound a threat gratuitously, Mr. Austin's statement is still open to criticism. Assuming the risk to Mr. Lie's chances to have been substantial, the United States decision to veto other candidates nevertheless had its serious drawbacks, from the points of view of Washington, the Secretary-General, and the Organization.

It put Washington in the awkward position of announcing that it was prepared to invoke the devil's weapon. It stimulated domestic criticism to the effect that the United States was "imitating Russia." [8] It strengthened the hand of the administration's opponents, some of whom had long clamored for a veto of the accreditation of the Chinese Communist government when that issue would again arise in the Security Council.[9] And, as earlier indicated, Mr. Austin's threat clashed with the many prior and then current efforts of the United States to limit and even sterilize the veto.

Mr. Austin's statement, further, tended to give the unjustified impression that the Secretary-General was excessively dependent upon and bound to a single Great Power. It lent plausibility to the Soviet contention that Mr. Lie was being imposed upon the Organization as a result of "crude pressure"[10] by the United States. It tended to obscure the fact that nine of the eleven members of the Security Council had voted for Mr. Lie's reappointment.

Finally, it might be said that the veto threat, insofar as it might actually have blocked the nomination of a candidate other than Mr. Lie, frustrated the desires of the majority of the Security Council and, perhaps, of the Organization. The majority, while initially favoring Mr. Lie, might, in the light of the Soviet veto, have preferred a candidate acceptable to both East and West — a candidate who could have been appointed according to the letter of Article 97. The United States had indicated it would veto certain candidates, not because it disputed their fitness, but solely because "the issue was now focused on principles rather than on personalities. The use of the veto to punish the Secretary-General for his efforts to resist aggression in Korea . . . made it impossible to consider new nominations on their merits."[11]

The United States view was one of great force. Nevertheless, it was suggested in some quarters that if the majority of the Security Council did not share it, the Council should have been permitted to effect a compromise upon a candidate other than Mr. Lie. There was some feeling that it was not the place of Washington to set itself up as the arbiter of the "unity of the free powers" — that these powers, as free powers, should have been left the prerogative of making their own choice, uninfluenced by Mr. Austin's veto threat, between the undesirability of yielding to the Soviet veto and the desirability of securing a Secretary-General acceptable not merely to the majority but to the totality of the Organization. Some of Mr. Lie's convinced supporters were said to have felt that while Mr. Austin was wholly in the right in insisting that Mr. Lie deserved the "united support of those members whose cause he has supported," this was for these members, and not for Mr. Austin, to decide.

If the necessity and wisdom of the United States stand may be questioned, its significance for the development of the political powers of the Secretary-General may not. With Mr. Austin's statement, the most powerful member of the United Nations put itself on record as viewing the office of Secretary-General, particularly as filled by Mr. Lie, as one so important as to concern that member's security and the security of other areas of the world. It defined that office as essential to the maintenance of the unity of those Powers which had supported the Organization's effort to uphold collective security. It recognized the magnitude of Mr. Lie's Korean role by describing him as "the steadfast advocate and executive of the unity of fifty-three nations in resisting armed aggression." It threatened to invoke the veto over the issue of the Secretaryship General, not long after having declined to invoke it over the issue of China's seat in the United Nations.[12] With Mr. Austin's statement, the day clearly had passed when the United States regarded the Secretary-General as a minor and sometimes irritating cog in the world's security machinery.

While the issue was never in doubt after Mr. Austin's declaration, it was still fought over. On October 29, fourteen nations joined in introducing an Assembly resolution to extend Mr. Lie's term for three years (they were later joined by a fifteenth co-sponsor, Brazil). That same day, the Soviet Union called for another meeting of the Security Council.

When the Council met the following morning, the representative of the U.S.S.R. moved that the Assembly be asked to postpone debate on the appointment of a Secretary-General, pending more thorough Council study of the problem. He was voted down by seven votes to one, China, Egypt, and India abstaining.

Mr. Jacob Malik then went on to sound the threat later elaborated by his chief, Mr. Vishinsky. If Mr. Lie were continued in office as the fifteen-nation resolution envisaged, the Soviet Union would view his appointment as illegal and would "not consider him as Secretary General." [13] The Council, long since inured to Soviet allegations of illegality, proceeded to authorize its President to write for the third and last time to the President of the Assembly that the Council could make no recommendation. As the Yugoslav delegate pointed out, the Soviet Union itself did not appear to take too seriously its charges of illegality, since it had voted for General Romulo, the nominee of the "illegal" delegate of China.

That evening Mr. Vishinsky called one of his rare press conferences. He was, he said, appealing to the reporters to advise world public opinion of this attempt to impose Mr. Lie, hastily and illegally, upon the Organization. To be sure, the United States had thwarted all efforts to reach agreement, but in other cases of disagreement among the Great Powers — Mr. Vishinsky chose the example of the Italian colonies — a solution eventually had been found. The fifteen-nation resolution, he declared, was an "artificial maneuver designed to circumvent the Charter." Mr. Lie was an "echoer of the views of the United States delegation." Sir Benegal Rau and Dr. Padilla had dropped out of the race because of the American veto threat. "Sir Benegal waved his arms and maybe his feet — he was so scared," the Soviet Foreign Minister related with his customary sarcastic vivacity. "Dr. Padilla said one thing — then another thing — and then he waved his arms, too." When a correspondent asked Mr. Vishinsky if he had any other candidate in mind, the Soviet Foreign Minister replied: "I would be glad to nominate you if I knew you would accept."

Mr. Vishinsky was less expansive when it came to defining the implications of the Soviet intention of not recognizing Mr. Lie as Secretary-General after February 1, 1951. There would, he admitted, "be some difficulties." Soviet delegates would sit beside Mr. Lie in United Nations meetings, but in effect would ignore his presence. In regard to dealing with the Secretariat, the channel of the Organization's communications, Mr. Vishinsky said, "I hope we will find other people who will be talkable to. If not, we will not address anybody." [14]

Mr. Vishinsky's threat, the British Minister of State noted, was "not a tactic calculated to impress representatives of free sovereign nations." [15] Nor did it overawe Mr. Lie into withdrawing his candidacy. When the period of the Secretary-General's extended term began, the Soviet bloc took to addressing its communications to the "United Nations Secretariat" rather than to the Secretary-General. But when it came to more important things, such as seeking the Secretary-General's recognition when Mr. Lie presided over the Assembly's committee for the coördination of the Organization's disarmament efforts, the Soviet delegate refrained from challenging his authority. And the U.S.S.R. gave signs of abandoning its nonrecognition policy by the fall of 1951.

The legal aspects of the debates of the General Assembly upon the extension of the Secretary-General's term have been discussed earlier. As for their political content, there was considerable praise of Mr. Lie by the majority and the bitterest criticism of him by the minority, while mixed opinions came from that third group which chose to abstain from voting either for or against extending his term.

The theme of the majority struck two notes. Most of the forty-six states that voted for Mr. Lie viewed him as an able and devoted Secretary-General. They felt that they could not permit him to be ousted because of his having opposed the Korean aggression. To have permitted Mr. Lie to be so rewarded would have dealt a hard blow to the moral position of the United Nations in Korea and impaired the independence and initiative of future Secretaries-General.

A few of the delegations that voted for Mr. Lie, such as India, seemed guided by narrower considerations. The Organization had to have a Secretary-General; this new version of the "double veto," the determination of the U.S.S.R. and the United States to block each other's proposals, if necessary, by invoking the veto, prevented the election of a Secretary-General in the prescribed manner. Therefore, in view of the impasse, the one way out was to extend the term of office of the present Secretary-General.

The five members of the Soviet bloc denied that their purpose was to punish the Secretary-General for his Korean stand. If that were the case, Mr. Vishinsky argued, why would he seek to replace Mr. Lie with General Romulo, who had been "more aggressive on that question"? Would it not be "ridiculous to punish Trygve Lie by replacing him by a 'Trygve Lie cubed' "? [16] Rather, the Soviet bloc was dissatisfied with Mr. Lie for other reasons. Mr. Lie had "agreed to the establishment of illegal organs such as the Interim Committee of the General Assembly, the Commissions on Korea, on the Balkans." [17] He had made a "public declaration in support of this aggressive treaty," the North Atlantic pact. His ten-point peace program was "permeated with servility and obsequiousness towards the United States. . . Trygve Lie has shown duplicity. [18] . . . he has taken a two-faced and double dealing attitude [19] . . . a lackey [20] . . . an obedient tool [21] . . . [whose] activities have shown him to be a servant of the State Department [22]. . . Mr. Lie is not fit for the office of Secretary-General." [23] Having thus ingratiated itself with Mr. Lie, the Soviet bloc suggested that "any decent man who feels himself fit for the job . . . would withdraw . . . because he had been faced with strong opposition based entirely on the principles of the Charter." [24]

The vote for the fifteen-nation joint resolution was 46–5–8 – a majority of well over two-thirds upon a question which needed only a simple majority. Eight states abstained. Nationalist China did not need to detail its reasons. Australia, while praising the Secretary-General, indicated it had "genuine doubts" [25] about the legality of the proceedings. The sonorous legal arguments of the Arab bloc were rather spoiled by the delegate of Iraq, who complained, in explaining his vote, that Mr. Lie "had not been entirely impartial" in the Palestine affair.[26]

However, support for extending Mr. Lie's term does not seem to have been as solid as this impressive margin would indicate. For in two votes taken upon alternative resolutions – a Soviet proposal to request the Security Council to continue consideration of the question, and an Iraqi proposal for the appointment of a seven-member committee to study the matter and report to the General Assembly within two weeks – the totals of affirmative and abstaining votes were twenty for the Soviet motion and twenty-two for the Iraqi plan.[27] Thus it would appear that one-third of the membership either opposed or refrained from wholeheartedly supporting the extension of the term of office of the Secretary-General.

The Secretary-General acknowledged the Assembly's decision in a brief and meaningful speech to the following plenary session. "I understand your vote," he declared, "to be a reaffirmation . . . of the independence and integrity of the office of Secretary-General of the United Nations. In the present circumstances, I feel that I am under an obligation to the United Nations not to refuse your mandate continuing me in office for a period of three years.[28]

"The United Nations cannot function effectively unless the Secretariat acts in loyal conformity with the decisions and recommendations of the organs. . . The United Nations cannot function effectively unless the Secretariat acts in the collective interest of the United Nations as a whole, and in the collective interest only. . .

"I shall do my part towards the maintenance of similar [coöperative] relations with all the Member governments — without exception — during the next three years. . .

"The United Nations road to peace requires universal collective security against armed aggression. . . That we must achieve, and I believe we shall achieve it. The Member nations have been taking historic strides in that direction before and during this session of the General Assembly.

"But more is required than this, essential as it is. . . There must be steady, persistent, continuous effort to bring about a reconciliation, one by one, of the conflicting interests that divide the world. I have worked hard during the last five years for the reconciliation of these conflicting interests. I shall continue to do so.

"The combination of conciliation and force in support of peace is also not enough. The United Nations must develop a bold and statesmanlike program on a world scale that will bring reasonable hope for an adequate standard of living and decent life to the two-thirds of the world's people who do not have either today.

"These are the United Nations goals for which I shall work in the next three years." [29]

Thus, in a few lines, Mr. Lie confirmed his determination to pursue an independent course; answered Soviet criticism of his having carried out the decisions of United Nations organs; pledged that he would seek friendly relations with all members, "without exception"; reaffirmed his support of the Organization's stand in Korea; hailed the Acheson plan as "historic"; served notice, particularly to the West, that past efforts at promoting East-West negotiation would be resumed; and laid down a challenge to the Assembly to develop a technical assistance program of the greatest magnitude.

His address was a well-proportioned and constructive conclusion to a struggle that had been disproportionate in its intensity and often destructive in its content.

Was the decision to extend Mr. Lie's term of office in the best interests of the Secretaryship General and of the Organization?

The Soviet Union made the decision as difficult as possible by promoting the candidacies of highly qualified individuals who by no stretch of the imagination could be seen as pro-Soviet. It left no doubt that Mr. Lie would continue to serve not only without Soviet confidence but in the face of Soviet hostility.

Since the Secretary-General is equally the servant of all the members, and since he has "an important role to play as a mediator," [30] it might in these circumstances be argued that Mr. Lie cannot properly fulfill his functions nor fully exploit the potentiality of his office. Would it not have been wiser to have appointed a man like Dr. Padilla, who might have assumed office with the blessings of all of the members and by procedures legally less precarious than those by which Mr. Lie was retained? Could Mr. Lie, for example, be received in Moscow today on a "peace mission" as he was received in the spring of 1950?

In all likelihood, he could be. The "realistic" policies of the Kremlin have in the past sustained more embarrassing and far-reaching reversals. If it suited Moscow's ends, if the Soviet Union believed Mr. Lie's mediation would redound to its benefit, there is little question but that it would receive the Secretary-General at least as cordially as Molotov received Ribbentrop.

Moreover, if the Soviet Union is to persist in violating the Charter, any Secretary-General of initiative and integrity will be forced to range himself beside those who defend it. Since a General Romulo as Secretary-General would support the Organization's effort in Korea as vigorously as Mr. Lie, there is no reason to assume that he would be more the *persona grata* to Moscow than is the present Secretary-General. But, should Soviet policy shift to support the principles of the United Nations, then Moscow would have no difficulty in supporting Trygve Lie.

If the Soviet Union had taken exception to Mr. Lie primarily in response to his activities in connection with an issue which had been resolved in, let us say, 1947, the case of those who would have replaced the Secretary-General might have been stronger. But to have dismissed Mr. Lie in the very midst of that struggle of the Organization in support of which he had incurred the Kremlin's wrath would have been as politically inept as it would, at any time, have been morally disappointing. In the last analysis, little good, for the office or for the Organization, could have come from dismissing the Secretary-General because he had antagonized a Great Power by the courageous and honest fulfillment of his duties.

As it was, the extension of the Secretary-General's term upheld the independence of the office, confirmed Mr. Lie's constructive interpretation of the breadth of its political powers, and, because of all that the members staked upon it, raised still higher the political stature of the Secretaryship General.

# CHAPTER 9

## *Secretary or General?*

The original term of office of the first Secretary-General of the United Nations expired in February 1951. Mr. Lie has been the first to explore the potentialities of the office. Has he taken full advantage of the powers granted him, are these powers adequate, and what is the trend of their usage?

As for his constitutional weapons — the Charter and those portions of the Report of the Preparatory Commission adopted by the General Assembly — these have been demonstrated to provide a legal springboard for a span of activity of considerable elasticity and vitality. That is not to say that they invest the Secretary-General with unlimited political potential. But that the Secretary-General has been able to advance his political activity to the present point indicates that his legal weapons are essentially adequate for the job.

The "essentially adequate" does not equate with the optimum. Mr. Lie's thoughts in this regard are of course of the greatest interest and significance. In response to the question, "Would you favor any revision in the prerogatives of the office if this were, say, 1956, and the Charter were up for review?" the Secretary-General, speaking unofficially and in a manner of merely thinking aloud, replied as follows: "I think the office of Secretary-General should be clearly defined. . . The Charter should actually say that he is more than the chief administrator. I think the experience gained now, the Secretary-General's right to state his opinion, should be clearly stated in the Charter. Article 99 should be detailed, its implications written out . . . Article 99 is an atomic bomb, or at least a 32-inch gun. . . Why can't I use the smaller rifles? Why just on world peace?" [1]

Unquestionably, the definition in the Charter of the political powers which a liberal interpretation would give to Articles 97, 98, and 99 would greatly strengthen the Secretary-General's hand. Such clarification could prove of particular value in time of challenge of the Secretary-General's initiative. What Mr. Lie has won through practice could be spelled out in the Charter, promoting a continued vitality and growth of the Secretary-General's political activity.

Whether the Secretary-General of 1956[2] would do well to press for such a definition of his powers of course will depend upon the possibilities of the hour. Were the situation like that of the present, discretion would probably call for no further textual prerogative, for to do so would be to run the risk of the Secretary-General's proposals being voted down. The five permanent members of the Security Council must be among the two-thirds majority of the member states ratifying any amendments in order to alter the Charter's provisions,[3] and their willingness and unanimous agreement to detail liberally the Secretary-General's political authority can hardly be assumed. And for proposals of the Secretary-General to fail of adoption would, far from expanding his authority, tend to delimit negatively the sphere of his initiative.

Has Mr. Lie gone as far as he could? Or as far as he should?

It is of course impossible to judge up to what point the member states (and perhaps public opinion) would permit the Secretary-General to advance his political initiative. The governments themselves do not know; nor can the Secretary-General. It is nonetheless clear that Mr. Lie has not thrown his whole weight onto many issues, that he has not attempted to exercise his potential to the full. His suggestions relating to atomic control, for example, the second of his ten-point program advanced in the spring of 1950, constituted his first entree into the atomic question; and on numerous other issues, he has said nothing at all. The Secretary-General's substantive participation in the formal proceedings of United Nations organs, moreover, has far from approached the maximum. While his organic interventions have been pioneering and often useful in themselves, they have not

been so steadily sustained as to constitute that purposeful guidance of the work of the United Nations which ideally may be
conceived. Mr. Lie has leaped into and out of the United Nations
debate — he has not been a constant element of it.

Whether Mr. Lie *should* have taken a wider initiative is a more
difficult question.

A general summation of his record of political activity presents
a cautious picture of his first two years in office. His annual reports and other declarations, though not mere milk and toast,
were relatively mild; his interventions in the proceedings of
United Nations organs were more important in their laying the
groundwork for future activity than in their substance; and his
private diplomatic initiative did not go into high gear until his
Palestine activity, which began at the end of 1947.

Since that time, Mr. Lie has demonstrated considerable boldness. His annual reports and public statements have been imaginative and courageous, his relations with organs constructive, and
his governmental activity, on occasion, daring. In 1950, particularly, the Secretary-General came forth with pointed proposals
and vigorous action.

Mr. Lie's initiative of 1950 was such that it satisfied even most
of his critics in what he calls the "world leader" school. Whether
that initiative should have been comparably bold earlier is debatable; it may well be that Mr. Lie's early record was overly
cautious, despite the understandable caution which the Secretary-
General must have felt in a new post, with his Great Power
sponsors split into two warring camps and the potentialities of
the position as yet to be tested. At any rate, there can be little
question that since the end of 1947 the Secretary-General has
taken a considerable measure of initiative and that his notable
activity of 1950, if sustained, carries him as far as he can reasonably be expected to go at the present time.

What promises to be the most fruitful future growth of the
political activity of the Secretary-General was initiated by
Mr. Lie in the spring of 1950. The seeds go back to Albert
Thomas, were nurtured by the international technical agencies,
the I.L.O. among them, and twice flowered in 1950 in the

Secretary-General's suggestions for the resolution of the Chinese
deadlock and the resumption of Great Power negotiations.

That growth is simply the right of the Secretary-General to
suggest the procedures for and the substance of conciliation of
differences among the member states. It is a matter of the Secretary-General's continuing to acquire, and the governments' continuing to accord, the authority to originate, develop, and pro-
pound proposals for the solution of international problems —
proposals which are informed with an objective, supranational
point of view. The member states of course retain their power of
putting forth what plans they like, but they do not deny similar
authority to the Secretary-General; moreover, though the Secretary-General may propose, the member governments preserve all
the power to dispose.

The advantages of such a development are described by John
J. McCloy, former President of the International Bank for Reconstruction and Development and now United States High
Commissioner for Germany — a man of direct experience and
eminent practicality — as follows:

In these days of knife-edged political tension, it is popular to think
of international organizations as simply forums for blunt and often ill-
tempered debate. The Bank's experience over a considerable period of
time indicates that this need not be the case. . .

It is true, of course, that economic matters traditionally arouse less
acrimony than things political. It is also true that one of the two great
protagonists in today's political struggles is not a Member of the
Bank. But there is another, equally fundamental, reason for such
success as the Bank has had in creating an effectively functioning
Organization. In the case of the Bank, as distinguished from the United
Nations and many other international agencies, the initiative in making
recommendations and proposing action has been vested in an international staff, whose loyalty is only to the Bank itself, rather than in a
group of national representatives expressing the viewpoints of their
respective governments. Responsibility for making final decisions rests,
of course, with the national representatives — the Bank's Executive
Directors — but they base their action and center their debates upon
staff recommendations. This means, in practice, that problems are
approached and decided primarily on the basis of an objective nonpolitical analysis of the issues involved rather than as a result of
political compromise.

I believe that there is a lesson here with broad implications. . .

Public debates in the General Assembly and the Security Council are an important means of bringing an enlightened world opinion to bear on vital issues. But I suggest that the debate might well be more temperate and illuminating, and solutions to the problems made easier, if the initiative for analyzing the issues and recommending appropriate action were vested in a non-political and objective international secretariat.[4]

Similar sentiments are expressed by a former high official in the League of Nations:

The Secretary-General should be a man of public affairs, rather than a civil servant. After all, as Secretary-General, you want him to be an international leader. You want him to put to the Assembly and the Council time after time the problems as they present themselves from the international point of view and not merely from the national points of view. There is such a thing as an international synthesis. It is something very different from the sum of the national views which get represented at the meetings. The fact that he was called Secretary-General displayed a very significant misconception of what his functions ought to be. He ought not to be a secretary at all. He ought to be the head. Choose a word. He ought to be the head of the great world organization — the executive.[5]

How the I.L.O. secretariat gave life to this concept, in contrast with the League, is set forth by C. Wilfred Jenks as follows:

The International Labor Office, under the leadership of Albert Thomas, developed a different tradition. The Director of the ILO and his representatives . . . make detailed proposals upon every question which comes before the Governing Body of the Conference, and explain and defend their proposals during the discussions. The Governing Body and Conference have complete freedom to approve, amend or reject these proposals; but on every question submitted for decision there is available for consideration a concrete proposal, based on the disinterested expert knowledge of an international staff with a wide variety of viewpoints and experience, which represents an attempt to interpret the requirements of general interest. In the absence of leadership of this kind, the difficulties of securing agreement at general international conferences are greatly increased, and often increased beyond the frequently narrow margin between hard-won success and demoralizing failure.[6]

There is no more persuasive advocate of leadership by the international executive than Edward J. Phelan, who is among the first to have conceived of and applied the concept. Mr. Phelan was associated with Albert Thomas from the earliest days of the I.L.O. In 1936, he wrote his well-known biography of Thomas as a purposeful illustration of what was then a substantially new phenomenon in world affairs; and *Yes and Albert Thomas* has exercised since a notable influence upon the development of international institutions. Mr. Phelan's present thoughts about the international executive are as advanced as his original contribution to the theory and practice of secretariat leadership was creative.

One of the most significant facts in the history of international organization, Mr. Phelan suggests, is that the I.L.O. survived the war, while the League and the Permanent Court of International Justice did not. The I.L.O. weathered the immediate postwar period, when there was considerable governmental and, particularly, Soviet pressure for its being replaced, primarily because it had succeeded in sinking its roots in a firm base of public support. "The I.L.O. wasn't for the governments to give away." [7] A crucial element in the development of this public support, Mr. Phelan submits, was the leadership given since the Organization's founding by the Directors of the I.L.O. In contrast, the Secretaries-General of the League had failed to give "manifest leadership. I think profoundly that the history of the League might have been entirely different if Drummond and Thomas had changed places."

If the United Nations is to succeed, Mr. Phelan affirms, it must become "imbedded deep into public opinion. . . It's a long process. To begin with, you can only form an international organization at the top. Representatives of governments come together to start it. They may come together again to destroy it. If meanwhile you can get roots in the populace— For the defense of international organization is a process of international education, which arrives at a broad basis of support below the governments, which governments cannot upset. . .

"The success of international organization depends more upon leadership than upon any one thing. This is a tendency which has now become quite apparent. . .

"Article 99 of the Charter is derived from the experience of the Directors of the I.L.O. There is no doubt at all that Article 99 is a reflection of Albert Thomas and his successors. But the United Nations should take further account of the I.L.O.'s experience. For the difference in the challenge to the Secretary-General and the Director General is not so great as is generally supposed. The technical questions the I.L.O. deals with are questions of very intense political controversy in the member countries. They are not technical questions as the common international labeling of a formula for quinine is a technical question. A lot of the so-called technical questions of the I.L.O. in reality are political questions. . .

"No I.L.O. meeting ever comes together like a Quaker's meeting and waits for an idea. The constitutions of Britain and the United States were never built up in such a fashion. International organization — any community organization — does not consist of plucking ideas out of the air. International organization involves presenting the drafts of policy to the international organs. A council or a committee or an assembly can only say two things — yes or no. Somebody has got to put the questions to them. The assembly cannot evolve policy. . . You must have an element of *international* leadership in international organization. What you have got in the Security Council is a multinational discussion, not an international discussion. You cannot have an international discussion without an international spokesman. There is a profound difference. That spokesman must be the Secretary-General. Mr. Lie, I think, ought to participate in the decisions of the Council. He ought to be in the discussion all the way. Nobody in the Security Council is putting up the international point of view.

"The leadership of the Secretary-General must be public and manifest. It filters down. And it makes all the difference to the members of the Council. Whether the Secretary-General whispers to the delegates in private or speaks out in public with the journalists there — this is a great difference. The Secretary-General's activity behind the scenes is useful. But multiple consultations decide nothing. They keep the Secretary-General informed and they exercise a gentle influence. This is not the same as influencing an international, collective decision.

"And the Secretary-General must lead not so much by public pronunciamentos as by participation in the debate of the governmental United Nations organs. Mr. Lie should make his public speeches part and parcel of the Security Council's discussion. Instead of Sir Gladwyn Jebb, a national representative, winning the publicity, the publicity should go to the Secretary-General, the international representative. . .

"Mr. Lie's weakness is that he has nothing between him and the General Assembly. Leadership means living with the people you lead. You mustn't get too far ahead or too far behind. You must be in the bunch and guide them. A weakness of the United Nations and of the Secretary-General is that there are months from one Assembly to the next. What the Secretary-General needs is a standing governmental executive committee. In a sense, he has three: the Security Council, the Economic and Social Council, and the Trusteeship Council. But he has none linking him with the Assembly. There is a need for an executive committee to carry out the decisions of the governments, and the Secretary-General should lead this committee. Members of the Senate pay attention to Senators. . . The General Assembly would pay attention to a committee of its members. The psychology governing this committee and the Assembly should and would be: 'You may not agree with the Secretary-General, but, be careful — he knows more about the subject than you do.' This is one of the keys to the influence of the I.L.O. Director General in the Governing Body. This is what Article 99 wants — secretariat leadership in committee, and not occasional Papal pronouncements. . . What is needed is leadership by the Secretary-General — leadership which is public and manifest."

The advanced measure of political initiative of the Secretary-General which Mr. Phelan so ably advocates obviously is not to be facilely achieved. For the Secretary-General to win a participatory role of the nature Mr. Phelan envisages would demand considerable resourcefulness on his part and forbearance on the part of the member states. And though there are, as Mr. Phelan points out, political aspects to the work of the I.L.O., the differences of degree in this respect and the absolute differences in other respects between the I.L.O. and the United Nations cannot be discounted.

The experience of economic and social agencies such as the Bank and the International Labor Organization — and the United Nations Economic Commission for Europe — cannot of course be directly applied to the political work of the United Nations. Objective proposals are less easily and accurately conceived in matters intensely political, for one thing. Moreover, the political difficulties of placing the prime power of policy proposal in the Secretary-General and his staff, in the fashion Mr. McCloy describes, are evidently enormous. It is hard to think of Mr. Vishinsky deferring his warmongering resolution and Mr. Austin his peace-essentials resolution in favor of an even-handed, substantial plan of the Secretary-General which might well fit the cold-war maneuvers of neither.

The Secretary-General of the United Nations, then, cannot expect to exercise full powers of policy proposal in the near future. It is a question of slow growth. But this is surely the direction of the growth.

Nor would the attainment of such powers involve his making proposals with respect to every problem coming before the Organization. Particularly in the case of political questions, the Secretary-General would have to speak out selectively, choosing to commit his influence only where his initiative gave some promise of success.

It may well be that, in some cases, the Secretary-General could both advance the international viewpoint and lessen the chances of overextending his initiative by submitting to the member states, not a single proposed solution to the problem in point, but rather two or more possible solutions. The decisive power of the governments would thus be emphasized, while the field of proposals in the general interest would be widened.

As Mr. Lie's suggestions concerning Chinese representation and Great Power negotiation demonstrate, a power of proposition is both possible and desirable. In it is the promise of an international executive whose political influence surpasses that of the present Secretary-General, of an executive building upon what we have seen to be the considerable and significant base of political activity already constructed with the materials of the Charter and the initiative of Secretary-General Trygve Lie.

# APPENDIX

## Notes on the
## Resignation of Joseph Avenol

The resignation of Joseph Avenol in August 1940 is the *cause célèbre* in the brief history of Secretaries-General. The circumstances of the resignation were tragic. They are instructive as well. For they provide a case study of the reactions of a Secretary-General in a period of the most extreme crisis. They further reveal much about M. Avenol's fundamental political biases — revelations which have a present importance for the evolution of the international executive.

M. Avenol dropped out of sight after his resignation. He stopped in Vichy for a short time, then made his way to a village in the Haute-Savoie, where he stayed for three years. Warned by friends that the Germans were about to deport him, he slipped over the Swiss border and was granted political refuge. He has lived for the most part since in a hamlet not far from Geneva, quite cut off from the associates of former years and from participation in the events of the present day. Other than attempting to clear his name by addressing letters to such colleagues of his League experience as Anthony Eden and Philip Noel-Baker — letters which significantly have evoked little or no response — M. Avenol has remained isolated. He describes his treatment as that of an outcast. That a former Secretary-General of the League could in fact widely be so regarded emphasizes the deeply controversial nature of his political history. An analysis of the meaning of his resignation must first of all begin with a fuller consideration of that history.

In addition to his attempt to bring about Italy's return to the League,[1] M. Avenol relates that his second major effort — one that was more procedural than political — was his plan, in the years before the outbreak of World War II, for concentrating the League's attention upon technical matters of economic and social coöperation. At that time, he states, "I knew that the Covenant was finished."[2] In the belief that the political machinery of the League was dying, the Secretary-General did what he could to expand, or at least save, its technical machinery. "I had had, you know, the great hope of creating out of the League a new organization, much more adapted to the world situation, since the League had become useless by the lack of employment of the political institutions of 1919."[3] Such technical coöperation was to have embraced nonmembers of the League, but M. Avenol denies that it was his intention to include the Axis powers. "The idea was to collaborate first of all with the United States. . . I knew there was nothing further to do with Germany and Italy. Russia was never interested in technical collaboration. The League for Russia was a coalition against Germany. But they were quite friendly. They changed their policy in 1939." The former Secretary-General suggests that the conception of the United Nations Economic and Social Council "is born of this idea. . . For a while, I had hope of succeeding, but the war. . ."[4]

M. Avenol's attempt to regroup the League on the basis of technical coöperation has been much criticized on grounds of facilitating the demise of the League as a political force. Vladimir Sokoline, former Soviet Under Secretary-General of the League of Nations, suggests, however, that it was not M. Avenol who initiated the policy of stripping the League of its political functions, but the United Kingdom, followed by France. The principal roles in the League, after all, were played by London and Paris. When London led the move to shift the center of consequential political negotiation from Geneva to the chancelleries — Munich is the striking example of this process — the Secretary-General would have had great difficulty in opposing the trend. It was not, M. Sokoline affirms, a question of M. Avenol's receiving directives from London or Paris — rather, both M. Avenol and his predecessor would hardly have been inclined to take up a policy which the Foreign Office and the Quai d'Orsay rejected, in that such a policy would not be adopted by League organs.

Moreover, M. Sokoline suggests, it may perhaps be that a conservative French finance expert of the old tradition, like M. Avenol, found the adoption of a program of accenting the League's technical preoccupations not overly difficult. M. Avenol tended to think in a fashion similar to that of his conservative counterparts in London and Paris; political retrenchment was "realistic" in the atmosphere of the period; technical concerns were occupationally congenial to him.

M. Sokoline indicates, in short, that the essence of M. Avenol's political activity may possibly be traced to two elements: the Secretary-General was at least in some degree of the ultraconservative French caste of his day; and, as such, he was susceptible to the policies of his conservative colleagues in the Foreign Office and the Quai d'Orsay — policies which were destructive of the League's political content. But to say all this, M. Sokoline adds, is perhaps to place M. Avenol in his political and personal context; it is not necessarily to credit the criticisms made against him.[5]

M. Sokoline's analysis has much to commend it. Broadly speaking, M. Avenol's political history would seem to be that of a man who was part of the trend of the 1930's which led away from the core of the Covenant's ideals. When war finally came, and when England, which had led this trend, reversed her course of appeasement and fought, M. Avenol found himself, after the fall of France, at odds with the League power to which hitherto he had been closest both in outlook and in daily relations. M. Avenol chose to adhere to the Pétain faction of Vichy. He thus failed to wash away his prewar compliance with appeasement policies; on the contrary, by his Vichy sympathies he compounded his faults and prepared himself to serve as a whipping boy for the sins of the prewar period, though his role in them was actually subsidiary.

This is not to say that M. Avenol's services to the League as financial expert par excellence, Deputy Secretary-General (1923–1933), and Secretary-General (1933–1940) were not considerable. He played, for example, a prominent role in the League's financial reconstruction of central Europe after the First World War; and his administration of the League, from the financial point of view, was able. Through his efforts, the magnificent Palais des Nations was completed. A former French Inspector General of Finance, M. Avenol was above all a techniciaι; he was neither a diplomat nor a politician. His usefulness as Secretary-General was limited accordingly. Though he did not underestimate the importance of his office, M. Avenol does not seem to have exploited its diplomatic potential as effectively as did Sir Eric Drummond.

M. Avenol and, still more, Sir Eric often have been accused of excessive intimacy with their respective foreign offices. The following implies more than that realistic appreciation of the importance of the Anglo-French views of which M. Sokoline speaks: "The League of Nations has failed. . . The Secretariat has its share of the responsibility because the Secretaries-General were accustomed to consider the chiefs of the Ministries of Foreign Affairs of their respective countries as their sole masters." [6] Both Secretaries-General assert the contrary most forcefully. Sir Eric asserts that his first concern was to demonstrate his independence of his government.[7] M. Avenol declares that he "was absolutely independent as regards his actions. It was not difficult, owing to the number of French Foreign Ministers and their differences of opinion. M. Avenol was not in their confidence, nevertheless they never tried to influence him." [8] These words of Miss Vera B. Lever, private secretary to M. Avenol, support the impression that M. Avenol did not enjoy relations with the Quai d'Orsay as friendly as those which Sir Eric enjoyed with the Foreign Office.

The facts surrounding M. Avenol's resignation are elusive. As careful an observer as Ranshofen-Wertheimer, in describing "the most painful episode in the League's history," [9] suggests that M. Avenol was moved "by acquiescence in the rising totalitarian forces not fully compatible with the spirit and letter of the Covenant." [10] He mentions the possibility that pressures by Vichy perhaps were exerted upon M. Avenol, and concludes that "it appeared as though he were bent upon the destruction of the machinery which had been entrusted to his care by the common confidence of all the member States and in the building up of which he had participated." [11]

Another former official of the League states that the question of Avenol's resignation turned upon the decision of Vichy France as to whether France would remain in the League or not. M. Avenol, it is said, asked Vichy its intentions, apparently intending to resign if Vichy declared that it planned to withdraw from the League; and Vichy, though deciding to remain a member, asked Avenol to resign nonetheless, in order that a French Secretary-General might not embarrass Pétain's government by indicating a French attachment to the League more fervent than Vichy deemed politic.

Still another former official of the League alleges: "The last Secretary-General went so far as to try to hand over the League of Nations to the Nazi and Fascist Ambassadors in the capital of Switzerland after the German invasion of France." [12] While this last accusation cannot be substantiated, it is reported on the highest authority that, in the brief period just after the fall of France, M. Avenol shared the view held by almost all Frenchmen that England too would soon collapse; and that the former Secretary-General openly contemplated how the League machinery might best be fitted into what then appeared to him to be the inevitable new order.

M. Avenol, for his part, declares with considerable indignation that the story of the trip to Bern is "absolutely false! Not a word of truth! Never had I a relation with Hitler! . . . and never anything with Mussolini after 1936." He denies that the British exerted pressure upon him to resign (as has also been alleged); the former Secretary-General asserts that his resignation "was my initiative." [13] As for the Vichy government's having requested him to resign, M. Avenol indicates, in a letter dated October 18, 1940, to Señor A. Costa du Rels, President of the Council of the League, that, while he wrote to Vichy pledging his adherence to Pétain and underlined that adhesion by offering to resign if Vichy so wished, Vichy did not call upon him to do so. M. Avenol acknowledges six factors which influenced him in his decision to resign.

1. "Since the Assembly, the Council, and the Committees cannot meet at the present time," M. Avenol wrote in his letter of resignation, "the constitutional powers of the Secretary-General are in fact in suspense. The duties which remain — principally the administration of a small body of officials and the management of the finances of the League of Nations — no longer justify the maintenance of a political High Direction, which is no longer consistent with the realities of the situation." [14]

2. Moreover, the chances of strengthening the League's technical activities had been lessened in the past by the League's political mission — that principal mission in which the League had failed; and "the functions of the Secretary-General defined by the Covenant have a highly political character which perpetuates this tendency of the past" and which might hinder saving the League's technical activity.[15] (Even after his resignation, M. Avenol sustained his interest in preserving the League's technical work, though there is considerable dispute whether his methods of doing so — especially his initial opposition to moving certain League services to Princeton — were best suited to that end.)

3. It would have been a great error, M. Avenol felt, to try to maintain as the symbol of the League "civil servants discredited by their idleness and uselessness." [16] "Without work, without purpose, and without direction (of the Council, Assembly, Committees, etc.), an organization [such as the Secretariat] can only degenerate." [17] Rather, the Secretary-General believed that the League ideal should be upheld during the war by a political committee named for the purpose by the competent organs of the League.[18] There is perhaps some contradiction between this reasoning and that set forth in the preceding paragraph.

4. Having had to dismiss the greater part of the Secretariat, M. Avenol writes, he could not see himself remaining as the "privileged beneficiary" of the economies he had been forced to make.[19]

5. His decision to resign, taken in June, was hastened by the shock of the severance of diplomatic relations between the United Kingdom and France. "The incident of Mers-el-Kebir [the attack

by the British upon the French fleet at Oran] had, in the isolation in which I found myself, deprived of all information, a decisive influence upon me." [20]

6. Avenol felt that, as a Frenchman, in a period both of great crisis for France and of impotence of the League, he ought to place his services at the disposition of France; and France to him meant Vichy. "In this heartbreaking hour, I found ease in the simplest duty: being faithful to my country." [21] Thus the Secretary-General wrote to Vichy on July 4, 1940, pledging his allegiance and expressing willingness to demonstrate that allegiance by resigning, should Marshal Pétain so wish. Vichy's reply of July 13, 1940, seems to have left the matter to M. Avenol's decision (though it has been suggested in other quarters that Vichy communicated its desire for his resignation by courier). At any rate, the Secretary-General announced his intention to resign as of September 1; and he journeyed on August 21 to Vichy, where he was welcomed by Marshal Pétain. (M. Avenol's sympathies with Vichy, it should be noted, were with the anti-Laval faction. He threw his support to Vichy like "many Frenchmen who decided, at that moment, to do their best . . . to hope, in spite of all appearances, in spite of the presence of Laval, to prevent the worst." [22])

Which of these six factors were the most important in bringing about M. Avenol's departure is difficult to establish. M. Avenol's critics incline toward discounting all but the last two. M. Avenol himself accents the Oran incident: "After that attack, those sinkings, I knew that I could not remain in the Secretariat." [23] But he seems to view his attitude toward Oran and Vichy primarily as the immediate, and certainly not the sole, cause of his resignation. "For a long time," the former Secretary-General wrote Arthur Sweetser, "the reasons which I summed up in my letter of resignation were on my mind, and I always said to myself: Not yet. I do not have the right to leave. The trials of my country, her dissensions with England, have now made it a point of honor to resign." [24]

The mechanics of M. Avenol's resignation have provoked much comment, and the relevant League documentation — particularly one text which declares an earlier document to be "null and void" [25] — lends an air of intrigue to the proceedings. One may also gain from a reading of the League documentation alone the impression that M. Avenol at one time after July 25, 1940, reconsidered his intention to resign. This apparently was not the case, although, possibly in response to a cable of Carl J. Hambro, then President of the Supervisory Commission, urging him not to resign, M. Avenol did offer to put himself informally at the disposal of the League, without salary or responsibility.[26] The affair of the "null and void" documentation and a number of other incidents of the period from August to September 1940, while perhaps indicative of mistrust between M. Avenol, on the one hand, and his successor, Sean Lester, and the British, on the other, appear to have been more questions of protocol than of high politics.[27]

The circumstances of M. Avenol's resignation raise fundamental questions concerning the role of the Secretary-General in a period of high crisis. At least three problems of a significance wider than those peculiar circumstances emerge.

1. Nationalistic reactions are as a rule relatively dormant in the international civil servant. In a period of war — especially at the outbreak of a war in which the home country of the international civil servant is involved — he may tend to be caught up in the special surge of patriotic feeling which characterizes such a period. Can the Secretary-General be insulated against the feelings of his countrymen?

2. M. Avenol suggests that his attitude was in part molded by his isolation, both from his Secretariat and the world. In the summer of 1940, he says, "I had no confidence at all in the people remaining in the Secretariat"; [28] "the incident of Mers-el-Kebir had, in the isolation in which I found myself, deprived of all information, a decisive influence upon me"; [29] "my country was invaded. . . there was no government to take an interest in me — my best friends before had been the British." [30] The reasons for M. Avenol's isolation aside (and it may be that in some measure the Secretary-General isolated himself), his experience would seem to underline the importance of the Secretary-General's possessing at once independence, a first-caliber staff with which he enjoys relations of mutual trust, and comprehensive channels of

information. M. Avenol's isolation possibly further indicates the disabilities of a town of the type of Geneva as the world organization's headquarters in time of crisis. Had Avenol been able to breathe the bracing air of London, for example, rather than the artificial atmosphere of Geneva, conceivably he might have reacted differently.

3. It is not difficult for the Secretary-General to be a source of loyal strength to the international institution of which he is the chief permanent officer when, in a period of crisis, that institution gives some promise of a successful response. What may be expected of him when his organization is in fact politically dead — when it gives no hope of meeting the crisis successfully? When, indeed, a crucial element of the crisis is the organization's impotence? The natural reply would seem to be that, if no one else, at least the Secretary-General should attempt to maintain the ideal which the international organization has failed to sustain. M. Avenol, however, specifically challenges this contention; he holds that this highly political mission should be entrusted to a special political agency of the organization created for the task. The case of M. Avenol, at any rate, recalls that the Secretaries-General are human too; that they are perhaps subject to loss of heart, or that at least they are capable of interpreting their duties at such an hour in a subjective way distinct from that in which the Secretary-General as an abstraction would be expected to see them.

The essence of the solution to these three problems would appear to turn upon the political philosophy of the Secretary-General. "We must understand that the organization of peace and coöperation between nations is the revolution of the twentieth century as the organization of democracy was the revolution of the eighteenth century. Ah, revolution must be carried forward by revolutionary-minded people! And revolutionary-minded people must be equipped with political ideals. Therefore an international organization such as the Secretariat of the League of Nations must recruit militants who are capable of sacrificing everything for the realization of the ideal of the League of Nations." [31] That the Secretary-General must also be sound in his judgment, realistic in his approach, diplomatic in his tactics, goes without saying. But the core of intelligent idealism cannot be overlooked.

The Secretary-General must first of all possess this; without it, his other qualities may be directed against the higher interests of the organization. That M. Avenol unblushingly could have chosen Pétain is of profound significance. The import of his choice is the greater in that it appears to have been a personally disinterested one, impelled by a sincere sense of duty to what he saw as France.

The case of M. Avenol demonstrates that the response of the international executive in a period of supreme crisis may be primarily determined by the degree of the executive's adherence to the organization's ideal — by the character of its comprehension of that ideal. This is by no means a surprising discovery. But it does reiterate with the greatest force that, in the choice of the Secretary-General, first things must be considered first: that above all the Secretary-General must be devoted to the international community which designates him.

# NOTES

# NOTES

## Introduction. The Legacy of the League

The first and second quotations at the beginning of the Introduction are from the Notes prepared by Lord Perth for the author, January 31, 1951; the final quotation is from an interview we had on February 14, 1951. For clarity's sake, Lord Perth is referred to throughout the text as Sir Eric Drummond, as he was known during his service as Secretary-General of the League of Nations, though his statements to the author were of course made long after he had succeeded to his earldom and the title of Lord Perth. The third quotation is an observation made to the author, January 3, 1950, by Mr. Hill, who was a high official of the League Secretariat. The comment by M. Thomas, first Director of the International Labor Organization, was made to Archibald Evans, formerly a member of Thomas' *cabinet*. The remark was made by Thomas in the course of his comments upon a small imbroglio with Sir Walter Citrine concerning the nature of a speech Thomas was to make to the Trade Union Congress, and was related to the author by Mr. Evans, February 16, 1950.

1. See David Hunter Miller, *The Drafting of the Covenant* (1928), II, 108, 110, 120–121, 143; and Florence Wilson, *The Origins of the League Covenant* (1928), pp. 175, 182.

2. Viscount Cecil, *A Great Experiment* (1941), p. 89.

3. It is interesting to note, however, that much of the substance of the power which was to have been given to the Chancellor in 1919 is essentially that power which was entrusted to the Secretary-General of the United Nations by Article 99 of the Charter. That article empowers him to bring to the attention of the Security Council, which is organized to function continuously, any matter which in his opinion threatens the maintenance of international peace. Similarly, "the intention was to . . . give him [the Chancellor] the power to summon meetings of the Council on his own initiative. When Venizelos refused, and it was decided to put a civil servant instead of what at the time was considered a great statesman at the head of the Secretariat . . . Articles XI and XV [were] slightly altered so as to make it clear that the Council could be summoned only on the initiative of some government member of the League" (C. Howard-Ellis, *The Origin, Structure and Working of the League of Nations*, 1928, p. 163, n. 2).

4. Sir Eric Drummond, interview of February 14, 1951.

5. For two analyses making the most of the political potentialities of these clauses, see Felix Morley, *The Society of Nations* (1932), pp. 309–314, 264–265, 486, 566; and André Cagne, *Le Secrétariat Général de la Société des Nations* (1936), pp. 54–66, 81–128.

6. League of Nations Covenant, Article VI. The obscurity of this provision perhaps reflects the uncertainty of the Covenant's authors regarding what would be the precise activities of the Secretary-General. In the very least, "that capacity" would seem to refer to the Secretary-General's supplying the Assembly and the Council with normal secretarial assistance, such as the preparation of the requisite documentation. What more the word "capacity" may imply evidently depends upon the interpretation of the Secretary-General's functions that is adopted. Whatever the nature of that capacity, however, the clause serves to emphasize the fact that the Secretary-General was to be secretary of the League's individual organs and head of a unified secretariat acting under his single direction, as well as Secretary-General of the League as a whole.

7. *Ibid.*, Article XI.

8. *Ibid.*, Article XV.

9. *Ibid.*, Article VI.

10. *Ibid.*, Article VII. Only with respect to diplomatic privileges and immunities was the constitutional endowment of the Secretary-General of the League broader than that of the Secretary-General of the United Nations. The Covenant's Article XI, in providing that "officials of the League when engaged on the business of the League shall enjoy diplomatic privileges and immunities," is more generous than the comparable Article 105 of the Charter: "Officials of the Organization shall . . . enjoy such privileges and immunities as are necessary for the independent exercise of their functions in connection with the Organization."

11. A former high-ranking League official, in *Proceedings of the Conference on Experience in International Administration* (1943), p. 9. The participants in the conference are unnamed.

12. Arthur Sweetser, interview with the author, September 22, 1949.

13. Martin Hill, interview with the author, January 4, 1950. This administrative concept did not exclude political responsibility, however. Though the League Secretary-General may be aptly compared with the permanent under-secretary of a British government office, his position necessarily was a more political one. For the permanent under-secretary shifts all political responsibility onto his secretary of state or minister, something the League Secretary-General could not do. Rather than a minister, the political entities to which he was responsible were the Assembly and Council. Because of the general nature of their resolutions, which were, so to speak, his political instructions, and because of the infrequency of their meetings, the Secretary-General was necessarily forced to take political decisions with which the permanent under-secretary is never confronted.

These considerations apply to the United Nations Secretary-General, but in a lesser degree. For he is more the minister and less the permanent under-secretary than was the Secretary-General of the League. He is a principal organ of the Organization, on a par with the General Assembly and the Security Council. Certain of his functions, such as those under Article 99, are exercised at his discretion, and in their exercise he is responsible to no other organ. Furthermore, to the extent that he is responsible to the General Assembly, Security Council, and other United Nations organs, these organs are in a better position to assert their prerogatives than were the League Assembly and Council, since these United Nations bodies are in session far more than were their League counterparts.

14. On the contrary, in the League's beginnings Sir Eric was fortunate in securing a staff of his own choice of a caliber which the governments after World War II were reluctant to turn over to the United Nations Secretary-General: men of outstanding ability like Jean Monnet, Sir Arthur Salter, and Salvador de Madariaga.

15. This latter example is illustrative and not invidious. The League Secretaries-General were paid about $2000 more a year than is their United Nations counterpart. The differential is much more substantial, considering the general rise in salary levels since 1920.

16. *Proceedings of the Conference on Experience in International Administration*, p. 11.

17. Assembly Rules of Procedure, League of Nations Doc. C.220M. (2.1931.V), rule 9.

18. Egon F. Ranshofen-Wertheimer, *The International Secretariat* (1945), p. 203.

19. J. V. Wilson, "Problems of an International Secretariat," *International Affairs*, vol. XX (1944). For similar assessment of Sir Eric's abilities, see Viscount Cecil, *A Great Experiment*, p. 89.

20. Arthur Sweetser, interview of September 22, 1949.

21. Martin Hill, interview of January 3, 1950. This view has been asserted particularly with respect to comparative activity in the Council and the Security Council. Here it should be recalled, however, that the Council considered a wide range of technical (economic and social) problems especially susceptible to Secretariat influence, as well as the "touchier" political issues within the Security Council's ambit.

22. Sir Eric Drummond, interview of February 14, 1951.

23. Sir Eric Drummond, Notes of January 31, 1951.

24. *Ibid.*

25. *Ibid.*

26. Interview with the author, August 3, 1951. It could be said that "all" Mussolini wanted was a great deal — in fact, recognition of his Ethiopian conquest. M. Avenol, however, is firm in the view that his plan would not

have involved League recognition of Italian aggression. For the arrangement with Mussolini, it seems, was not for the Assembly's Credentials Committee to alter the status *de jure* of Ethiopia; rather, the Italian government made its return to the League dependent upon the presence or absence *de facto* of an Ethiopian delegation. Thus the question that would arise, the Secretary-General suggested, was whether the Ethiopian delegation submitted credentials which were valid or not. If the credentials of the Ethiopian delegation were deemed invalid, Ethiopia actually would be deprived of its representation at that Assembly, though, presumably, its legal right to dispatch a properly accredited delegation would in law subsist. M. Avenol's hope that the Credentials Committee would declare the Ethiopian delegation's credentials invalid, however, was not then realized. (See League of Nations, *Official Journal*, 17th Year, No. 11, 93rd Session of the Council, First Meeting, Doc. 18/IX/1936, p. 1139, for an explanation by the Secretary-General of his visit to Mussolini. That M. Avenol's initiative was prompted by no particular solicitude for Italy's status, legal or otherwise, in Ethiopia is indicated by the Secretary-General's comments upon a British draft resolution submitted to the Council in the spring of 1938. In a memorandum of April 3, 1938, M. Avenol forcefully criticized the British proposal that the question of the recognition of the Italian position in Ethiopia was then one to be settled by each member of the League for itself in the light of its own interests and obligations.)

27. Report of the Committee of Thirteen, League of Nations Doc. A.16.1930, and in the *Official Journal* of 1930, Minutes of the 4th Committee, Appendix II.

28. Sir Eric Drummond, interview of February 14, 1951. Support for Sir Eric's view may be found in Cagne, *Le Secrétariat Général*.

29. The word "organic" as herein employed refers to the formal relations of the Secretary-General with the organs of the Organization.

30. Sir Eric Drummond, Notes of January 31, 1951. Sir Eric's stress of the additional powers entrusted to the United Nations Secretary-General by Article 99 must be qualified, however, in the light of two resolutions of early League Assemblies which endowed the League Secretary-General with powers of a nature remarkably similar to those of Article 99 — powers which the League Secretaries-General apparently neglected to exploit.

The First Assembly adopted on December 10, 1920, a Report on the Implementation of Article XVI of the Covenant which in part read:

"It shall be the duty of the Secretary-General to call the attention of the Council to any facts which in his opinion show that a member of the League has become a Covenant-breaking State within the meaning of Article XVI;

"Upon receiving such an intimation, the Council shall, on the request of any of its members, hold a meeting with the least possible delay to consider it."

The Second Assembly adopted on October 4, 1921, Interpretive Resolutions regarding Article XVI, one of which prescribed that "if a breach of the

Covenant be committed, or if there arise a danger of such breach being committed, the Secretary-General shall at once give notice thereof to all members of the Council. Upon receipt . . . of such a notice by the Secretary-General, the Council will meet as soon as possible" (as quoted in William E. Rappard, *The Quest for Peace*, 1940, pp. 227, 237). That the Secretary-General should have let these resolutions rust unused is the more surprising, since their origins may in some measure be traced to his initiative (*ibid.*, p. 220).

Sir Eric explains that he viewed these resolutions as being governed by the first clause of Article XVI ("Should any member of the League resort to war in disregard of its covenants"), and, in the absence of war, did not bring them into play (interview of February 14, 1951).

It is true that the resolutions specifically appertained to Article XVI and to that degree were not as sweeping as Article 99. But the 1921 resolution speaks of a "danger" to the peace, as well as an actual breach of it. However, while Article 99 is part of the United Nations Charter, the resolutions in question were of course not part of the Covenant and so were proportionately less potent.

These explanations notwithstanding, the resolutions quoted come close to the substance of Article 99 and, along with the powers which would have been entrusted constitutionally to the Chancellor, provide that article with fascinating antecedents. This reoccurrence of the theme of Article 99 in the brief history of international administration indicates that the Charter's expression of it is not so revolutionary an innovation as is generally supposed.

31. *Organisation of the Secretariat and of the International Labour Office* (Noblemaire Report), adopted by the Second Assembly of the League, as quoted by Ranshofen-Wertheimer, *The International Secretariat*, p. 385.

32. E. J. Phelan, *Yes and Albert Thomas* (1936), p. 253. Thomas' constitutional endowment, it should be noted, was no greater than that of the Secretary-General of the League. Article 394 of the Treaty of Versailles provides:

"There shall be a Director of the International Labour Office who shall be appointed by the Governing Body, and, subject to the instructions of the Governing Body, shall be responsible for the efficient conduct of the International Labour Office and for such other duties as may be assigned to him.

"The Director or his deputy shall attend all meetings of the Governing Body."

33. Phelan, *Yes and Albert Thomas*, p. 251.

34. *Ibid.*, p. 125.

35. *Ibid.*, p. 250.

36. *Ibid.*, p. 53.

37. *Ibid.*, pp. 41, 109.

38. *Ibid.*, p. 138.

39. *Ibid.*, p. 54.

40. *Ibid.*, pp. 113, 114.

41. Two qualifications may be attached to this assessment of Thomas' service, the first more of an explanation than a reservation. Much of his success in steering his conventions through the I.L.O. Conference may be traced to the fact that the support of the workers' delegates was often almost automatic — they regarded Thomas as one of their own — and to the presence, in the early days, of governmental delegates who represented social democratic regimes friendly to Thomas' view. Secondly, if one measures the results of his leadership, not by the conventions which he influenced the conference to adopt, but by the ratifications of those conventions by the governments, his success appears to be less striking.

42. "As to the policy of Albert Thomas," Sir Eric Drummond relates, "he was a complete master in his own domain. He was full of initiative. . . I do not feel that his method could have been applicable or successful if applied to the League, nor would mine have been, if applied to the Labour Office" (Notes of January 31, 1951). "We agreed," Sir Eric adds, "that each of us was right in his own sphere. . . In labour matters, Thomas could be the whole limelight; nobody minded. It was different with political affairs" (interview of February 14, 1951). (I presented this quotation to Edward J. Phelan, former Director General of the I.L.O., in an interview on August 16, 1951. Mr. Phelan responded to Sir Eric's suggestion that "nobody minded": "But they did mind. They minded so much that they wanted to put the I.L.O. out of business. . . But once Thomas was able to build down, once he was able to count upon the support not only of two or three top people of the trade unions but of the rank and file, then he had something solid.")

Yet there is, of course, some force in what Sir Eric says. The attitude and resolutions of League organs, moreover, were not always such that they encouraged a more public initiative on the part of the Secretary-General. "We recommend with special urgency," the Second Assembly resolved, "that in the interests of the League, as well as in its own interests, the Secretariat should not extend the sphere of its activities; . . . that it should . . . prepare the ground for . . . decisions without suggesting what these decisions should be; . . . that once these decisions have been taken, it should then confine itself to executing them in the letter and in the spirit" (as quoted by Morley, *The Society of Nations*, p. 197).

The atmosphere in the United Nations has been more congenial to the Secretary-General's initiative. Owing to this, to his more substantial constitutional endowment, and to his personal inclinations, the U.N.'s first Secretary-General has outstripped the Secretary-General of the League in political activities.

## Chapter 1. San Francisco, the Charter, and the Preparatory Commission

The prefatory quotation is from the interview of February 14, 1951, with Sir Eric.

1. Dr. Leo Pasvolsky, interview of February 3, 1950.

2. It is interesting to note that the International Civil Aviation Organization follows this scheme of two permanent officers. There is a President of the Council, who presides over ICAO's executive organ, and a Secretary-General, who acts as the organization's chief executive officer (Convention on International Civil Aviation, Articles 51, 54, 59, 60). The pros and cons of entrusting the chairmanship of the main political organ of the world organization to either the Secretary-General or an officer analogous to the President who would serve with the Secretary-General are ably discussed in the report of a committee of former high League officials which met under the chairmanship of Sir Eric Drummond (Royal Institute of International Affairs, *The International Secretariat of the Future*, 1944, pp. 32–33).

The Secretary-General of the United Nations, in the person of the Director of the Political Division of the Department of Security Council Affairs, has presided over governmental subcommittees of the Interim Committee of the General Assembly. The notable contribution of the Secretariat to the success of these subcommittees was acknowledged by the Interim Committee (see Clive Parry, "The Secretariat of the United Nations," *World Affairs*, July 1950, p. 362).

The *Articles of Agreement of the International Bank for Reconstruction and Development* (Article V, section 5) and the *Articles of Agreement of the International Monetary Fund* (Article XII, section iv) provide that the chiefs of their operating staffs shall be respectively President and Managing Director of their executive bodies.

3. "What was his [FDR's] chief ambition? . . . [It was] to create the beginnings at least of a functioning world machinery to keep peace in perpetuity. I have heard it said that, if he had finished out the fourth term, he would have been the happiest man alive to take on some job as that held now by Trygve Lie, Secretary-General of the United Nations" (John Gunther, *Roosevelt in Retrospect*, 1950, p. 81).

4. Mrs. Franklin D. Roosevelt, in a letter to the author, March 2, 1950.

5. F. L. McDougall, in a letter to the author, November 17, 1950. Mr. McDougall, now Counselor of the Food and Agriculture Organization, discussed the question with the late President at the White House in September 1942.

6. Benjamin V. Cohen, former Counselor of the Department of State, interview of February 3, 1950.

7. Field Marshal Jan Christiaan Smuts, in a letter to the author transmitted by Mr. H. W. A. Cooper, December 15, 1949.

8. They were, in fact, unanimously adopted by Commission I (United Nations Conference on International Organization, *Documents,* vol. 6, p. 173, minutes of the 4th meeting). Differences in policy appeared in sub-Commission voting.

9. Preparatory Commission, *Report,* 1946, Doc. PC/20, p. 87.

10. *Ibid.*

11. Herbert V. Evatt, *The United Nations* (1948), p. 138.

12. UNCIO, *Documents,* vol. 7, pp. 162–163, Committee I/2, 17th meeting.

13. *Ibid.,* p. 556, draft report of Subcommittee I/2/D.

14. *Ibid.,* p. 162, Committee I/2, 17th meeting.

15. *Ibid.,* pp. 168–169, Committee I/2, 18th meeting. The vote was 18 to 11.

16. L. M. Goodrich and E. Hambro, *Charter of the United Nations* (1949), p. 502.

17. Dr. Leo Pasvolsky, interview of February 3, 1950.

18. UNCIO, *Documents,* vol. 7, p. 163, Committee I/2, 17th meeting.

19. *Ibid.,* pp. 168–169, Committee I/2, 18th meeting. The vote was 16 to 13.

20. *Ibid.,* vol. 6, p. 234, Report of the Rapporteur of Commission I.

21. Disagreement with this view is implied in the remarks of no less experts on international organization than Lord Cecil and Lord Cranborne. "Speaking personally," Viscount Cranborne said, "I suggest that it will be necessary in the new organization, that the chief permanent official . . . who will be an international official and therefore not open to the same embarrassment as the Ministers of individual states, should be empowered to bring before its members, on his own initiative, any potentially dangerous development at an early stage before the aggressor has time to gird himself for war. Unless there is some provision of that kind it will, I believe, be impossible this time, as it was the last time, to keep the situation under control." Lord Cecil observed in the same debate, "The advantage of [a very similar] procedure is that it removes the necessity of any single power appearing as the hostile critic of any other power. That would be done as a matter of routine by the Secretariat" (Parliamentary Debates, House of Lords, April 15, 14, 1943, as quoted in *The International Secretariat of the Future,* p. 27). The first Secretary-General of the League of Nations shares these views regarding the value and potential of an Article 99 (interview of February 14, 1951).

The remarks quoted, while provocative and suggestive of the sources which gave birth to Article 99, are not presently as relevant as they might be, in that states seem only too ready to assume the role of hostile critic of other states and to hail other states before the Security Council.

22. Executive Committee of the Preparatory Commission, Committee 6, 4th meeting, Doc. PC/EX/SEC/9.

23. Preparatory Commission, *Report*, Doc. PC/20, p. 87.

24. Summary Record of the 47th meeting of the Committee of Experts, Doc. S/Procedure/100. The summary records of the committee are "restricted" and are quoted by permission of the Secretary-General.

25. *Ibid.*, 48th meeting, Doc. S/Procedure/103.

26. *Ibid.*

27. Dr. Alexander W. Rudzinski, in a letter to the author, July 13, 1950. The comments in the preceding paragraph are also from this letter.

28. Of which paragraph 1 reads: "Any Member of the United Nations may bring any dispute or any situation of the nature referred to in Article 34 to the attention of the Security Council or of the General Assembly." (Article 99, it will be recalled, does not extend to the Assembly.)

29. Charter of the United Nations, Article 11, paragraph 3.

30. See above, n. 22. Professor Lauterpacht points out that Article 99 presents "considerable potentialities" for bringing to the Security Council's attention violations of human rights so grave that they threaten the maintenance of international peace and security. Moreover, he notes, "The clause of domestic jurisdiction of Article 2, paragraph 7, presents no impediment in the way of the exercise of this particular function of the Secretary-General. The matters referred to in Article 99 are not, by definition, essentially within the domestic jurisdiction of any State" (Hersch Lauterpacht, *International Law and Human Rights*, 1950, p. 187).

31. See pp. 89–90.

32. Ambassador Warren Austin, in speaking to the General Assembly about the "unprecedented political responsibilities" entrusted to the Secretary-General by Article 99, seemed to endorse this investigatory power when he said: "We need not await its [Article 99's] full implementation to recognize that the power of the Secretary-General to study conditions which in his opinion threaten the peaceful relations of the United Nations, and to make recommendations based on these findings, represents a significant departure from the usual concepts of international organization and national sovereignty" (Official Records of the Second Part of the First Session of the General Assembly, Plenary Meetings, p. 902).

33. The Dumbarton Oaks text, roughly the same, is: "The Secretary-General should act in that capacity in all meetings of the General Assembly, of the Security Council, and of the Economic and Social Council, and should make an annual report on the work of the Organization." The Trusteeship Council is not mentioned, since it was a creation of San Francisco.

34. UNCIO, *Documents*, vol. 7, pp. 555–556, Subcommittee I/2/D, draft report. This draft report reads, "to cover all functions of the Secretariat, political as well as administrative." The Netherlands delegate objected to

the word "political," since, in his view, "the Secretariat would not have political functions" (*ibid.*, pp. 161–162, Committee I/2). The offending phrase does not appear in the Report of the Rapporteur of Committee I/2.

35. *United Nations Secretariat*, United Nations Studies 4, Carnegie Endowment for International Peace (1950), p. 175.

36. Preparatory Commission, *Report*, Doc. PC/20, p. 13, rule 48, and p. 9, rule 12.

37. Summary Report of the 16th meeting of Committee 1, Doc. PC/EX/A/2.

38. It is not unusual for the Secretary-General to preside at the opening meetings of other United Nations bodies, however. Mr. Lie presided over the first meeting of a body which derives from a resolution of the Fifth Session of the General Assembly, the Committee of Twelve, established to explore coördination or merging of the Atomic Energy and Conventional Armaments Commissions (*New York Times*, February 15, 1951, p. 4). He likewise opened the first meeting of the Assembly's Collective Sanctions Committee (*New York Times*, International Air Edition, February 17, 1951, p. 2).

39. Preparatory Commission, *Report*, Doc. PC/20, p. 26, rule 15.

40. *Ibid.*, p. 25, rule 4. The provisional rules of procedure, as amended by the Council, further provide that the President must call a meeting of the Security Council if the Secretary-General wishes to bring a matter to its attention under Article 99 (Doc. S/96/Rev. 3, rule 3).

41. The extent of the Secretary-General's discretion is illustrated by Professor Eagleton's comments on the Security Council's handling of the Hyderabad case: "At one point discussion of the question was not completed. According to the Rules of Procedure, it should have been brought up at the next succeeding meeting of the Council. It was not, however, because, as the Secretariat explained in reply to an inquiry, the Indian delegation stated it did not have a speaker available to discuss the subject. The Rules state that the Secretariat arranges the agenda in consultation with the President of the organ, and in this case the Secretariat not only controlled the agenda but even disposed of the matter (rightly or wrongly), by not including it for further discussion" (Clyde Eagleton, ed. *Annual Review of United Nations Affairs*, 1949, p. 46).

The Hyderabad case is of interest with regard to another agenda matter. Hyderabad appealed to the Security Council when Indian troops invaded its territory. The Secretary-General, however, was not sure that Hyderabad was a state within the meaning of Article 35 and thus entitled to bring a dispute before the Council. Mr. Lie therefore passed on Hyderabad's request to the President of the Council, noting his indecision regarding Hyderabad's status. The President accepted the item as valid for the Council's agenda.

42. However, rule 17 of the unamended provisional rules did provide that "the Security Council may invite members of the Secretariat or any person, whom it considers competent for the purpose, to supply it with

information or to give their assistance in examining matters within its competence" (Preparatory Commission, *Report*, Doc. PC/20, p. 26).

43. *Ibid.*, p. 30, rule 9.

44. *Ibid.*, rule 10.

45. *Ibid.*, rule 24.

46. *Ibid.*, pp. 50–51, rules 5, 6, and 16.

47. See James Reston's article in the *New York Times* of April 19, 1946, commenting upon Mr. Lie's Iranian intervention.

48. The Assembly's reciprocal of this clause is Article 15, paragraph 2: "The General Assembly shall receive and consider reports from the other organs of the United Nations."

49. In this, the Charter follows League precedent. Compare Article VI of the Covenant.

50. The Dumbarton Oaks draft of what came to be Article 97 provided: "There should be a Secretariat comprising a Secretary-General and such staff as may be required. The Secretary-General should be the chief administrative officer of the Organization. He should be elected by the General Assembly, on the recommendation of the Security Council, for such term and under such conditions as are specified in the Charter."

51. See the "Report to the President on the Results of the San Francisco Conference by the Chairman of the United States Delegation, the Secretary of State" (1945), as reproduced in the *Hearings before the Committee on Foreign Relations, U. S. Senate, 79th Congress, on the Charter of the United Nations* (1945), p. 130.

The Report of the Rapporteur of Committee I/2 does not indicate that the Soviet-proposed amendment providing for five deputies was accepted by the other sponsoring Powers. In view of the poor quality of the San Francisco summary records, however, it is likely that the "Report to the President" is more accurate.

The quality of the San Francisco records emphasizes the undesirability of making summary rather than verbatim records of international meetings. Considering the hindrance summary records are to accurate scholarship and precise treaty interpretation, which so often rely upon the *travaux preparatoires*, the sums saved by replacing verbatim with summary documentation represent misplaced thrift.

52. UNCIO, *Documents*, vol. 7, pp. 389–391, Report of the Rapporteur of Committee I/2.

53. *Ibid.*

54. *Ibid.*, vol. 8, p. 353, Committee II/1, Report of the 7th meeting.

55. *Ibid.*, vol. 7, pp. 389–390, Report of the Rapporteur of Committee I/2.

56. *Ibid.*, vol. 8, pp. 332–333, Committee II/1, Report of the 5th meeting. These arguments were put forth before the sponsoring Powers offered their

revised version, which envisaged five deputies who would be eligible for reëlection. These concessions by the sponsoring Powers did not succeed in winning over the opposition.

57. *Ibid.*, vol. 7, p. 388, Report of the Rapporteur of Committee I/2.

58. *Ibid.*, p. 204, Report of the 22nd meeting of Committee I/2.

59. *Ibid.*, pp. 387–389, 343–347, Report of the Rapporteur of Committee I/2.

60. By a vote of 36–2–1; *ibid.*, pp. 389, 347.

61. *Ibid.*, vol. 2, pp. 691–693, Report of the Rapporteur of Committee III/1. Belgium, Canada, the Netherlands, and Australia took the lead in opposing this application of the veto.

62. General Assembly, First Session, 17th Plenary Meeting, Doc. A/64, p. 14.

63. UNCIO, *Documents*, vol. 7, p. 389, Report of the Rapporteur of Committee I/2. Professor Kelsen points out that the wording "shall be appointed" is faulty — that the Secretary-General actually is elected by the General Assembly just as the members of the International Court are elected. A collegiate organ like the Assembly, he notes, can appoint an organ only if the latter is subordinate to the creating collegiate organ. The Secretary-General is subordinate to the Assembly, however, in certain of his functions only. Nor, of course, are all his functions administrative. (Hans Kelsen, *The Law of the United Nations*, 1950, p. 296.)

64. Doc. A/64, p. 14.

65. Executive Committee of the Preparatory Commission, 6th meeting of Committee 6, Doc. PC/EX/SEC/13.

66. The Preparatory Commission probably included this reference to the Security Council in response to the San Francisco understanding that the Secretary-General's tenure would be the subject of an agreement between the Council and the Assembly (see pp. 33, 41–42). While the Assembly adopted this portion of the Commission's report (Doc. A/64, p. 14), by the same resolution it prescribed, without consulting the Security Council, that the first Secretary-General should be appointed for five years.

The Assembly's initiative was a constitutional development of importance. Though it conflicted with the intentions of the drafters of Article 97 (if the bare summary record from San Francisco may be taken as an accurate reflection of that intention), a good constitutional rationale may be made out for it. For it is the General Assembly which is empowered by the Charter to make recommendations concerning the "powers and functions of any organs" (Article 10), which establishes the regulations under which the staff shall be appointed (Article 101), and whose concern with the administration of the Organization is emphasized by Article 17, which provides that it shall consider and approve the Organization's budget. The Security Council lacks comparable powers.

On the other hand, the political and security functions of the Secretary-General may be said to justify the Security Council's participation in the determination of his tenure. Moreover, by the terms of the General Convention on Privileges and Immunities, the Security Council has the right to waive the Secretary-General's immunity (see Section 20, as quoted in Kelsen, *The Law of the United Nations*, p. 315).

67. Preparatory Commission, *Report*, Doc. PC/20, p. 87.

68. See Ranshofen-Wertheimer, *The International Secretariat*, p. 51.

69. Preparatory Commission, *Report*, Doc. PC/20, p. 81. The Report itself named no figure; the above scale was suggested in the Commission's Executive Committee discussions (Doc. PC/EX/SEC/40), and was adopted by the First Session of the General Assembly (Doc. A/64, p. 14).

70. Doc. PC/EX/SEC/40.

71. Or so one would ideally think. The Security Council's treatment of the question in the fall of 1950 produced several election casualties. Electioneering was open, and the substance of the Council's "private" consideration of candidates daily appeared in the press.

72. The Charter of course may be amended. The process is so cumbersome and hazardous, however, that any flexibility introduced by Articles 108 and 109 is more academic than actual.

73. *United Nations Secretariat*, p. 22.

74. *Ibid.*

75. Thomas J. Hamilton, in the *New York Times*, June 23, 1950, p. 14:5.

76. See pp. 106, 169.

77. "In view of the grave political responsibilities which, in addition to multifarious administrative duties, are imposed upon the Secretary-General . . . particularly . . . [by] Article 99," the British memorandum ran, "it is felt necessary to raise the question whether there should not be express provision for the suspension or dismissal of the Secretary-General. . . It is of course most unlikely that he will conduct himself in a manner calling for such a measure; and, if the case did arise, an appropriate method of removing him from office could under normal circumstances probably be found without any express provision. Indeed, a method other than suspension or dismissal might well be preferable in the interest of the credit of the Organization. But the procedure might take considerable time. It is necessary to face the possibility that some decline in the Secretary-General's physical or mental condition, or some mental disease, might deprive him of the capacity of appreciating the situation with which he has to deal" (Doc. PC/EX/SEC/45).

78. Executive Committee of the Preparatory Commission, Summary Report of the 6th meeting of Committee 6, Doc. PC/EX/SEC/13.

79. Dr. Leo Pasvolsky, interview of February 3, 1950.

80. The Organization retains express legal control over the Secretary-General, however, to the extent that the Security Council is empowered, by the General Convention on Privileges and Immunities, to waive his immunity. The Secretary-General and his officials are immune from legal process for all acts performed in their official capacity (Section 18 of the Convention); and the Secretary-General and the Assistant Secretaries-General are entitled to the privileges and immunities accorded to diplomatic envoys (Section 17). The Secretary-General has the "right and duty" to waive the more restricted privileges and immunities of the staff in any case in which, in his opinion, the immunity would impede the course of justice and could be waived without prejudice to the interests of the United Nations. (See Kelsen, *The Law of the United Nations*, pp. 314–318, and Lawrence Preuss, "Immunity of Officers and Employees of the United Nations for Official Acts: The Ranallo Case," *American Journal of International Law*, vol. XLI, 1947).

The most publicized case relating to immunities is that of Valentin A. Gubitchev, a Soviet national accused by the United States of espionage. Upon his arrest, his immunities as a member of the Secretariat were hastily waived by the Secretary-General, who demonstrated a quick appreciation of the political explosiveness of the question.

81. By analogy with the Advisory Opinion of the International Court of Justice Concerning the Competence of the General Assembly Regarding Admission to the United Nations (International Court of Justice, *Reports*, 1950, p. 4), it would seem that the recommendation of the Security Council with respect to the appointment of the Secretary-General must be positive. A failure to make a positive recommendation does not leave it to the Assembly to appoint the Secretary-General, despite what might be thought to be a negative recommendation; rather, in the absence of a positive recommendation, there is no recommendation at all for the Assembly to act upon.

82. The Canadian Minister of External Affairs seems to have thought that this is precisely what the Assembly proposed to do (Doc. A/P.V./297, p. 264). If so, its resolution effectively obscured its intentions. Nothing whatever is said of revoking or amending its prior resolution, which set the term at five years (resolution of January 24, 1946, Doc. A/64, p. 14). Nothing is said of establishing a new term of eight years. The text of the resolution which the Assembly adopted November 1, 1950, is as follows (Doc. A/1464/Add.1):

"The General Assembly,

"Having received communications from the President of the Security Council, dated 12 October and 25 October 1950, stating that the Security Council has been unable to agree on a recommendation to the General Assembly regarding the appointment of a Secretary-General,

"Considering the necessity to ensure the uninterrupted exercise of the functions vested by the Charter in the office of the Secretary-General,

"Considering that the Security Council recommended to the first regular session of the General Assembly the appointment of Mr. Trygve Lie as

Secretary-General, and that, on 1 February 1946, the General Assembly appointed Mr. Trygve Lie as Secretary-General for a five-year term,

"Decides that the present Secretary-General shall be continued in office for a period of three years."

83. Doc. A/1464/Add.1. But see above, pp. 33, 41–42. Were the San Francisco understanding regarding the Security Council's role in determining the Secretary-General's term adhered to, the legality of either method of extension would appear the more questionable.

84. This view was submitted, for example, by the delegates of the Philippines (Doc. A/P.V./297, p. 263), of Canada (*ibid.*, p. 264), and of Greece (Doc. A/P.V./296, p. 253).

85. As to the legal value of such a recommendation, see F. Blaine Sloan, "The Binding Force of a Recommendation of the General Assembly of the United Nations," *British Year Book of International Law* (1948), p. 5. While all recommendations of the Assembly do not have binding force, Mr. Sloan suggests, those directed to the Secretary-General do. Mr. Sloan's view, essentially correct, is perhaps too sweeping. Would, for example, a recommendation of the Assembly to the Secretary-General with regard to the exercise of his powers under Article 99 be binding upon him?

86. This view was held, for example, by the delegates of Greece (Doc. A/P.V./296, p. 253), of Ecuador (*ibid.*, p. 256), of Uruguay (*ibid.*), and of Peru (Doc. A/P.V./297, p. 275).

87. The delegate of France made this statement (Doc. A/P.V./296, p. 255). For a similar view, see the opinion of the delegate of the United Kingdom (Doc. A/P.V./297, p. 276).

88. Argument of the delegate of the U.S.S.R. (Doc. A/P.V./296, pp. 258, 250). Rule 140 of the Assembly's rules of procedure, Mr. Malik pointed out, reads: "When the Security Council has submitted its recommendation on the appointment of the Secretary-General, the General Assembly shall consider the recommendation and vote upon it by secret ballot in private meeting." The force of Mr. Malik's procedural argument was augmented by the fact that the Assembly considered the question under an agenda item entitled, "Appointment of the Secretary-General of the United Nations" (Doc. A/P.V./296).

89. The delegate of the U.S.S.R. (Doc. A/P.V./298, pp. 283, 282).

90. *Ibid.*, p. 286.

91. *Ibid.*, p. 290.

92. See p. 33. Professor Kelsen, in view of the San Francisco understanding there cited, and noting that "the Charter of the United Nations does not distinguish between the 'appointment' of the Secretary-General and the determination of his term of office," holds that, "consequently, not only the 'appointment' but also the determination of the term of office must be established by a cooperation of the Security Council and the General As-

sembly." He thus views as illegal any form of unilateral determination by the General Assembly of the Secretary-General's term. "It is true," he acknowledges, "that the Security Council in its decision concerning the appointment of the first Secretary-General, adopted at its fourth (private) meeting on January 29, 1946, did not refer to the term of office. But this cannot constitute a precedent to the effect of depriving the Security Council of a power conferred upon it by the Charter." (Hans Kelsen, *Recent Trends in the Law of the United Nations*, New York: Frederick A. Praeger, Inc., 1951, pp. 950–951.)

However, whether such a power actually was "conferred upon it [the Security Council] by the Charter" is at least debatable. The Charter does not expressly confer such a power. One may, for the persuasive reason Professor Kelsen advances, choose to find the implication of such a conferral in Article 97, but it is interesting to note that both the General Assembly and the Security Council each twice have found otherwise. The law of the matter does not lend itself to categorical definition — the meaning of Article 97, especially to the organs whose business it is to interpret it, is not so plain. As for the *travaux preparatoires*, which clearly support Professor Kelsen's view, these are of limited value. The few relevant lines consist of a suggestion and an assurance by one or two delegates, to which no exception is reported, but which received no positive or express endorsement by the committee, by vote or otherwise. The quality of the San Francisco summary records does not add to the weight to be attributed to them; and, were the records less sparse and more accurate, the juridical value of most, and particularly this form of, *travaux preparatoires* is in any case variable. Professor Kelsen further perhaps understates the force of the 1946 precedent of the Security Council's not participating in determining the length of the Secretary-General's term, and he fails to take account at all of the similar precedent of 1950. (See above, pp. 42, 189.)

93. "Report to the President on the Results of the San Francisco Conference by the Chairman of the United States Delegation, the Secretary of State," *Hearings before the Committee on Foreign Relations,* p. 130.

94. The question of the legality of the Secretary-General's continued tenure could be authoritatively adjudicated upon by the International Court of Justice. The Security Council, the General Assembly, an organ of or, possibly, a specialized agency authorized by the Assembly could request an advisory opinion of the Court, or the issue might arise incidentally to the Court's consideration of another question. Practically speaking, there would seem to be no chance that the Security Council or the General Assembly would take so rash a step; nor is it certain that it would be within the competence of the specialized agencies to request an advisory opinion on the question. Should the issue arise in an indirect fashion, the Court might well contrive to side-step ruling upon it.

95. With regard to the application of the opinion of the International Court of Justice concerning the nature of the recommendation which the

Security Council must extend prior to the election of new members, the Syrian delegate pointed out that, "in [that] matter . . . it is quite conceivable that, if the Security Council did not make the required recommendation, there would be no direct harm to the Organization because the question of the admission of an applicant State was delayed. . . But in the matter of the Secretary-General, Article 97 should be applied so as to ensure an appointment, because the Organization cannot continue its work without a Secretary-General. There is that difference between the two cases, and because of it we cannot apply in the matter of the Secretary-General the legal opinion pronounced by the International Court of Justice in connexion with the question of admission to membership" (Doc. A/P.V./298, p. 285).

96. The delegate of Egypt (*ibid.*, p. 284).

97. The delegate of Syria (*ibid.*, p. 281).

98. Resolution of January 24, 1946, Doc. A/64, p. 14. With regard to the legality of the Syrian proposal, however, it is relevant to note that, at San Francisco, Uruguay suggested the election of the Secretary-General by the General Assembly from a panel of three candidates to be submitted by the Security Council. The Uruguayan plan, after some discussion, was not adopted (UNCIO, *Documents*, vol. 8, pp. 318–319, Report of the 4th meeting of Committee II/1).

99. Doc. A/P.V./298, p. 277.

100. Except for the suggestions of Egypt and Syria.

101. Whether the General Assembly alone would have the power to prescribe this is not altogether clear. It might otherwise be argued that the outgoing Secretary-General has the power to arrange for such rotation. Rotation, if perhaps politically expedient, would be administratively weak. Its political possibilities would in some degree be dependent upon the nationality and personality of the Executive Assistant to the Secretary-General, since, under such an arrangement, he might actually be charged with running the Secretariat. The General Assembly has directed that "there shall always be one Assistant Secretary-General designated by the Secretary-General to deputize for him when he is absent or unable to perform his functions" (Doc. A/64, p. 14).

According to the terms of an understanding among the Secretary-General and the Assistant Secretaries-General, when the Secretary-General is absent from headquarters the Assistants rotate as Acting Secretary-General in the order of their listing in the Report of the Preparatory Commission (Doc. PC/20, p. 88): Security Council Affairs, Economic Affairs, Social Affairs, Trusteeship and Information from Non-Self-Governing Territories, Public Information, Legal, Conferences and General Services, and Administrative and Financial Services. In practice, the Secretary-General tends to name whom he chooses.

102. Preparatory Commission, *Report*, Doc. PC/20, pp. 84–85.

103.  See Ranshofen-Wertheimer, *The International Secretariat,* pp. 45–46, 352–354.

104.  Preparatory Commission, *Report,* Doc. PC/20, p. 86.

105.  *Ibid.,* p. 85.

106.  The Secretary-General himself, unlike the League Secretaries-General, who spent too much of their time on personnel matters (Ranshofen-Wertheimer, *The International Secretariat,* p. 45), is relieved of the greater part of personnel responsibilities by the Bureau of Personnel.

107.  Preparatory Commission, *Report,* Doc. PC/20, p. 85.

108.  The First Session of the General Assembly adopted provisional staff regulations which do not overly limit the Secretary-General's discretion (Doc. A/64, pp. 18–19; as amended, Doc. SGB/3/Add.5).

109.  The Supervisory Commission of the League of Nations, true enough, was not expressly authorized by the Covenant, but rather evolved from a modest committee appointed by the Council into the organization's major instrument of governmental control over the Secretariat's internal administration (see Ranshofen-Wertheimer, *The International Secretariat,* pp. 23–25). Presumably, the United Nations could create such a commission under Article 7, paragraph 2, of the Charter; but the fact that the delegates at San Francisco, well aware of the advantages and disadvantages of a supervisory commission, did not create one belies any intention of their doing so.

The record of the Supervisory Commission is a mixed one (*ibid.*). Moreover, the desirability of vesting predominant appointive power in the Secretary-General has been disputed (*ibid.,* p. 46). The appointive powers of the League Secretaries-General were in fact quite broad; the Supervisory Commission impinged upon them, and impinged still more upon other staff policies, indirectly, through its supervisory budgetary functions. Nevertheless, it is reasonable to assume that the United Nations Secretary-General, loosely responsible to the General Assembly, is a good deal more at ease in appointive and staff relations than were his League predecessors, who in appointive matters were responsible to the Council (not the Assembly), on the one hand, and on the other, were susceptible to the indirect budgetary influence of the Assembly's Supervisory Commission (after the Ninth Assembly).

This somewhat greater appointive independence of the United Nations Secretary-General appears to be desirable at least from the political point of view. It has been suggested that the Secretary-General would be relieved of external political pressures with regard to the choice of staff if the appointive power were taken out of his hands (Ranshofen-Wertheimer does not commit himself to such suggestions, but summarizes them, *ibid.,* p. 46). This is obviously true; but that pressure, in the United Nations experience, has not been so important as to obviate it at the price of stripping the Secretary-General of the extremely useful right of choosing his associates.

110. "The statement of Article 7, paragraph 1, that the 'Secretariat' is an organ of the United Nations is not in conformity with the provisions of the Charter, which does not organize the Secretariat as a collegiate body able to act, like the General Assembly, the three Councils, or the International Court. The organ designated by the term 'Secretariat' is the Secretary-General. It is upon the Secretary-General, not upon the Secretariat, that the Charter confers definite functions. Article 102, it is true, provides that treaties shall 'be registered with the Secretariat and published by it.' But the functions determined by this Article are functions of the Secretary-General, who alone is responsible for them. The Secretariat is the office of the Secretary-General just as the 'Ministry' is the office of a cabinet minister. The members of the staff of the Secretariat . . . are organs of the United Nations but subordinate to the Secretary-General, just as the employees of a ministry are organs of the state but subordinate to the cabinet minister" (Kelsen, *The Law of the United Nations*, pp. 136–137).

111. Article II: "The action of the League under this Covenant shall be effected through the instrumentality of an Assembly and a Council, with a permanent Secretariat."

112. See Josef L. Kunz, "The Legal Position of the Secretary-General of the United Nations," *American Journal of International Law*, vol. XL (1946).

113. Statute of the International Law Commission, Article 17, Doc. A/CN.4/4.

114. Similarly, the Fifth Session of the General Assembly asked the Secretary-General to submit one or more preliminary draft conventions and proposals to the special committee which it created to explore the question of the establishment and statute of an international criminal court.

115. Paul-Henri Spaak, first President of the General Assembly, in a congratulatory speech upon inaugurating the first Secretary-General (General Assembly, Official Records of the First Part of the First Session, Plenary Meetings, p. 324).

## Chapter 2. Trygve Lie, and How He Came to Be Secretary-General

The first quotation at the head of the chapter is from a letter to the author from Field Marshal Smuts. "The President" is of course Franklin D. Roosevelt. The comment by Dr. Evatt was made in the course of the discussions of the Executive Committee of the Preparatory Commission regarding the site of the permanent headquarters (21st meeting, Doc. PC/EX/73). The statement from the *New York Times* appeared in an editorial of January 30, 1946 (p. 24:3), the day after the Security Council decided to nominate Trygve Lie.

1. "A candidate for Secretary-General seriously proposed at one time during the long negotiations in London by Philip Noel-Baker was General

Eisenhower. The United States, assuming that the seat of the United Nations would be in this country, took no part in furthering the appointment of an American as Secretary-General" (an informed source, in a letter to the author).

2. Since the United Kingdom was so prominent in the affairs of the League, Thomas J. Hamilton suggests, it was natural that one of its citizens should have been appointed the first Secretary-General. "The U.N., however, was created in the belief that the five Great Powers should control it and that no one of them should have preponderant influence. Obviously, therefore, the actions of the Secretary-General had to be acceptable to them all, and by the same token it was impossible to give an office of such importance to a citizen of any one of them" ("The U.N. and Trygve Lie," *Foreign Affairs*, vol. XXIX, no. 1, October 1950).

3. For what it is worth, the relevant statement of Dr. Juliusz Katz-Suchy, permanent representative of Poland to the United Nations, made in the course of the 1950 debates on the continuance of Mr. Lie in office, is interesting: "It is not true that we once voted for Mr. Trygve Lie, as the representative of Bolivia states, because we thought he would be the servant of Soviet policy. The views of the former Foreign Minister of Norway are well enough known, and were well enough known at the time, to refute the statement of the representative of Bolivia. Those who voted in favour of Mr. Lie in 1946 saw in this Organization a centre for harmonizing the activities of nations with different political and social structures. It is the fact that Mr. Lie has failed to live up to that impartiality which is required of a Secretary-General of the United Nations that forces' us to withdraw that confidence which we reposed in him five years ago" (Doc. A/P.V./297, p. 271).

4. General Assembly, Official Records of the First Part of the First Session, Plenary Meetings, p. 610. Sources for the foregoing election sketch are private conversations of the author with persons of unimpeachable authority.

5. A composite based mainly on *World Biography* (New York, 1948); secondary sources were *International Who's Who* (London, 1949) and *International World Who's Who* (New York, 1948–49).

6. As quoted by Drew Middleton in "World Watchman — Trygve Lie of the UNO," *New York Times Magazine*, March 3, 1946, p. 11.

7. The reader may note that sources are not given, here and at other points, for certain quotations of Mr. Lie. These quotations have been verified, but the author is not at liberty to document the sources.

8. The reader will understand that the countries to which Mr. Lie refers cannot be disclosed.

9. The Soviet Union was reported to have presented to the Acting Secretary-General, on February 27, 1951, an *aide memoire* advancing the view

that the London agreement among the permanent members allocating the Assistant Secretaryships General continues in force (*New York Times*, International Air Edition, March 1, 1951, p. 2).

## *Chapter 3. Relations with the General Assembly*

1. The reports cover the period from July 1 to June 30 (excepting the 1946 report). They are communicated to the members at least forty-five days before the opening of the Assembly's regular session, which as a rule takes place on the third Tuesday of each September. The Secretary-General may also make "such supplementary reports as are required" (General Assembly, *Rules of Procedure*, Doc. A/520, rule 41).

The three Councils also make reports to the Assembly's regular session. The Council annual reports are in fact largely drawn up by the Secretariat and afford the Secretary-General an additional, though lesser, opportunity to present his suggestions. See the Carnegie Endowment's *United Nations Secretariat*, p. 39.

2. Secretary of State George C. Marshall, speaking in the general debate at the opening of the second Plenary Assembly, September 1947, said: "Our point of departure for the deliberations of this Assembly might well be the annual Report of the Secretary-General . . . a noteworthy document. It records realistically the progress and development of the United Nations and its failures" (General Assembly, Official Records of the Second Session, Plenary Meetings, p. 19). General Marshall's comment is a typical one.

3. Secretary-General, *Report* (1948), Doc. A/565, Introduction (July 5, 1948), p. x.

4. *Ibid.* (1949), Doc. A/930, Introduction, p. ix.

5. *Ibid.*, p. xii.

6. *Pravda*, September 16, 1948.

7. Secretary-General, *Report* (1948), Doc. A/565, Introduction, pp. xvii, xviii.

8. *Ibid.* (1949), Doc. A/930, Introduction, pp. xiv, xv.

9. Paul-Henri Spaak, speech at First Session (General Assembly, Official Records of the First Part of the First Session, Plenary Meetings, p. 324).

10. A completely reliable source notes that the United States Department of State has a standing group of approximately thirty persons, which, upon the report's publication, proceeds to analyze it meticulously, chapter by chapter, day by day.

11. General Assembly, *Rules of Procedure*, Doc. A/520, rule 12.

12. Press release SG/97.

13. Charter of the United Nations, Article 24, paragraph 1. However, by the terms of the Acheson plan ("United Action for Peace"), adopted by the

Fifth Session of the General Assembly, the Assembly has assumed a much larger part in the Organization's security functions.

14. "With his staff of experts in political, economic, social and legal fields, and the flow of information on political, economic and social conditions throughout the world, he is in a privileged position to advise the Councils and the General Assembly on the urgency and priority of projects proposed by the Members or by the Specialized Agencies" (Advisory Committee on Administrative and Budgetary Questions, report of April 1948, Doc. A/534, p. 2). See also the Carnegie Endowment's *United Nations Secretariat*, pp. 26–30.

15. Preparatory Commission, *Report*, Doc. PC/20, provisional rules of procedure, rule 48: "The Secretary-General may at any time, upon invitation of the President, make to the General Assembly either oral or written statements concerning any question which is being considered by the Assembly." His right of intervention in Assembly committees was broader: "The Secretary-General or a member of the Secretariat designated by him may make to any committee or sub-committees any oral or written statement which the Secretary-General considers desirable" (rule 97).

16. The rule (63 of the rules of procedure) was altered to the Secretary-General's satisfaction by the Assembly upon the recommendation of its special Committee on Procedures and Organization. The committee met at Lake Success in September 1947 to consider revision of the provisional rules, and adopted the Secretary-General's recommendations for the amendment of rule 48 (later 63 in the permanent rules) without discussion (Doc. A/AC.12/SP.7; the Secretary-General's draft appears in Doc. A/AC/12/12). Appearances are deceiving, however, for though no discussion implies easy passage (as in fact was the case at this stage), the vote upon the issue had been assured by considerable lobbying beforehand by the Executive Office. (The lobbying and its results were facilitated by the decision of the Security Council in the spring of 1946 to grant the Secretary-General unrestricted right of intervention. The record of this latter decision is a good deal more revealing and is analyzed on pp. 84–87.)

17. In an interview with the author.

18. An exception was Mr. Lie's forthright drawing of the Assembly's attention to the dangers of the continued existence of the Franco regime (General Assembly, Official Records of the Second Part of the First Session, Plenary Meetings, p. 700).

19. Verbatim Record of the 219th Plenary Meeting, Doc. A/P.V./219, pp. 68–70, 72. Mr. Lie similarly mentions Palestine, Indonesia, and Kashmir. Thus he likewise appealed — by implication, to the more recalcitrant parties — for coöperation with the United Nations effort.

20. Verbatim Record of the 276th Plenary Meeting, Doc. A/P.V./276, pp. 126–136. (The Mexican resolution was adopted by the Third Session.)

21. Second Session of the General Assembly, Sixth Committee, Proceedings, September-November 1947.

22. Summary Record of the 225th meeting of the Sixth Committee, Doc. A/C.6/SR.225, pp. 87–88.

23. Summary Record of the 250th meeting of the Sixth Committee, Doc. A/C.6/SR.250, p. 278.

24. As it was referred to by Lord MacDonald, the delegate of the United Kingdom (Summary Record of the 287th meeting of the Third Committee, Doc. A/C.3/SR.287, p. 101). Throughout the discussion, the delegates referred to the "draft resolution submitted by the Secretary-General" as a matter of course. The Secretary-General's draft appeared as Doc. A/1411.

25. Summary Record of the 135th, 136th meetings of the Second Committee, Doc. A/C.2/SR.135–136, pp. 117ff. The Secretary-General's draft appeared as Doc. A/1404. Again, through the discussion, the Secretary-General's draft was directly referred to, and there seemed no question of its requiring the sponsorship of a member state.

26. Summary Record of the 56th meeting of the Joint Second and Third Committee, Doc. A/C.2&3/SR.56, p. 73. The Secretary-General's amendment appeared as Doc. A/C.2&3/L.35.

27. Summary Record of the 156th meeting of the Fourth Committee, Doc. A/C.4/SR.156, p. 81.

28. Summary Record of the 189th meeting of the Fourth Committee, Doc. A/C.4/SR.189, p. 307.

29. Summary Record of the 231st meeting of the Sixth Committee, Doc. A/C.6/SR.231, p. 131.

30. See, among innumerable examples, the Summary Records of the 257th and 258th meetings, Docs. A/C.5/SR.257–258, pp. 124, 133, respectively.

31. See the Proceedings of the *Ad Hoc* Political Committee, 30th meeting, Third Session, Part II, and the Report of the Special Committee (Doc. A/959).

32. Fourth Session, 252nd Plenary Meeting, Doc. A/1130.

33. The budgetary powers and processes of the Secretary-General and the related activities of the Advisory and Fifth Committees are in themselves a large area of the whole extent of the field of international administration and can hardly be adequately dealt with in a few pages. Thus there is no attempt here at a thoroughgoing analysis, but only a sketch touching upon the political aspects of the budgetary process and only as incidentally upon the administrative and technical elements as is necessary to the coherence of our political emphasis.

34. Ranshofen-Wertheimer, *The International Secretariat*, pp. 223–227. The Supervisory Commission, a body appointed by the Assembly, asserted

progressively stronger control over the budgetary and administrative work of the League.

35. Dr. Katz-Suchy (Poland), for example, noted "a dangerous tendency in the Department of Public Information to disseminate propaganda that reflected local views alone" (Official Records of the Second Session of the General Assembly, Fifth Committee, Summary Records of Meetings, 16 September–18 November 1947, p. 15). M. Roland Lebeau (Belgium), in urging cuts in the Department's budget, asserted that the case of the United Nations is better served by silence (*ibid.*, p. 117) — a thesis which Benjamin A. Cohen, Assistant Secretary-General for Public Information, resisted strongly, with Mr. Lie's support (*ibid.*, p. 127).

Although Mr. Lie takes part in the proceedings of the Fifth Committee, as indicated, the length and frequency of his participation, and, for that matter, his preoccupation with financial and administrative affairs altogether, is a good deal less than was the comparable concern of the League Secretaries-General. Much the greater part of such work has been delegated to the Assistant Secretary-General for Administrative and Financial Affairs. This is all to the good, since it frees the Secretary-General for his external, political activities. With the Secretary-General of the League, on the other hand, "instead of taking a leading part in the Assembly, three quarters of his time in the course of the Assembly year after year was taken by defending his budget" (*Proceedings of the Conference on Experience in International Administration*, p. 11). Moreover, the League Secretaries-General devoted a disproportionate amount of their energies to personnel problems (see E. F. Ranshofen-Wertheimer, "The Position of the Executive and Administrative Heads of the United Nations International Organizations," *American Journal of International Law*, XXXIX, 1946, 323–330).

36. This consideration of the Secretary-General's financial activities is by no means exhaustive. One further matter particularly merits mention, among the many which have gone unmentioned: the Secretary-General may advance upon his own discretion such sums, up to $2,000,000, as he sees necessary from the Working Capital Fund to meet "unforeseen and extraordinary expenses" relating to the maintenance of peace and security or to economic rehabilitation; for commitments totaling above that amount, the prior concurrence of the Advisory Committee is required. He may loan up to $3,000,000 under similar conditions to the specialized agencies. (The foregoing authorization is generally adopted by each Assembly for the coming year.)

It should be noted, also, that the Secretary-General's financial and administrative practices are subject to further limitations than those of the Advisory and Fifth Committees. He is governed by the financial regulations of the United Nations, a code of financial practices adopted by the General Assembly (Doc. A/1331), and the Organization's accounts are audited by a Board of Auditors appointed by the Assembly. Recommendations of the auditors with which the Secretary-General is not in sympathy are "arbitrated" by the Advisory Committee.

For a useful analysis of the Secretary-General's budgetary and financial functions, see *The Budget of the United Nations,* United Nations Studies 1, Carnegie Endowment for International Peace (1947), particularly pp. 7, 12–24.

37. The Secretary-General is of course further concerned with those Assembly resolutions dealing with the administration of the Secretariat. In the Fifth Committee's production of such resolutions, he plays a prominent part.

38. General Assembly, Fourth Session, Resolutions, Doc. A/1251.

39. General Assembly, First Special Session, Resolutions, Doc. A/307.

40. General Assembly, Third Session, Resolutions, Doc. A/900.

41. A tribute to the Secretary-General's conscientiousness in attempting to execute the Assembly's resolutions relating to this latter question was paid by the delegate of Greece in the course of the Assembly's debates on continuing the Secretary-General in office: "I should like to add to these reasons of a legal character the gratitude that we feel towards Mr. Lie for all his efforts in trying to facilitate the implementation of the resolutions adopted by the General Assembly in 1948 and 1949 on the question of Greek children. It is certainly not the fault of the Secretary-General . . . that this problem has not yet been resolved" (General Assembly, Fifth Session, Doc. A/P.V./296, p. 253).

The Fifth Session of the Assembly adopted a resolution setting up a standing committee of the representatives of three states which, "in consultation with the Secretary-General," is to facilitate the repatriation of the Greek children (Doc. A/1536).

42. Ranshofen-Wertheimer, *The International Secretariat,* p. 6.

43. General Assembly, Fourth Session, Resolutions, Doc. A/1251.

44. *New York Times,* International Air Edition, February 13, 1951, p. 4.

45. General Assembly, Fifth Session, Resolutions, Doc. A/1481.

46. In an address to the First Committee (Summary Record, Doc. A/C.1/SR.354, p. 64). The verbatim quotation in the *New York Times* ran, "under the Secretary General" (International Air Edition, October 10, 1950, p. 4).

47. Summary Record of the 362nd meeting of the First Committee, Doc. A/C.1/SR.362, p. 116. "The appointment of military experts was not the responsibility of the Secretary-General," said Abba Eban, Israel's permanent representative to the United Nations.

48. *New York Times,* International Air Edition, October 11, 1950, p. 4.

49. Transcript of the Secretary-General's press conference of December 21, 1950 (press release SG/135, pp. 5, 3).

Mr. Lie expanded upon his attitude toward the Acheson plan in a speech five days later over the Norwegian State Broadcasting System. "The will to . . . stop any disturber of the peace has never been stronger within the United Nations than it is today. The General Assembly gave expression to this attitude early last autumn when by an overwhelming majority it passed what one perhaps may describe as a new universal plan for preparedness, called 'United Action for Peace.'

"This was a decision of the widest importance. . . The United Nations as an organization has been considerably strengthened through these new decisions so that it will be able to act in nearly all situations with increased efficiency."

50. In this respect, the Secretary-General follows League precedent. The League Secretaries-General were similarly influential in the selection of Assembly officers. See Morley, *The Society of Nations*, pp. 566, 313.

51. Comment of an informed Secretariat source.

52. It is perhaps symptomatic of the intimacy of the Secretary-General's Assembly role that the section of the Secretariat for General Assembly Affairs is part of his Executive Office, headed by his Executive Officer; and that his Executive Assistant, Mr. Cordier, is *de facto* parliamentarian of the Assembly.

## Chapter 4. Relations with the Security Council

1. See p. 28. Rule 15 did restate the provisions of Article 99 and of course entitled the Secretary-General to address the Council in connection with his functions thereunder (Preparatory Commission, *Report*, Doc. PC/20, p. 26). That is probably why no article was included setting forth his rights of communication.

2. Committee of Experts, Summary Record of the 47th meeting, Doc. S/Procedure/100.

3. "The Secretary-General or his deputy may at any time, upon the invitation of the President of the Council, or of the Chairman of the Committees of the Council, and subsidiary bodies, make either oral or written statements concerning any question under consideration" (rule 24 in the provisional rules; rule 28 in the permanent rules).

4. "The Secretary-General may at any time, upon the invitation of the President, make to the General Assembly either oral or written statements concerning any question which is being considered by the Assembly" (rule 48 of the provisional rules, altered to become rule 63 in the permanent rules).

5. Committee of Experts, Summary Record of the 47th meeting, Doc. S/Procedure/100.

6. *Ibid.*, 48th meeting, Doc. S/Procedure/103.

7. *Ibid.*, 50th meeting, Doc. S/Procedure/105.

8. *Ibid.*, 51st meeting, Doc. S/Procedure/106. The phrase "at any time" appeared in the original draft of the rule adopted. The delegate of the United States, Professor Joseph E. Johnson, suggested "at least" dropping this phrase, since its retention, without the "invitation" clause, "might be interpreted as giving the Secretary-General more extensive rights than a representative on the Council." For the Secretary-General, if he could intervene "at any time, might, if he wishes, speak up without awaiting recognition by the President — which no representative may do." Professor Johnson won this point (Committee of Experts, Summary Record of the 50th meeting, Doc. S/Procedure/105).

9. Rule 23.

10. Committee of Experts, Summary Record of the 51st meeting, Doc. S/Procedure/106.

11. The Council of the League of Nations evolved another variation of the rapporteur system. The Council would appoint from among its members a disinterested representative, or, in the case of a very important dispute, two or three representatives, who would be charged with drafting a proposed solution to the problem under consideration. While only governmental delegates, and not the Secretary-General, could be appointed as rapporteur, the influence of the Secretary-General was great. "The rapporteur," Sir Eric Drummond notes (interview of February 14, 1951), "usually was entirely dependent upon the Secretariat. He was generally the national of a small state, amenable to the Secretariat's suggestions. We were always proposing solutions to him. He could adopt them or reject them. When the proposals came forward, they were his." In the Upper Silesian case, for example, the Secretariat drew the line of partition. But the solution was the rapporteur's responsibility.

12. The words of a supremely informed and reliable source.

13. According to an informed source.

14. Article 24, paragraph 1.

15. The words are those of two high-ranking Secretariat officials close to Mr. Lie.

16. Quoted from verbatim record (Security Council, Doc. S/P.V./70), September 20, 1946.

17. The United States resolution and those of the U.S.S.R. and the Netherlands on the subject were all defeated. The delegate of Poland then suggested a resolution noting that the Security Council remained seized of the Greek question. The Australian representative replied that "it is not necessary to retain an item on the agenda in order to keep it under observation. . . Any Member of this Council can draw attention to a matter. We have the good offices and the undoubted powers of the Secretary-General to keep the matter under observation." The Polish resolution was defeated.

18. Address to the General Assembly of September 28, 1950, press release SG/121, p. 1.

19. See the proceedings of June 25, 1950 (43rd meeting of the 5th Year, Security Council Official Record No. 15). Also, Doc. S/1495, a letter from United States Deputy Representative Gross to the Secretary-General transmitting the text of the message which Mr. Gross had telephoned to Mr. Lie earlier that morning.

20. Doc. S/1496.

21. Proceedings of June 25, 1950 (see note 19, above).

22. *Ibid.*

23. Executive Committee of the Preparatory Commission, Committee 6, 4th meeting, Doc. PC/EX/SEC/9.

24. Transcript of the press conference of the Secretary-General, July 14, 1950, at Lake Success.

25. Press release SG/159, p. 3 (April 16, 1951).

26. Doc. S/39. The following illustrates the tone and contains the key reasoning of the memorandum: "I feel it is desirable to present to you my views with respect to the legal aspects of the question. . . I submit the views herein expressed for such use as you may care to make of them. . . It is . . . arguable that, following withdrawal by the Iranian representative, the question is automatically removed from the agenda. . . Since the Council has not chosen to invoke Article 34 in the only way it can be invoked, that is, through voting an investigation, and has not chosen to invoke Article 36, paragraph 1, by deciding that a dispute exists under Article 33 or that there is a situation of a like nature," and since no member brings the item up as a situation or dispute under Article 35, "it may well be that there is no way in which it [the Council] can remain seized of the matter."

The Secretary-General's position may have been a legally cogent one, but its political wisdom is debatable. For its effect, had this advisory opinion been followed by the Council, would have been to make it more difficult for a small state to have a hearing before the Council. As the Italo-Ethiopian and, perhaps, Iranian cases demonstrate, a Great Power in dispute with a lesser one tends to demand as a condition of further negotiations that the latter withdraw its accusations submitted to the international security organization. The majority view in the Iranian case frustrates such pressure.

27. W. H. Lawrence, in the *New York Times*, April 17, 1946, p. 1:8.

28. All of the preceding quotations are from the verbatim text of the 33rd meeting, Doc. S/P.V./33. The Council thereupon adjourned. In the Committee of Experts, the 8 to 3 split reappeared. The committee did not agree upon what Mr. Gromyko described as an "objective and detailed analysis of the juridical aspect of the question" (36th meeting, Doc. S/P.V./36). "There was general agreement that Mr. Lie had every right to state his opinion, there was no general agreement with him about his opinions

in the matter" (*New York Times*, April 18, 1946, p. 14:2). As far as is known, the Iranian item is still on the Council's agenda.

29. James Reston, in the *New York Times*, April 19, 1946, p. 14:3. Mr. Reston reports, but does not engage in, this criticism.

30. *Ibid*.

31. Dr. Alexander Rudzinski, letter of July 13, 1950.

32. Evatt, *The United Nations*, p. 139.

33. Security Council, 91st meeting, Doc. S/P.V./91, January 10, 1947. Australia held the powers of the Council to be limited to those specifically granted in Chapters V, VI, VII, VIII, and XII, and argued that these did not embrace the authority to accept the responsibilities of the instruments for the Provisional Regime of the Free Territory of Trieste, the Free Port of Trieste, and of the Permanent Statute for the Free Territory of Trieste, nor did it impose upon the members the obligation to accept or carry out the decisions of the Security Council pursuant to these instruments.

34. *Ibid*. The Secretary-General held that the provision of Article 24 conferring upon the Council "primary responsibility for the maintenance of world peace and security" was "a grant of power sufficiently wide to enable the Security Council to approve the documents in question," and invited the Council's attention to the discussion of the 14th meeting of Committee III/1 at San Francisco, wherein it was "clearly recognized by all the representatives that the Security Council was not restricted to the specific powers set forth."

35. Doc. A/AC/21/13, p. 6, as quoted by Oscar Schachter in "The Development of International Law through the Legal Opinions of the United Nations Secretariat," *British Year Book of International Law*, XXV (1948), 100.

36. Doc. A/AC/21/13, p. 7, quoted *ibid*.

37. *New York Times*, March 10, 1948, p. 3:1.

38. *New York Times*, March 11, 1948, p. 17:2.

39. General Assembly, Second Session, Provisional Staff Regulations, Doc. SGB/3/Add. 5, regulation 1.

40. Security Council, Doc. S/1446. Strictly speaking, it is incorrect to present the memorandum in the context of legal opinions formally delivered to a session of the Council; rather, it was "unofficially" circulated to all Council members (see letter dated 8 March 1950 from the Secretary-General to the President of the Security Council transmitting the memorandum, Doc. S/1466).

41. *New York Times*, January 21, 1950, p. 4:2.

42. The background of the memorandum is aptly filled out by quoting Mr. Lie's letter of transmission addressed to the President of the Security Council (Doc. S/1466, March 8, 1950):

"During the month of February I had a number of informal conversations with members of the Security Council in connexion with the question of representation of States in the United Nations. In view of the proposal made by the representative of India for certain changes in the rules of procedure of the Security Council on this subject, I requested the preparation of a confidential memorandum on the legal aspects of the problem for my information. Some of the representatives on the Security Council to whom I mentioned this memorandum asked to see it, and I therefore gave copies to those representatives who were at that time present in New York.

"References to this memorandum have now appeared in the press, and I feel it appropriate that the full text now be made available to all members of the Council. I am therefore circulating copies of this letter and of the memorandum unofficially to all members and am also releasing the text of the memorandum to the press." (India had suggested that all the members of the United Nations be polled whenever the credentials of any Security Council member were challenged.)

43. Doc. S/1466.

44. *New York Times*, March 9, 1950, p. 16.

45. Trygve Lie, in a public statement of March 10, 1950 (*New York Times*, March 11, 1950, p. 4).

46. Article 18, paragraph 2, of the Charter provides: "Decisions of the General Assembly on important questions shall be made by a two-thirds majority of the members present and voting." However, the Charter does not indicate whether voting upon amendments to and parts of such questions demands a two-thirds majority. Considerable difference of opinion and inconsistency in practice arose, leading to the Assembly's requesting the Secretary-General for an opinion.

47. See the discussions of the Sixth Committee, 213th and 214th meetings, Docs. A/C.6/SR.213–214.

48. The report appeared as Doc. A/1356.

49. Doc. A/C.6/SR.214, p. 10, and Doc. A/C.6/SR.213, p. 6.

50. The United States, on the other hand, denied the competence of the Council to consider the matter. The Secretary-General took the view that the question, as an international economic problem, was within the Council's jurisdiction. The Council, however, finally agreed with the United States position (Docs. E/AC.6/25, E/AC.6/23, E/743, E/764).

51. *New York Times*, International Air Edition, October 29, 1950, p. 3. The Economic and Social Council at the same time requested another opinion regarding the difficulties of the representative of the World Federation of Trade Unions in obtaining a visa. The Secretary-General also delivered an opinion on the question of whether consultants to the Council have consultative rights (and corresponding diplomatic privileges) in relation to the General Assembly. By his latter opinion, the Secretary-General notably

broadened the consultative status of nongovernmental organizations by affirming that their rights extended, in some degree, to include a consultative relationship with the Assembly.

52. Headquarters Agreement between the United Nations and the United States of June 26, 1947, Doc. A/371. Section 11 provides that the United States shall "not impose any impediments to transit to and from the headquarters district" of, among others, representatives of organizations enjoying consultative status.

A similar issue arose in 1947 over the detention on Ellis Island of the correspondent of a Greek Communist newspaper. The Secretary-General drew the Headquarters Agreement to the attention of the United States Mission to the United Nations, and the correspondent was released. (See the *New York Times*, December 22, 23, 24, 25, 31, 1947, and January 1, 9, 10, 13, 1948, for an account of this and similar cases.)

The Secretary-General has a variety of administrative powers under the Headquarters Agreement, some of which might give rise to political events (see Kelsen, *The Law of the United Nations*, pp. 350–356, 486–487).

53. Press release PM/473.

54. See Schachter, "The Development of International Law through the Legal Opinions of the United Nations Secretariat," p. 103.

55. *Ibid.*, pp. 104, 95.

56. See the address of Dr. Ivan S. Kerno, Assistant Secretary-General for Legal Affairs, before the Bar Association of the District of Columbia, Washington, May 10, 1949, reprinted in the Association's pamphlet under the title, "Legal Activity of the Secretary-General".

57. Schachter, "The Development of International Law through the Legal Opinions of the United Nations Secretariat," p. 95. Mr. Schachter's excellent analysis also deals with a number of cases not considered here.

58. For a discussion of the similar implications of the Secretary-General's discretion with regard to the registration of treaties, see S. Rosenne, "Recognition of States by the United Nations," *British Year Book of International Law*, XXVI (1949), 443–444.

59. Press release SG/104, and Security Council Proceedings of June 25, 1950, 43rd meeting of the 5th Year, Record no. 15.

60. Thomas J. Hamilton suggests that the Secretary-General's statement "probably resulted in winning the votes of India and his native Norway for the cease-fire resolution" ("The U.N. and Trygve Lie," p. 68).

61. *New York Times*, June 27, 1950, p. 4.

62. Transcript of press conference of July 14, 1950.

63. Lev Oshanin, in the Moscow *Literary Gazette* of July 9, 1950.

64. Security Council, Doc. S/1652.

65. General Assembly, Doc. A/1595, Section A(7), December 2, 1950.

66. *Ibid.*, Section A(9).

67. *Ibid.*, Section A(11).

68. Oslo press conference, *New York Herald Tribune*, Paris Edition, August 15, 1950, p. 1.

69. Oslo statement, *New York Herald Tribune*, Paris Edition, August 14, 1950, p. 1.

70. From an address delivered under the sponsorship of the United Nations Association of Chicago; *New York Times*, September 8, 1950, p. 1.

71. Statement to the University of Chicago Round Table, August 6, 1950; press release SG/111.

72. United Nations Association of Chicago address.

73. Secretary-General, *Report* (1950), Doc. A/1287, Introduction.

74. Address by the Secretary-General at a dinner given in his honor by Thomas J. Watson, December 5, 1950 (press release SG/131).

75. Address by the Secretary-General over the Norwegian State Broadcasting System, December 26, 1950 (official United Nations translation from Norwegian).

76. Press release SG/131.

77. Address by the Secretary-General of December 26, 1950.

78. Transcript of a press conference of August 7, 1950. See also his "inaugural address," November 1, 1950 (Doc. A/P.V./299, p. 291).

79. Mr. Lie's statement was made at the 54th meeting of the Council, August 28, 1946, and was prefaced with an espousal of the principle of universality, recommending to the General Assembly the admission of all current applicants (including Albania and the Mongolian People's Republic).

The following are a few excerpts from the Secretary-General's statement to the Council (Doc. S/P.V./54): "I think it may be useful at this point [which was just after Herschel Johnson offered his resolution] to call the attention of the Security Council to a number of pertinent facts. [Mr. Lie then cited a number of United Nations endorsements of the principle of universality.] A single exception was made in the case of Spain under the present Spanish Government. . . I do not quarrel with that decision in any way. . . [Universality] is one subject on which there has never been any serious difference of opinion. For this reason, in my capacity as Secretary-General of the United Nations, I wish to support the admissions to membership of all the States which are applying today."

It is not clear from the records, and it may perhaps not have been clear to the Secretary-General at the time he made his statement, that the Soviet Union would in effect oppose the admission of the applicants en bloc. The reiterated opposition of a large number of members, all of the Great Powers at one time or another included (though never at the same time), has not, however, deterred the Secretary-General from forcefully restating his position.

80. Security Council, 186th meeting, August 18, 1947 (Doc. S/P.V./186). The seven states to have been admitted at once were Albania, Eire, Mongolian People's Republic, Pakistan, Portugal, Transjordan, and Yemen. (Agreement was reached upon Pakistan and Yemen.) The five states to be admitted once the peace treaties came into force would have been Austria, Bulgaria, Hungary, Italy, and Rumania.

In his espousal of universality of membership, Mr. Lie has gone so far as to look forward to the admission of Germany and Japan. In July 1950, in a statement to a group of visiting Japanese political and business leaders, he affirmed:

"The United Nations is not an alliance against anybody. It is a world organization, and it aims and should continue to aim at universality of membership.

"I hope the time will come when every nation in the world will be a member of the United Nations. And that includes Germany and Japan when the peace settlements are completed" (press release SG/109). Three months earlier the Secretary-General had expressed similar sentiments in the course of his "ten-point" memorandum.

The Secretary-General's assurance that "the United Nations is not an alliance against anybody" takes on political point, if it loses in legal standing, by a consideration of Articles 107, 53, and, to a lesser extent, Articles 23 and 106 of the Charter. These articles imply that the United Nations is an alliance against the "enemy states" of the Second World War, or, at least, that the Charter authorizes alliances against these states; and they underline the preferred position of the principal members of the anti-Axis alliance by assigning to them permanent seats on the Security Council and other special security functions.

81. Security Council, 338th meeting, July 15, 1948 (Doc. S/P.V./338).

82. Security Council, 331st meeting, July 7, 1948 (Doc. S/P.V./331).

83. 338th meeting.

84. 331st meeting.

85. Two illustrations of the textual bases of service provisions are: The resolution of the Assembly's Second Special Session creating the office and setting forth the duties of the Mediator authorized "the Secretary-General . . . to provide the Mediator with the necessary staff to assist in carrying out the functions assigned to the Mediator by the General Assembly." The resolution of the Security Council in the case of Indonesia imposes more extensive duties upon the Secretary-General: "The Secretary-General [is] requested to act as convenor of the Committee of Three and arrange for organization of its work" (207th meeting, October 3, 1947, Docs. S/P.V./207, S/574).

86. The Executive Office of the Secretary-General is responsible for the coördination of all United Nations missions, approves the appointment of

their principal substantive officers, and receives their reports directly. For a description of the composition and competence of the Secretary-General's Missions Coördination Committee, which is under the chairmanship of Mr. Cordier, see the useful *Organization of the Secretariat* (U.N. Doc. ST/AFS/2, June 8, 1951, pp. 66–67).

The Principal Secretary of a mission may act as the Secretary-General's personal representative — this is an *ad hoc* matter, depending upon the needs of the situation and the capabilities of the Secretary. Initially, missions were topped with a Secretary and a special personal representative of the Secretary-General. In the case of Palestine, for example, Assistant Secretary-General Jackson acted as Mr. Lie's representative. Later, the trend was toward viewing the Principal Secretary both as chief of mission and as personal representative of the Secretary-General. With the Korean invasion, however, the former procedure was adopted, Mr. Lie appointing Colonel Katzin as his personal representative.

87. Protocol may signify substance as well as form, and in that light the following excerpt from Aide Memoire No. 1 of the Interim Report (Doc. S/1196, January 10, 1949) is instructive: "His Excellency, Dr. Lozano [Colombia] . . . and His Excellency, Mr. Colban, Personal Representative of the Secretary-General, met with the Prime Minister [Mr. Nehru] yesterday." The report goes on to describe an interview in which Mr. Colban's contribution was of the same order as that of Dr. Lozano.

Mr. Colban, a former League official of distinction and an expert on both minorities and disarmament, was particularly fitted for his Kashmir post. He is a good example of the type of Principal Secretary through whom the Secretary-General may exert considerable influence.

88. See Chapter 2, note 7.

## Chapter 5. Political Aspects of the Secretary-General's Relations with Nonpolitical Organs

1. The rules of procedure of the Economic and Social Council (Doc. E/1662)˙ provide:

Rule 30. "The Secretary-General, or his representative, may, subject to rule 47, make oral as well as written statements to the Council, its committees, or subsidiary bodies concerning any question under consideration."

Rule 47. "The President shall direct the discussion . . . accord the right to speak . . . subject to these rules, shall have control of the proceedings of the Council and over the maintenance of order at its meetings. . .

"Debate shall be confined to the question before the Council, and the President may call a speaker to order if his remarks are not relevant to the subject under discussion."

The rules of procedure of the Trusteeship Council (Doc. T/1/Rev.2) provide:

Rule 26. "The Secretary-General, or his deputy acting on his behalf, may at any time, upon the invitation of the President or of the Chairman of a committee or a subsidiary body of the Trusteeship Council, make oral or written statements concerning any question under consideration."

Rule 53. "No representative may address the Trusteeship Council without having previously obtained the permission of the President. The President shall call upon speakers in the order in which they signify their desire to speak. The Chairman of a subsidiary body, or a rapporteur, or the Secretary-General, however, may be accorded precedence. The President may call a speaker to order if his remarks are not relevant to the subject under discussion."

The analogous rules of these Councils in their original wording, before amended to read as above, were more restrictive of the Secretary-General's rights, unqualifiedly limiting him to intervention at the invitation of the President (see Kelsen, *The Law of the United Nations*, p. 305).

2. General Assembly, Third Session, Resolutions, Doc. A/900, Resolution 212.

3. *New York Times*, April 14, 1950, p. 9.

4. Article 63, paragraph 2.

5. The agreements referred to detail reciprocal consultation and coöperation between the United Nations and the agencies, and spell out essentially similar coördinating devices of a loose character between the Organization and the agencies. It is interesting to note that these agreements empower the Secretary-General (as contrasted with the Organization) to enter into additional agreements. Article 18 of the agreement between the United Nations and the International Labor Organization, entitled "Implementation of the Agreement," illustrates like clauses to be found in the agreements: "The Secretary-General and the Director may enter into such supplementary arrangements for the implementation of this Agreement as may be found desirable in the light of the operating experience of the two organizations."

For an able analysis of the treaty-making power of the United Nations and that of the Secretary-General, see Clive Parry in the *British Year Book of International Law*, XXVI (1949), 140–142. With regard to the Secretary-General's treaty-making power, the case of Mr. Lie's adhering, on the Organization's behalf, to the International High-Frequency Broadcasting Agreement of April 1949 is notable. The Secretary-General, though taking the view that he had the capacity to accede in the Organization's name in view of the exclusively administrative character of the Broadcasting Agreement and the terms of the agreement whereby the International Telecommunications Union was brought into relationship with the United Nations, reported his action to the General Assembly afterward (see J. L. Brierly, *Report on the Law of Treaties*, U.N. Doc. A/CN.4/23, pp. 24–25, 28).

The case perhaps illustrates that modicum of initiative with which the Secretary-General is endowed by the fact that the General Assembly and most other United Nations organs are not continuously in session (see p. 229, n. 13).

6. Economic and Social Council, Third Session, Doc. E/245/Rev.1, p. 24, Resolution 13. For a full discussion of the coördinating process, see the "Report of the Secretary-General on action taken in pursuance of the agreements between the United Nations and the Specialized Agencies" (Doc. E/1317).

For an excellent critical analysis of the potential of the Secretary-General's coördinating role, see *Coördination of Economic and Social Activities*, United Nations Studies 2, Carnegie Endowment for International Peace (1948), pp. 7, 13, 30–32, 42, 46, 47, 53–59, 62–99.

7. Earlier still, it was called the Coördination Committee (Doc. E/1317, p. 105). The former name was seen as not quite considerate enough of the station of the Directors General, the latter as implying a complete surrender of coördinating functions by the Economic and Social Council. The Secretary-General was agreeable to the final change of title.

8. Statement of an informed official of the Secretariat.

9. *New York Times*, June 7, 1950, p. 4.

10. Remark of an informed official of the Secretariat.

11. Article 96 of the Charter provides that the General Assembly or the Security Council may request the Court to give an advisory opinion on any legal question, and that "other organs . . . and specialized agencies . . . may also request advisory opinions of the court on legal questions arising within the scope of their activities." The Secretariat is of course an organ, and presumably the Secretary-General could be empowered by the Assembly to request an advisory opinion of the Court. As it stands, he has the "advisory opinions" of his Legal Department.

The Secretariat (Registry) of the Court is not regarded as part of the United Nations Secretariat and is autonomously administered by the President and the Registrar. The powers of the General Assembly with regard to the Registry are the same as those relating to the Secretariat. The Court draws up its own budget, which the Secretary-General may transmit to the Assembly with comment but without change.

12. Other international instruments have embodied clauses modeled upon those in the peace treaties which endow the Secretary-General with the function of appointing the odd member of the arbitral tribunal. For example, the resolution (Doc. A/1604) of the Fifth Session of the General Assembly on the treatment of Indians in South Africa provides that, in certain circumstances, a three-member commission shall be constituted to aid India and South Africa in their negotiations. One member is to be named by India and the other by South Africa. If these two fail to agree upon the third, he is to be named by the Secretary-General.

Of more practical importance may be the resolution (Doc. A/1757) adopted by the Fifth Session of the Assembly providing that the negotiations between France and Libya concerning frontier delimitations between Libyan and French territory may be assisted by a third person. Failing agreement upon that person by the two parties, he shall be appointed by the Secretary-General. This same resolution provides that, with regard to the delimitation of the boundaries of the Trust Territory of Somaliland, the Secretary-General shall, in case of differences among the parties concerned and upon the request of any such party, appoint a United Nations Mediator to recommend a settlement.

13. Interpretation of Peace Treaties (second phase), Advisory Opinion; I.C.J., *Reports*, 1950, pp. 227–230. The vote was 11 to 2.

14. See Yuen-li Liang, "Notes on Legal Questions Concerning the United Nations," *American Journal of International Law*, XLIII (July 1949), 460–478.

15. Reparation for Injuries Suffered in the Service of the United Nations, Advisory Opinion; I.C.J., *Reports*, 1949, p. 179.

16. Article 102:

"1. Every treaty and every international agreement entered into by any Member of the United Nations after the present Charter comes into force shall as soon as possible be registered with the Secretariat and published by it.

"2. No party to any such treaty or international agreement which has not been registered in accordance with the provisions of paragraph 1 of this Article may invoke that treaty or agreement before any organ of the United Nations."

17. See Schachter, "The Development of International Law through the Legal Opinions of the United Nations Secretariat," pp. 127–132.

18. *Ibid.*, pp. 122–127. See also Yuen-li Liang, "Notes on Legal Questions Concerning the United Nations," *American Journal of International Law*, XLIV (January 1950), and Parry, "The Treaty-Making Power of the United Nations," p. 118.

19. General Assembly, Doc. A/1372.

20. General Assembly, Doc. A/1316.

21. Reservations to the Convention on Genocide, Advisory Opinion; I.C.J., *Reports*, 1951, pp. 15ff. The Court further held that if a party to the Convention objects to a reservation which it considers to be incompatible with the object and purpose of the Convention, it can in fact consider that the reserving state is not a party to the Convention; that if, on the other hand, a party accepts the reservation as compatible, it can consider that the reserving state is a party to the Convention. Again by a vote of 7 to 5, the Court lastly held that an objection to a reservation made by a signatory state which has not yet ratified the Convention can have legal effect only upon ratification, and that an objection made by a state which is entitled to sign or accede to the Convention, but which has not yet done so, is without legal effect.

The Court's criterion of the compatibility of a reservation with the object and purpose of the Convention is a new one. The practice of the Secretary-General has been to the effect that, without the consent of all the parties, a reservation proposed in relation to a multilateral convention cannot become effective and the reserving state cannot become a party thereto. The difficulties into which the Court's opinion might lead the Secretary-General are forcefully stated in the joint dissenting opinion (*ibid.*, pp. 45–46).

22. General Assembly, First Part of the First Session, Resolutions, Doc. A/64, pp. 18–19; as amended by the Second Session, Doc. SGB/3/Add.5.

Regulation 29 authorizes the Secretary-General to implement the staff regulations by issuing staff rules. These rules, which may be found in the *United Nations Administrative Manual*, emphasize the Secretary-General's administrative authority. For example, rule 140 (II, 421) provides:

"(a) The Secretary-General may impose disciplinary measures on staff members whose conduct is unsatisfactory.

"(b) Disciplinary measures include written censure, suspension without pay, transfer to an inferior post, dismissal with regular notice, or summary dismissal.

"(c) No staff member shall be subjected to a disciplinary measure until the case has been referred for advice to the Joint Disciplinary Committee, provided that the referral to the Joint Disciplinary Committee may be waived by mutual agreement of the staff member concerned and the Secretary-General."

23. The provisional staff regulations, for example, can hardly be said greatly to hobble the Secretary-General's administrative independence: "All members of the staff are subject to the authority of the Secretary-General, and are responsible to him in the exercise of their functions" (regulation 1). "The whole time of members of the staff shall be at the disposal of the Secretary-General" (regulation 17). "The Secretary-General may terminate the appointment of a member of the staff . . . if the necessities of the service require the abolition of the post, or if the services of the individual concerned prove unsatisfactory" (regulation 21).

24. The Secretary-General's bulletin (Doc. SGB/13) outlining the duties of the Assistant Secretary-General was as follows:

"8 April 1946

"To: Members of the Staff of the United Nations
"1. There is hereby delegated to the Assistant Secretary-General in charge of Administrative and Financial Services the authority to act for the Secretary-General as follows:

"(a) Recruitment, classification, and training of personnel;

"(b) Personnel relations, including health and welfare activities;

"(c) Budgetary, fiscal, and organizational matters.
"2. The scope of this delegation includes authority to modify 'by direction of the Secretary-General' the existing Secretary-General's Bulletins on such

subjects. The Secretary-General's Bulletins may be interpreted and explained by Administrative Instructions which will be signed by the Assistant Secretary-General in charge of Administrative and Financial Services.

"Trygve Lie
"Secretary-General"

25. The comment of a high-ranking member of the Secretariat who comes into contact with all of the Assistant Secretaries-General in the course of his duties.

26. It should further be recalled that the Assistant Secretaries-General are not created by the Charter as entities coördinate with the Secretary-General. The decision on the San Francisco deputies expressly precluded this and so tended to reduce the stature of the future assistants.

27. Administrative Instruction No. 64, July 1, 1949 (Doc. AI/64).

28. See Chapter 4, note 86.

29. Remark by a source close to the work of the Executive Office.

30. Coördination is effected by the Executive Office of the Secretary-General "through meetings of the top-ranking directors of departments. They are called together once or twice a week to talk over the work. . . Each department reports to Mr. Cordier's office every day, and every evening he reports to the Secretary-General on the top developments. That report is then processed and goes to the top people in each department. Thus, all the departments get the same information on top-level developments within the Organization" (summary of remarks by Mr. Cordier to the Institute for the Annual Review of United Nations Affairs, *Annual Review of United Nations Affairs*, 1949, p. 97).

31. How effectively the Executive Office performs its functions is a question I am not competent to answer. A top official of the office, well known for his uncompromising ability, expresses the view that "things are working perfectly now. The Secretary-General is effectively coördinating and expediting. . . We are very much pleased with our coördinating effort. . . We are now getting the results we want." The able study of the Carnegie Endowment (*United Nations Secretariat*) does not wholly share his views.

32. Whereas the Covenant provided that "the Secretaries and staff shall be appointed by the Secretary-General with the approval of the Council" (Article VI), Article 101 of the Charter leaves the appointment of staff up to the Secretary-General subject only to regulations to be established by the Assembly. The practical advantages of the position of the United Nations Secretary-General need not be overstressed, however, for the power of the League Council over appointments, while exerting a cautionary influence upon the Secretary-General, was not actively exploited. See Ranshofen-Wertheimer, *The International Secretariat*, pp. 43–44.

33. The comment of an informed member of the Secretariat.

34. An additional criterion would have been the percentage of the budget contributed by a state. There is, of course, nothing wrong with geo-

graphical distribution as such; it is, indeed, a highly desirable and, in some large measure, necessary element of a healthy Secretariat. Certain countries simply do not possess the skilled personnel which the Secretariat positions demand, however, and to employ persons primarily on the basis of nationality would inevitably impair the quality of the Secretariat's work.

35. See the *New York Times,* July 27, 1949, p. 6:5.

36. *New York Times,* July 28, 1949, p. 8:3.

37. For a lively and critical commentary upon the Secretariat's competence and administration, see Walter Crocker, "Some Notes on the United Nations Secretariat," *International Organization,* November 1950. For a more profound and theoretical study, see the Carnegie Endowment's *United Nations Secretariat.*

38. The resolution adopted by the Security Council at its 286th meeting on April 21, 1948 (Doc. S/P.V./286), provided that "the Government of India should agree that a nominee of the Secretary-General of the United Nations will be appointed to be the Plebiscite Administrator." Mr. Lie selected Admiral Chester W. Nimitz.

39. General Assembly, Second Part of the First Session, Resolutions, Doc. A/64/Add.1, p. 92: "The Secretary-General of the United Nations shall appoint the Executive Director, in consultation with the Executive Board."

40. The Final Report of the United Nations Economic Survey Mission for the Middle East, Doc. AAC/25/6 (Resolution 212 of the Third General Assembly), "requests the Secretary-General to appoint a Director of United Nations Relief for Palestine Refugees to whom he may delegate such responsibility as he may deem appropriate."

41. The General Assembly "requests the Secretary-General, after consulting with the United Nations Commission for the Unification and Rehabilitation of Korea and the Advisory Committee to appoint the United Nations Agent General for Korean Reconstruction; and authorizes the Agent General to appoint one or more Deputy Agents General in consultation with the Secretary-General" (Doc. A/1595, pp. 4–5).

42. The Fifth General Assembly "requests the Secretary-General to establish an *Ad Hoc* Commission composed of three qualified and impartial persons chosen by the International Red Cross or failing that, by the Secretary-General himself, with a view to settling the question of the prisoners of war" (Doc. A/1749).

43. Mr. Lie appointed Dr. Bunche Acting Mediator upon the assassination of Count Bernadotte, without authorization, but in consultation with the President of the Security Council. The Secretary-General's cable read: "In light tragic news concerning Count Bernadotte I empower you to assume full authority Palestine mission until further notice" (Doc. S/1003). The President informed the Security Council of Mr. Lie's cable, saying, "I trust that I can assume they [there was another cable] have the endorsement of all the members of the Security Council" (358th meeting, September 18,

1948, Doc. S/P.V./358). There was no objection from any quarter to Mr. Lie's initiative.

44. General Assembly, Fourth Session, Resolution 319: "The High Commissioner should be elected by the General Assembly, on the nomination of the Secretary-General, for a term of three years from January 1, 1951."

45. It is well known that Mr. Lie was instrumental in the selection of Count Bernadotte. Adrian Pelt, Commission for Libya and, until his election to that post, Assistant Secretary-General for Conferences and General Services, was nominated by a five-man Assembly committee, almost the very first act of which was to consult with Mr. Lie. His influence in the appointment was "significant" (the assessment of a responsible and high-ranking member of the Secretariat in a position to make an informed judgment).

Another illustration, this concerning the selection of a governor for Trieste, was reported by the *New York Times* (April 24, 1947, p. 9:1): "Since the search for an administrator for Trieste began, Mr. Lie said, he has been approached by various delegations for an opinion of the candidates. From personal experience he has been able to comment favorably upon all of the Scandinavian candidates."

46. Provisional Summary Record of the 171st meeting of the Social Committee, August 10, 1950, Doc. E/AC.7/SR.171.

## Chapter 6. *The Secretary-General's Relations with Governments*

The author is not free to document the two remarks by Mr. Lie at the beginning of this chapter (see Chapter 2, note 7). The comment by Mr. Hill was made during our interview of January 3, 1950; that of Mr. Hamilton during our interview of August 25, 1949.

1. "Governmental" as here employed denotes the Secretary-General's activity in relation to individual governments, rather than governments (actually, states) in their collective capacity as four of the United Nations principal organs (the General Assembly, the Security Council, the Economic and Social Council, and the Trusteeship Council).

2. Preparatory Commission, *Report*, Doc. PC/20, p. 86.

3. See Chapter 2, note 7.

4. Conversation with the author. A governmental point of view is illustrated by the following excerpt from an address by United States Ambassador Warren Austin to the General Assembly:

"Less obvious, but perhaps equally important, is the function of the Secretary-General and his staff to serve as a cohesive and coördinating force in the preparation of studies and proposals for the several organs, by suggesting compromises or techniques for dealing with matters under discussion, and by acting as intermediary or conciliator. Many of these activities will never be part of the official record, but the ability of the Secretary-General and his staff to function effectively in this matter will have an important bearing on the development of the United Nations" (Official Records of the Second Part of the First Session of the General Assembly, p. 903).

5. See, for example, "Report of the Secretary-General on action taken in pursuance of the agreements between the United Nations and the Specialized Agencies" (Doc. E/1317).

6. *New York Times*, January 10, 1948, p. 4:5.

7. See p. 116. The preceding, where sources are not indicated, is based upon conversations with informed United Nations officials and delegates.

8. *New York Times*, January 11, 1949, p. 11:1.

9. *Ibid.*, November 9, 1948, p. 1:6.

10. *Ibid.*, November 10, 1949, p. 1:4. The *Times* quotes from a statement issued on the Secretary-General's behalf.

11. The General Assembly adopted unanimously on November 3, 1948, a Mexican-proposed "Appeal to the Great Powers to renew their efforts to compose their differences and establish a lasting peace." For the description by the former Australian Minister of External Affairs of the background of the letter, see Herbert V. Evatt, *The Task of Nations* (1949), pp. 81–84.

12. *New York Times*, March 19, 1949, p. 2:2.

13. Transcript of his press conference of June 8, 1950, Note to Correspondents No. 156, p. B–2.

14. Address by the Secretary-General at the National Convention of B'nai B'rith, Washington, D. C., March 21, 1950; press release SG/64.

15. *New York Times*, March 11, 1950, p. 1.

16. Transcript of his press conference of June 8, 1950 (see note 13).

17. *New York Times*, June 18, 1950, p. 22.

18. Transcript of his press conference of May 3, 1950, Note to Correspondents no. 128, p. 3.

19. Interview with the author, August 7, 1950.

20. Transcript of his press conference of May 26, 1950, Note to Correspondents no. 145, p. B–1.

21. *Ibid.*

22. With Peiping's intervention in Korea, however, the United Kingdom's view underwent another change. Britain voted to postpone consideration of Peiping's admission, pending developments in Korea.

23. Transcript of his press conference of July 14, 1950, p. 2.

24. From the text of a letter sent by the Secretary-General to each of the member states on June 6, 1950 (*United Nations Bulletin*, vol. VIII, no. 12, June 12, 1950).

25. Transcript of his press conference of May 26, 1950, Note to Correspondents no. 145, p. B–1. The phrase "an exploring mission" is also from this transcript.

26. Address of March 21, 1950, to B'nai B'rith; press release SG/64.

27. *New York Times*, April 14, 1950, p. 1.

28. Transcript of his press conference of May 17, 1950, p. 2.

29. Transcript of his press conference of May 18, 1950.

A year later Mr. Lie revealed another of the subjects of his Moscow conversations. In a speech at a state dinner in his honor given by the Greek government in Athens, Mr. Lie declared:

"I know how much Greece has suffered by the loss of so many of her children taken away during the guerrilla warfare. . .

"I share your feelings and I have devoted a great deal of time and effort to this question. I will continue to use every means in my power to resolve it. Insofar as children in Yugoslavia are concerned, I talked in Belgrade with Dr. Homberg of the Swedish Red Cross Delegation and with the highest officials of the Yugoslav Government about the matter. I cannot say what the outcome will be, but if my advice is followed the situation will be improved.

"During my visit to Prague in April last year and my stay in Moscow in May, I had discussions with the highest officials of both governments about Greek children in Czechoslovakia and other Eastern European countries. But I am sorry to say that, until now, these have been without result" (April 18, 1951, press release SG/162).

30. Transcript of his press conference of June 8, 1950, p. C–3.

31. Letter of June 6, 1950, to the member states.

32. Transcript of his press conference of May 26, 1950, p. 1.

33. *Ibid.*, p. 4. Mr. Lie first visited Moscow in 1921 as secretary of a delegation of the Norwegian Labor Party. The delegation was received by Lenin. Mr. Lie thus was in a position to contrast the Moscow of 1950 with the Moscow of 1921 and to note the interim progress.

34. *Ibid.*, p. 2.

35. *Ibid.*, p. 1.

36. *New York Times*, May 27, 1950, p. 2.

37. *Ibid.*, June 8, 1950, p. 2.

38. Transcript of his press conference of June 8, 1950, p. 1.

39. Transcript of his press conference of May 26, 1950, p. 1.

40. *New York Times*, June 21, 1950, p. 1.

41. Transcript of his press conference of July 14, 1950, p. 1.

42. Letter and memorandum of June 6, 1950.

43. Transcript of his press conference of June 8, 1950, pp. B–2, B–3. The Secretary-General's plan for periodic meetings was fresh in the sense of drawing attention to a hitherto neglected provision of the Charter, but it was by no means original with the Secretary-General. The body of Mr. Lie's suggestion is to be found in Article 28.

44. Transcript of his press conference of June 8, 1950, p. 2.

45. Preparatory Commission, *Report*, Doc. PC/20, p. 87.

46. *New York Times*, July 9, 1950, p. 1.

47. *Ibid.*, June 14, 1950, p. 2.

48. A formal statement issued at his press conference of February 6, 1950.

49. *New York Times*, February 11, 1950, p. 5.

50. Interview with the author, August 7, 1950. That the Secretary-General since has perhaps taken a step in Secretary Acheson's direction, while clinging to this thesis, may be indicated by the following declaration to an Athens press conference on April 18, 1951 (press release SG/164):

"In spite of everything that has happened and is still happening, I think there is a good chance that processes of negotiation, mediation and concili-ation, for which the United Nations stands, will preserve the peace.

"In my opinion the chance is better now in some ways than it was before, because the United Nations — and I include Member States like Greece supporting its actions — is a much stronger force for collective security than it was before Korea.

"Negotiation and conciliation are more likely to succeed in the present situation when backed by strength instead of weakness."

51. A criticism akin to that of questioning the desirability of negotiations was voiced by Sir Carl Berendsen in the course of the Assembly's debate on continuing Mr. Lie in office. "I am in strong disagreement with certain aspects of the ten points which he laid before the world on his return from Moscow. My principal — though not my only — criticism of that plan, a criticism which to me is conclusive, is that it places the two contesting groups in this great struggle for freedom, order and justice in the world on the same moral plane. That, it seems to me, is an error which is so gross as to be destructive of everything that flows from it" (Doc. A/P.V./296, p. 253).

52. Doc. A/P.V./312, p. 86. The verbatim records referred to in this section are provisional, with the exception of A/P.V./308.

The U.S.S.R., while ostensibly accepting the Secretary-General's plan for periodic meetings, proposed a number of amendments to the majority resolution which were easily voted down.

53. Doc. A/P.V./308, pp. 436–441. Rule 5 of the provisional rules of procedure of the Security Council empowers the Secretary-General to pro-pose that the Council shall, in accordance with Article 28, paragraph 3, meet at a place other than the seat of the Organization.

54. Doc. A/P.V./309, p. 27.

55. Doc. A/P.V./310, p. 18.

56. Doc. A/P.V./311, p. 28.

57. *Ibid.*

58. *Ibid.*, p. 30.

59. Doc. A/P.V./310, p. 3.

60. Doc. A/P.V./309, p. 10.

61. *Ibid.*, p. 12.

62. *Ibid.*, p. 19.

63. Doc. A/P.V./312, pp. 72–75.

64. *Ibid.*, p. 81.

65. See Chapter 2, note 7.

66. Walter Kerr, in an article cabled from Paris, in the *New York Herald Tribune*, November 14, 1948, p. 1:7.

67. Thomas J. Hamilton, in the *New York Times*, March 9, 1950, p. 16:3.

68. General Assembly, Second Part of the Third Session, Records of the Plenary Meetings, Doc. A/P.V./200, pp. 18–20.

69. Yakob Viktorov, "The Distorted Mirror in the Form of a Report," *Pravda*, September 16, 1948.

70. This apparently refers to the Secretary-General's legal opinion which held the Security Council competent to act in Korea, despite the absence of the U.S.S.R. and despite Soviet allegations revolving about the presence of the Nationalist representative.

71. *Pravda*, July 13, 1950.

72. Dr. Alexander Rudzinski, letter of July 13, 1950.

73. *New York Times*, March 15, 1950, 15:1.

74. *Ibid.*, March 9, 1950, 16:3.

75. *Ibid.*, March 11, 1950, p. 1.

76. Interview with the author, September 22, 1950.

77. Notes of January 31, 1951.

78. The statement of a prominent delegate to the United Nations, associated with the Organization from its earliest days, in an interview with the author.

79. "I do not feel able," Sir Eric Drummond writes, "to make any comparison between my methods of approach and those of Mr. Trygve Lie. It must be remembered that the atmosphere of the League of Nations and of the United Nations are completely incomparable. In the days of the League previous to the Manchurian trouble the countries were really anxious to secure a just settlement of any political disputes that arose, and the influence of the Great Powers was exerted to that end. . . The situation in the United Nations today is unhappily very different, and a different method of approach by the Secretary-General is therefore probably required" (Notes of January 31, 1951).

80. I present this provocative view because of its interest and the importance of the person in the United Nations who expressed it, and not because it is one that I necessarily share, in whole or in part.

# 272  Notes to Chapter 7

## Chapter 7. The Secretary-General and World Public Opinion

Mr. Lie's remark, quoted at the beginning of the chapter, was made at a dinner given in his honor by Thomas J. Watson on December 5, 1950 (press release SG/131). The second comment was made to the author by a high official of the United Nations.

1. Preparatory Commission, *Report*, Doc. PC/20, p. 87.

2. States parties to the United Nations General Convention on Privileges and Immunities, however, are legally bound to exempt the United Nations "from customs duties and prohibitions and restrictions on imports and exports in respect of its publications" (Section 7, as quoted in Goodrich and Hambro, *Charter of the United Nations*, p. 653).

3. Transcript of the Secretary-General's press conference of July 14, 1950, pp. 11–12.

4. Edward J. Phelan, "The New International Civil Service," *Foreign Affairs*, 1932–33.

5. Address by the Secretary-General to B'nai B'rith, March 21, 1950 (press release SG/64).

6. Address by the Secretary-General at the Commencement exercises of Hofstra College, Hempstead, New York, June 12, 1949 (press release SG/2).

7. Address by the Secretary-General at the dinner given in his honor by the American Association for the United Nations, September 29, 1949 (press release SG/22).

8. Address by the Secretary-General at Bergen, Norway, August 8, 1949 (press release SG/15).

9. Press release SG/113.

10. See the speech of the delegate of the Ukrainian S.S.R. to the General Assembly, in which he cited this very case (Doc. A/P.V./297, p. 267).

11. Statement of April 14, 1951, to an official banquet in the White Palace in Belgrade (press release SG/161). In the same address, Mr. Lie declared that he was "sure that under all circumstances Yugoslavia will never bow to foreign domination." He also hailed the Acheson plan as "the second great advance of the past few months toward a United Nations system of collective security."

12. See pp. 55–56.

13. A distinguished American journalist, in a conversation with the author.

14. *Pravda*, September 16, 1948.

15. *New York Times*, April 16, 1948, p. 22:6.

16. In a statement of March 10, 1950, quoted in the *New York Times*, March 11, 1950, p. 4:3.

## Chapter 8. The Extension of Mr. Lie's Term

The quotations from Mr. Vishinsky were taken from a speech made to the General Assembly (Doc. A/P.V./296, p. 261), and from a press conference of October 30, 1950 (reported in the *New York Times,* October 31, 1950, p. 4). Sir Carl Berendsen's remark was made in a speech to the General Assembly (Doc. A/P.V./296, p. 254).

1. *New York Times,* October 26, 1950, p. 1.

2. *Ibid.,* December 17, 1949, p. 6.

3. Thomas J. Hamilton, in the *New York Times,* June 23, 1950, p. 4.

4. Sir Benegal Rau, in a speech to the General Assembly (Doc. A/P.V./ 298, p. 288).

5. *New York Times,* International Air Edition, October 25, 1950, p. 4.

6. *New York Times,* October 26, 1950, p. 1.

7. In a speech by M. Chauvel to the General Assembly (Doc. A/P.V./ 296, p. 254).

8. See, for example, an editorial of that title in the *New York World Telegram and The Sun* of October 30, 1950, p. 18.

9. See David Lawrence, "Today in Washington," *New York Herald Tribune,* October 31, 1950, p. 8:3.

10. In a speech by Mr. Vishinsky to the General Assembly (Doc. A/P.V./296, p. 262).

11. Warren R. Austin, in a speech to the General Assembly (Doc. A/P.V./296, p. 252).

12. Legally speaking, there is of course an important distinction between the two cases. The question of the validity of the credentials of a delegation to a United Nations organ — the question in the Chinese affair — is procedural and not subject to veto, while the recommendation of a candidate for the Secretaryship General is a substantive matter, subject to the unanimity rule. The advocates of vetoing the admission of the Peiping representatives could not be bothered with such a distinction; but had they taken note of it, they might have suggested that the United States, by invoking the so-called "double veto," might have defined the issue as substantive. This would have compounded American intransigence, and was a course to which no commitment was made.

13. *New York Times,* October 31, 1950, p. 1.

14. *Ibid.* See also the *New York Herald Tribune* and *The Times* (London) of the same date, p. 1 and p. 4, respectively.

15. In a speech to the General Assembly (Doc. A/P.V./297, p. 277).

16. Doc. A/P.V./296, p. 259.

17. The delegate of Czechoslovakia (Doc. A/P.V./297, p. 274).

18. The delegate of the U.S.S.R. (Doc. A/P.V./296, p. 261).

19. The delegate of the Ukrainian S.S.R. (Doc. A/P.V./297, p. 266).

20. The delegate of the Byelorussian S.S.R. (*ibid.*, p. 276).

21. The delegate of Poland (*ibid.*, p. 272).

22. The delegate of the Byelorussian S.S.R. (*ibid.*, p. 275).

23. The delegate of Poland (*ibid.*, p. 271).

24. *Ibid.*, p. 272.

25. Doc. A/P.V./298, p. 290.

26. *Ibid.*, p. 289.

27. *Ibid.*

28. The following exchange at the Secretary-General's press conference of December 21, 1950 (press release SG/135, p. 6), is revealing in this regard:

"QUESTION: Time after time at previous press conferences you told us that you would not be a definite candidate for the post of Secretary-General, yet you accepted the candidacy. Could you tell us something about that?

"THE SECRETARY-GENERAL: It is quite true that I would have been more happy if I had been able to go home and rest for a year or two and think and write during that period. Because of the circumstances, I had to accept. I was put into a corner from which I could not get out because it was not a question of my personal feelings and thinking; there were some principles involved, and I could not fail to take up the duty and responsibility which I was called upon to take up. . .

"You know what principles were at stake; I told you. I talked about some of them in my — if you can call it so — inauguration speech which I gave the same day I received the 46 votes in the General Assembly."

29. Doc. A/P.V./299, pp. 291–292.

30. Preparatory Commission, *Report*, Doc. PC/20, p. 86.

## Chapter 9. Secretary or General?

1. See Chapter 2, note 7.

2. Article 109, paragraph 3, of the Charter provides that the question of calling a general conference of the members for the purpose of reviewing the Charter shall be placed on the agenda of the tenth annual session of the General Assembly, if such a conference has not been held earlier under the provisions of paragraph 1 of the article. The first paragraph permits the calling of such a general conference by a two-thirds vote of the Assembly and any seven members of the Security Council. The conference envisaged under paragraph 3 requires a majority vote of the Assembly and of any seven members of the Council.

3. Article 108.

4. John J. McCloy, "The Lesson of the World Bank," *Foreign Affairs*, XXVII (July 1949), 559.

5. *Proceedings of the Conference on Experience in International Administration*, pp. 10–11.

6. C. Wilfred Jenks, "Some Problems of an International Civil Service," *Public Administration Review*, III (Spring 1943), 94. See also Mr. Jenks' remarkable article, "Some Constitutional Problems of International Organizations," *British Year Book of International Law*, XXII (1945), especially pp. 42–44. In this article, Mr. Jenks suggests that the concept of international leadership which Thomas embodied be termed "parliamentary" and that of Sir Eric Drummond "secretarial." Though I have found it convenient to use "political" and "administrative" in place of these, Mr. Jenks' terminology is perhaps more apt.

For a defense of the "secretarial" concept, see J. V. Wilson, "Problems of an International Secretariat," and Maurice Bourquin, *Dynamism and the Machinery of International Institutions* (1940), pp. 42–43.

The Constitutions of the Food and Agriculture Organization and of the United Nations Educational, Scientific and Cultural Organization embody, in Articles VII and VI, respectively, the "parliamentary" view of the Director General's role.

7. This and subsequent remarks of Mr. Phelan are extracted from an interview of August 16, 1951.

## *Appendix. Notes on the Resignation of Joseph Avenol*

1. See Introduction, pp. 9–10, and note 26 of the Introduction, above.

2. Joseph Avenol, interview with the author, August 3, 1951.

3. M. Avenol to Dr. Frank Boudreau, in a letter of September 8, 1940.

4. Interview of August 3, 1951. The Bruce Report (League Doc. A.23.1939) embodied M. Avenol's plan and was ratified by the League Assembly. See also M. Avenol's letter of resignation of July 25, 1940 (Doc. C.121.M.111.1940), in which the Secretary-General speaks of the belief he had held in "certain inevitable reforms which would enable the League . . . to regroup the forces which were moving away from it," and in which he summarizes the hopes he had had for reëstablishing "collaboration between States Members and non-Member States on questions which were of concern to all alike."

5. Vladimir Sokoline, interview with the author, August 6, 1951.

6. Carnegie Endowment, *Proceedings of the Exploratory Conference*, p. 65.

7. Sir Eric Drummond, Notes of January 31, 1951.

8. Vera B. Lever, in a letter to the author, August 9, 1951.

9. Ranshofen-Wertheimer, *The International Secretariat*, p. 381.

10. *Ibid.*, p. 378.

11. *Ibid.*, pp. 379, 381.

12. Carnegie Endowment, *Proceedings of the Exploratory Conference,* p. 65. See also pp. 50, 56–57.

13. Interview of August 3, 1951.

14. July 25, 1940; League Doc. C.121.M.111.1940.

15. Letter of M. Avenol to C. J. Hambro, August 8, 1940 (my translation).

16. Letter of M. Avenol to Anthony Eden, January 5, 1941 (my translation).

17. M. Avenol to Arthur Sweetser, letter of September 1, 1940.

18. Joseph Avenol, interview with the author, August 13, 1951. M. Avenol appears to have consulted with Mr. Hambro about this or a similar possibility (letter from Mr. Hambro to M. Avenol of September 26, 1939; memorandum of the Secretary-General of October 2, 1939, which speaks of the creation of a special control commission to be formed by the Central Committee of twenty-four states which earlier would be set up in accordance with the Bruce Report; letter of M. Avenol to Mr. Hambro, November 3, 1939).

19. M. Avenol to Mr. Eden, letter of May 29, 1945 (my translation); similarly, in a letter to Mr. Hambro, August 8, 1940.

20. Letter to Mr. Eden of May 29, 1945 (my translation); the same reaction is expressed in letters of M. Avenol to Mr. Eden, January 6, 1941; to Dr. Frank Boudreau, September 8, 1940; and to Mr. Sweetser, September 1, 1940.

21. Letter of M. Avenol to Mr. Eden, January 6, 1941 (my translation).

22. Letter of M. Avenol to Mr. Eden, May 29, 1945 (my translation).

23. Interview of August 3, 1951.

24. Letter of M. Avenol to Mr. Sweetser, September 1, 1940 (my translation).

25. League Doc. C.136.M.125.1940, which declared Doc. C.131.M.120.1940 void.

26. Cable from Mr. Hambro to M. Avenol, July 26, 1940; letter of M. Avenol to Mr. Hambro, August 8, 1940; letter of M. Avenol to Sr. Costa du Rels, August 16, 1940 (Doc. C.131.M.120.1940); telegram to League members from M. Avenol, August 20, 1940 (Doc. C.127.M.116.1940); letter of M. Avenol to Sr. Costa du Rels, August 30, 1940.

27. Publicly available sources concerning M. Avenol's resignation and his administrative and political policies of the period are minimal. The following are the relevant League documents: C.121.M.111.1940; C.127.M.-116.1940; C.131.M.120.1940; C.132.M.121.1940; C.134.M.123.1940; C.136.-M.125.1940; C.152.M.139.1940.X; and C.C.1204. The last cited is composed of two interesting annexes attached to M. Avenol's letter of August 16, 1940, to Sr. Costa du Rels, the President of the Council. League Internal Circulars

41.1940, 43.1940, 49.1940, and 50.1940 throw some light on policy with regard to the extensive cutbacks in personnel. For M. Avenol's replies to criticism directed at him at the last League Assembly, see the *Journal de Genève*, April 16, 1946, p. 2, and the *Tribune de Genève*, April 12, 1946 ("Une lettre de M. Joseph Avenol").

It is ironic to note that plans were made as early as April 1939 by the Secretary-General and the Supervisory Commission to evacuate the Secretariat to Vichy, of all places, should Geneva appear endangered by the war (see *L'Europe nouvelle*, 22 Année, no. 106, April 22, 1939, p. 442). An advance mission was actually sent from Geneva to Vichy in the spring of 1940, before there was any question of Vichy's becoming the capital of unoccupied France.

28. Interview of August 13, 1951.

29. Letter of M. Avenol to Mr. Eden, May 29, 1945 (my translation).

30. Interview of August 13, 1951.

31. Carnegie Endowment, *Proceedings of the Exploratory Conference*, p. 65.

# Selected Bibliography

## United Nations Documents

United Nations Conference on International Organization (UNCIO). *Documents.* Volumes 1, 2, 3, 5, 6, 7, 8, 9, 15. London and New York, 1945.

Preparatory Commission of the United Nations. *Report.* Doc. PC/20, 23 December 1945. London: H. M. Stationery Office, 1946.

——— *Report of the Executive Committee.* Doc. PC/EX/113/Rev.1, 12 November 1945. London: H. M. Stationery Office, 1945.

——— *Summary Records of Meetings, 24 November–24 December, 1945.*

General Assembly. *Resolutions Adopted . . . during the First Part of Its First Session.* Doc. A/64, 1 July 1946. London: Church House, Westminster, 1946.

——— *Resolutions Adopted . . . during the Second Part of Its First Session.* Doc. A/64/Add.1, 31 January 1947. New York: Lake Success, 1947.

——— *Rules of Procedure.* Doc. A/520/Rev.1, 1 January 1950. New York: Lake Success, 1950.

Security Council. *Provisional Rules of Procedure.* Docs. S/96/Rev.3 and S/96/Rev.3/Add.1, 27 January 1948. New York: Lake Success, 1948.

Economic and Social Council. *Rules of Procedure.* Doc. E/1662, 5 April 1950. New York: Lake Success, 1950.

Trusteeship Council. *Rules of Procedure.* Doc. T/1/Rev.2, 5 December 1949. New York: Lake Success, 1949.

Secretary-General. *Report on the Work of the Organization, 1 January–15 June 1946.* Doc. A/65. New York: Lake Success, 1946.

——— *Report on the Work of the Organization, 15 June 1946–30 June 1947.* Doc. A/315. New York: Lake Success, 1947.

——— *Report on the Work of the Organization, 1 July 1947–30 June 1948.* Doc. A/565. New York: Lake Success, 1948.

——— *Report on the Work of the Organization, 1 July 1948–30 June 1949.* Doc. A/930. New York: Lake Success, 1949.

——— *Report on the Work of the Organization, 1 July 1949–30 June 1950.* Doc. A/1287. New York: Lake Success, 1950.

———— *Organization of the Secretariat*. Doc. ST/AFS/2, 8 June 1951. New York: United Nations, 1951.

Department of Public Information. *Yearbook of the United Nations, 1946–47*. New York: Lake Success, 1948.

———— *Yearbook of the United Nations, 1947–48*. New York: Lake Success, 1949.

———— *Yearbook of the United Nations, 1948–49*. New York: Lake Success, 1950.

### Other Official Publications and Documents

*Commentary on the Charter of the United Nations*. Cmd. 6666. London: H. M. Stationery Office, 1945.

*Commentary on the Report of the Preparatory Commission of the United Nations*. Cmd. 6734. London: H. M. Stationery Office, 1946.

Committee of Enquiry on the Organisation of the Secretariat, the International Labour Office, and the Registry of the Permanent Court of International Justice (Committee of Thirteen). *Report of the Committee*. League of Nations Doc. A.16.1930. Geneva, 1930.

Covenant of the League of Nations. Adopted 1919. Geneva: Information Section, 1936.

*Dumbarton Oaks Documents on International Organization*. United States Department of State, Doc. 2257. Washington: Government Printing Office, 1945.

Eagleton, Clyde, *Covenant of the League of Nations and Charter of the United Nations: Points of Difference*. United States Department of State, Doc. 2442. Washington: Government Printing Office, 1945.

*Hearings before the Committee on Foreign Relations, U. S. Senate, 79th Congress, on the Charter of the United Nations*. Washington: Government Printing Office, 1945.

International Court of Justice (I.C.J.). *Reports of Judgments, Advisory Opinions, and Orders, 1949; 1950; 1951*. Leyden: A. W. Sijthoff's Publishing Company, 1949, 1950, and 1951, respectively.

*Organisation of the Secretariat and of the International Labour Office*. Report submitted by the Fourth Committee and adopted by the Second Assembly on the conclusions and proposals of the Committee of Experts appointed in accordance with the resolutions approved by the First Assembly at its meeting of December 17, 1920 (Noblemaire Report). League of Nations Docs. C.424.M.305.1921.X and A.140(a).1921. Geneva, 1921.

*Report to the President on the Results of the San Francisco Conference by the Chairman of the United States Delegation, the Secretary of State*. United States Department of State, Publication 2349. Washington: Government Printing Office, 1945. (Also reprinted in *Hearings before the Committee on Foreign Relations*, 1945.)

*Report of the United Nations Conference on International Organization.* Ottawa: Department of External Affairs, 1945.

## Unofficial Publications

BOOKS

Basdevant, Suzanne. *Les Fonctionnaires internationaux.* Paris: Recueil Sirey, 1931.

Bourquin, Maurice. *Dynamism and the Machinery of International Institutions.* Geneva Studies XI, no. 5, 1940.

Boyd, Andrew. *United Nations Organization Handbook.* London: Pilot Press, Ltd., 1946.

Burton, Margaret E. *The Assembly of the League of Nations.* Chicago: University of Chicago Press, 1941.

Cagne, André. *Le Secrétariat Général de la Société des Nations.* Paris: Éditions Jel, 1936.

Cecil, Robert, Viscount Cecil. *A Great Experiment.* London: Jonathan Cape, 1941.

Conwell-Evans, T. P. *The League Council in Action.* London: Oxford University Press, 1929.

Eagleton, Clyde, ed. *Annual Review of United Nations Affairs.* New York: New York University Press, 1949.

Evatt, Herbert V. *The Task of Nations.* New York: Duell, Sloan and Pearce, 1949.

—— *The United Nations.* Cambridge: Harvard University Press, 1948.

Fakher, Hossein. *The Relationships among the Principal Organs of the United Nations.* Geneva: Imprimerie Centrale, 1950.

Goodrich, L. M., and E. Hambro. *Charter of the United Nations.* Boston: World Peace Foundation, 1949.

Hambro, C. J. *How to Win the Peace.* London: Hodder and Stoughton, Ltd., 1943.

Hill, Martin. *Immunities and Privileges of International Officials.* Washington: Carnegie Endowment for International Peace, 1947.

Hill, Norman L. *International Administration.* New York: McGraw-Hill Book Company, 1931.

Howard-Ellis, C. *The Origin, Structure and Working of the League of Nations.* London: George Allen and Unwin, Ltd., 1928.

Jessup, Philip. *A Modern Law of Nations.* New York: The Macmillan Company, 1949.

Kelsen, Hans. *The Law of the United Nations.* London: Stevens and Sons, Ltd., 1950.

—— *Recent Trends in the Law of the United Nations.* New York: Frederick A. Praeger, Inc., 1951.

King, John Kerry. *The Privileges and Immunities of the Personnel of International Organizations.* Odense, Denmark: Strandberg Bogtryk, 1949.

Lauterpacht, Hersch. *International Law and Human Rights.* London: Stevens and Sons, Ltd., 1950.

Miller, David Hunter. *The Drafting of the Covenant.* 2 vols. New York: G. P. Putnam's Sons, 1928.

Morley, Felix. *The Society of Nations.* London: Faber and Faber, Ltd., 1932.

Phelan, Edward J. *Yes and Albert Thomas.* London: Cresset Press, Ltd., 1936.

Purves, Chester. *The Internal Administration of an International Secretariat.* London: Royal Institute of International Affairs, 1945.

Ranshofen-Wertheimer, Egon F. *The International Secretariat: A Great Experiment in International Administration.* Washington: Carnegie Endowment for International Peace, 1945.

Rappard, William E. *The Quest for Peace.* Cambridge: Harvard University Press, 1940.

Royal Institute of International Affairs. *The International Secretariat of the Future: Lessons from Experience by a Group of Former Officials of the League of Nations.* London: Oxford University Press, 1944.

Walters, F. P. *Administrative Problems of International Organization.* Barnett House Paper No. 24; London: Oxford University Press, 1941.

Wilson, Florence. *The Origins of the League Covenant.* London: The Hogarth Press, 1928.

Zimmern, Alfred. *The League of Nations and the Rule of Law.* London: Macmillan and Company, 1939.

ARTICLES AND PAMPHLETS

Barrett, George. "Trygve Lie, Man of Controversy," *New York Times Magazine*, May 14, 1950.

Boudreau, Frank G. "International Civil Service — The Secretariat of the League of Nations," in *Pioneers in World Order*, edited by Harriet Eager Davis. New York: Columbia University Press, 1944.

*Budget of the United Nations.* United Nations Studies 1; New York: Carnegie Endowment for International Peace, 1947.

Butler, H. B. "Some Problems of an International Civil Service," *Public Administration*, vol. X, 1932.

Coördination of Economic and Social Activities. United Nations Studies 2; New York: Carnegie Endowment for International Peace, 1948.

Crocker, Walter R. "Some Notes on the United Nations Secretariat," *International Organization*, November 1950.

Drummond, Sir Eric. "The Secretariat of the League of Nations," *Public Administration*, vol. IX, 1931.

Evans, Archibald. "The International Secretariat of the Future," *Public Administration*, vol. XXII, 1945.

Finer, Herman. *The United Nations Economic and Social Council.* Boston: World Peace Foundation, 1946.

Fischer, Alfred Joachim. "UNO's Tryvge Lie," *New Republic*, vol. CXIV, no. 12, March 25, 1946.

Hamburger, Philip. "The Idea Is Everything" (profile of Trygve Lie), *New Yorker*, October 11, 19, 1948.

Hamilton, Thomas J. "The U. N. and Trygve Lie," *Foreign Affairs*, vol. XXIX, no. 1, October 1950.

———"The Secretary-General's Job," *Freedom and Union*, vol. V, no. 2, February 1950.

Howe, John M. "The Geographic Composition of International Secretariats," *Columbia Journal of International Affairs*, vol. II, no. 2, Spring 1948.

Jenks, C. Wilfred. "Some Problems of an International Civil Service," *Public Administration Review*, vol. III, no. 2, Spring 1943.

———"Some Constitutional Problems of International Organizations," *British Year Book of International Law*, vol. XXII, 1945.

Kaplan, Robert. "Some Problems in the Administration of an International Secretariat," *Columbia Journal of International Affairs*, vol. II, no. 2, Spring 1948.

Kerno, Ivan S. "Legal Activity of the Secretary-General," reprint of speech, published by the Bar Association of the District of Columbia, 1949.

Kunz, Josef L. "The Legal Position of the Secretary-General of the United Nations," *American Journal of International Law*, vol. XL, 1946.

Laves, Walter H. C. "The United Nations: Reorganizing the World's Governmental Institutions," *Public Administration Review*, vol. III, Summer 1945.

Laves, Walter H. C., and Donald C. Stone. "The United Nations Secretariat," *Foreign Policy Reports*, vol. XXII, no. 15, October 15, 1946.

Leonard, L. L. *The United Nations and Palestine*. New York: Carnegie Endowment for International Peace, 1950.

Liang Yuen-li. "Notes on Legal Questions Concerning the United Nations," *American Journal of International Law*, vol. XLIII, no. 3, July 1949.

——— "Notes on Legal Questions Concerning the United Nations," *American Journal of International Law*, vol. XLIV, no. 1, January 1950.

McCloy, John J. "The Lesson of the World Bank," *Foreign Affairs*, vol. XXVII, no. 4, July 1949.

Middleton, Drew. "World Watchman — Trygve Lie of the UNO," *New York Times Magazine*, March 3, 1946.

Moore, Bernard. "Role and Functions of the Secretariat," in *Annual Review of United Nations Affairs*. New York: New York University Press, 1949.

Morley, Shephard. "The Real Trygve Lie: Stalin's Tool in the UN?" *Plain Talk*, October 1947.

O'Connell, D. P. "The British Commonwealth and State Succession after the Second World War," *British Year Book of International Law*, vol. XXVI, 1949.

Parry, Clive. "The Secretariat of the United Nations," *World Affairs*, July 1950.

——— "The Treaty-Making Power of the United Nations," *British Year Book of International Law*, vol. XXVI, 1949.

Pelt, Adrian. "Peculiar Characteristics of an International Administration," *Public Administration Review*, vol. VI, 1946.

Phelan, E. J. "The New International Civil Service," *Foreign Affairs*, 1932–33.

Preuss, Lawrence. "Immunity of Officers and Employees of the United Nations for Official Acts: The Ranallo Case," *American Journal of International Law*, vol. XLI, 1947.

*Proceedings of the Conference on Experience in International Administration*. Washington: Carnegie Endowment for International Peace, 1943.

*Proceedings of the Exploratory Conference on the Experience of the League of Nations Secretariat*. Washington: Carnegie Endowment for International Peace, 1942.

Ranshofen-Wertheimer, Egon F. "The International Civil Service of the Future," *International Conciliation*, no. 418, February 1946.

———— "The Position of the Executive and Administrative Heads of the United Nations International Organizations," *American Journal of International Law*, vol. XXXIX, 1945.

———— "Problems of Postwar Reconstruction," *American Political Science Review*, vol. XXXVII, October 1945.

Rosenne, S. "Recognition of States by the United Nations," *British Year Book of International Law*, vol. XXVI, 1949.

Schachter, Oscar. "The Development of International Law through the Legal Opinions of the United Nations Secretariat," *British Year Book of International Law*, vol. XXV, 1948.

Secretan, Jacques. "The Independence Granted to Agents of the International Community in Their Relations with National Public Authorities," *British Year Book of International Law*, vol. XVI, 1935.

Shalom, Nessim. "Coördination of the Programs of the Specialized Agencies," in *Annual Review of United Nations Affairs*. New York: New York University Press, 1949.

Stone, Donald C. "Organizing the United Nations," *Public Administration Review*, vol. VI, 1946.

Stoneman, William H. "The Secretary-General," *The Norseman*, vol. IV, no. 2, March–April 1946.

Tead, Ordway. "The Importance of Administration in International Action," *International Conciliation*, no. 407, January 1945.

"U. N. and the Agencies; I: Staffing Problems," in *Planning*, vol. XV, no. 298, May 23, 1949.

"U. N. and the Agencies; II: The Secretariat's Role," in *Planning*, vol. XVI, no. 307, January 2, 1950.

*United Nations Secretariat*. United Nations Studies 4; New York: Carnegie Endowment for International Peace, 1950.

Werner, M. R. "Trygve Lie," *United Nations World*, vol. I, no. 1, February 1947.

Wilson, J. V. "Problems of an International Secretariat," *International Affairs*, vol. XX, October 1944.

*INDEX*

# INDEX

Acheson, Dean, 106, 150, 154, 159, 160, 161, 166
Acheson Plan, powers of Secretary-General under, 80–81; Lie's comments on, 82, 203, 251–52 n.49, 272 n.11; security functions of Assembly under, 247 n.13
Administrative Committee on Coördination, 121–22, 262 n.7
Administrative theory of Secretaryship General, 169, 171–72, 275 n.6
Admission of new members, Lie's proposals on, 113, 151, 258 n.79, 259 n.80; I.C.J. advisory opinion on, 124, 258 n.79
Advisory Committee on Administrative and Budgetary Questions, 75–77, 128, 249 n.33, 250 n.36
Advisory opinions, see International Court of Justice; Secretary-General of United Nations, legal opinions of
Aghnides, Thanassis, 76
Annual report, in Article 98, 20, 26; importance of, 30, 247 n.2, n.10; Lie's use of, 30; Lie's introductions to, 63–67; criticism of third report by Pravda, 65, 168, 182–83; procedure of, 247 n.1
Arce, José, 72, 97
Argentina, 175
Assistant Secretaries-General, recommendation of Preparatory Commission on, 31; rotation as Acting Secretary-General, 43, 243 n.101; Big Three apportionment of, 56–59; appointment by Secretary-General, 58; interventions in Assembly committees, 71; in budgetary matters, 78; as Secretary-General's cabinet, 131–32; in negotiations with governments, 132, 166; experimental Assistant Secretaryship General for General Coördination, 31, 133; in draft-

ing of ten-point memorandum, 163; Soviet view on Big Five allocation of, 246 n.9; stature of, 265 n.26
Atomic energy, in ten-point memorandum, 151, 206; Commission on, 236 n.38
Atilio Bramuglia, Juan, 142–43
Attlee, Clement, 150, 156
Auriol, Vincent, 150, 153
Austin, Warren R., relations with Lie, 166; support of Lie's reappointment, 188, 190, 192, 194–198; on Article 99, 235 n.32; on investigatory powers of Secretary-General, 235 n.32; on Secretary-General's diplomatic activity, 267 n.4
Avenol, Joseph, administrative role, 8, 218, 222; relations with League organs, 8; public activities, 8; declining diplomatic influence, 8, 218; resignation, 8, 215–224, 275 n.5; on role of Secretary-General, 8; appointment as Secretary-General, 8, 9; negotiations with Mussolini, 9, 216, 219, 229 n.26; relations with Britain, 37, 217, 221, 222; Ethiopian plan, 9–10, 216, 229 n.26; position on refugee problem, 80; relations with French government, 216–219; plan for reforming League, 216, 275 n.4; personality of, 217–218; compared with Drummond, 218

Bajpai, Sir Girja, 193
Barthou, Jean Louis, 9
Belgium, 165, 250 n.35
Berendsen, Sir Carl, 187, 270 n.51
Berlin blockade, Lie's efforts to resolve, 71, 142–144; committee of neutrals, 142–43; Evatt-Lie letter, 143, 166, 180, 181
Bernadotte, Count Folke, Lie's relations with, 115, 116; relations